Praise for

Rare Mamas

"*Rare Mamas* is more than a book; it's a lifeline for parents navigating the uncharted territory of raising a child with a rare disease. Nikki McIntosh has taken her personal experience and transformed it into a powerful, practical guide filled with care, wisdom, and actionable strategies. Her voice is one of strength and hope, offering a much-needed sense of community for those who often feel alone in their journeys. This book is an essential resource, and I believe it will make a real difference for so many families."

—**MONTEL WILLIAMS,** TV host, podcast host, and author

"As a TV producer who tells the stories of rare families—and the mother of a child with a rare disease—I only wish this book had existed when we began our journey. *Rare Mamas* is the kind of honest, compassionate support every rare parent deserves."

—**CARRI LEVY,** rare mom, co-creator and senior producer of the series *Behind the Mystery: Rare and Genetic Disease*

"*Rare Mamas* is the anchor and compass parents need after receiving a life-changing diagnosis for their child. There hasn't been a roadmap to deal with such complexities . . . until now. It offers the vital guidance, unwavering support, and a deep understanding that will empower you to navigate the unique and challenging journey of rare disease. *Rare Mamas* isn't just a book—it's the lifeline you've been desperately searching for."

—**BRITTANY COCILOVA,** supervising producer of the series *Behind the Mystery: Rare and Genetic Disease*

"As a rare disease patient, I've seen firsthand the relentless advocacy my mom had to shoulder. This book is the guide she deserved but never had."

—**ILANA JACQUELINE,** rare disease patient and author of *Medical Gaslighting* and *Surviving and Thriving with an Invisible Chronic Illness*

"Nikki McIntosh wrote the book we've all needed with the power of retrospect as well as a pithy gaze at her family's life now. She knows that rare parents enter this rare life at diagnosis but never leave, because our children can't. Nikki reminds us that the energy of connection will give us endurance, and love will fuel our resilience when we forget to live for ourselves and give everything we can for our child. What I appreciate most about this book is the practical—giving us reminders, heads ups, and answers when we ask what now? In my own Rare Mama journey, I learned as I went alone. I wish I'd had this book earlier."

—**PATTI M. HALL,** author of *Loving Large: A Mother's Rare Disease Memoir*

"*Rare Mamas* is the book I wish I'd had when my daughter got her diagnosis, when I was feeling overwhelmed, when I was scared, and when I felt isolated. Nikki shares so much wisdom in the voice of a trusted guide, who's also a cheerleader and best friend. Knowing there are others traveling a similar path provides the dose of courage we all need when our worlds are turned upside down by a rare disease diagnosis. From practical strategies to emotional support, *Rare Mamas* is an indispensable manual to refer to when you need a compassionate guide who truly understands. This book doesn't just offer solutions—it offers validation, inspiration, and the reassurance that even in the rarest of journeys, you are never alone."

—**JESSICA FEIN,** author of *Break Taking: A Memoir of Family, Dreams, and Broken Genes* and host of podcast *I Don't Know How You Do It*

"*Rare Mamas* is a heartfelt and practical guide that offers clarity, strength, and unwavering support for parents facing the overwhelming journey of rare disease. The author is incredibly well-spoken and relatable, drawing from lived experience and deep empathy to speak directly to the hearts of caregivers. With compassion and wisdom, she shares empowering strategies that help mothers feel less alone, more equipped, and grounded in their inner strength as they advocate for their children. This book is a must-read companion for any parent navigating this complex path."

—**CAROL GELBARD,** LCSW, psychotherapist and former director of emotional wellness at the Neuromuscular Disease Foundation

"Rare mamas are less rare than we would like them to be. Millions of rare families manage everyday life with a level of uncertainty that would scare most. But as Nikki tells us in her beautiful book, Rare Mamas are a special breed, a group that will never stop fighting. We can all learn so much by just watching them live; they are true warriors for health and happiness!"

—**DR. KATIA MORITZ,** director of documentary *Undiagnosed* and parent to two rare young adults

"This book is the companion I wish my friend had when her child was diagnosed with a rare disease—a source of support and a roadmap all in one."

—**BRITTANY DANIEL,** actress

"With raw honesty and emotional vulnerability, Nikki opens a door into the journey of being a rare mama and guides readers through complex emotions and challenges. She lights the path for other rare mamas with grace, wisdom, and a deep well of compassion. Her empowering, and practical advice provides guidance in navigating the often-overwhelming journey of rare disease care. Nikki writes from the trenches. Her voice is authentic and fierce, yet loving and compassionate. *Rare Mamas* is not just a book . . . it is a lifeline for rare mamas!"

—**MELISSA HIOCO,** director of community engagement for STXBP1 Foundation, and rare mama to Alex

NIKKI MCINTOSH

Rare Mamas

EMPOWERING STRATEGIES FOR NAVIGATING YOUR CHILD'S RARE DISEASE

WONDERWELL

Published by Wonderwell Press
Austin, Texas
www.gbgpress.com

Distributed by River Grove Books

Design and composition by Greenleaf Book Group
Cover design by Greenleaf Book Group
Rare Mamas logo by Gabriel Corral

Publisher's Cataloging-in-Publication data is available.

Print ISBN: 978-1-963827-21-7

eBook ISBN: 978-1-963827-22-4

First Edition

For Mason and Miles,
the ones who made me a mama
and fill my heart with love.

And for my own mama, Myrna,
a beautiful, bright soul
and the greatest guide in motherhood
God could have blessed me with.

Everything I know about unconditional love,
I learned for you and from you.
This book is for you, with endless love.

Contents

INTRODUCTION

I See You, Friend

Did you just receive life-changing news that your child has been diagnosed with a condition, illness, or disease? A rare one on top of that? Are you swimming in questions, confusion, and fear? As you read these lines, are you thinking of the million other things you need to do? Do you feel like you're alone on an island or in a sea of people, but no one can relate?

Or have you been on this rare disease road for a little while, and you're running out of stamina? Do you wonder why it's so hard, if you're doing it right, and how you're going to keep going?

I was in your shoes (and still am), and I'm here to tell you that no one should go this road alone. The truth is you're not alone. According to the National Organization for Rare Disorders (NORD), 30 million Americans have a rare disease.[1] That's one in ten Americans. According to Global Genes, one out of every two patients diagnosed with a rare disease is a child.[2] Therefore, it can be approximated that there are around 15 million children in the United States under the age of eighteen who have a rare disease. This represents a significant segment of the nation's population. Worldwide, there are an estimated 175 million children living with a rare disease. This means there are literally millions of rare mothers out there treading down this road.

I am one of them.

My younger son was diagnosed with a severe rare disease at eighteen months old. I was hurled into a world I knew nothing about. His medical needs were beyond my competency. I was just an ordinary girl trying to live her life when my world took on extraordinary circumstances. I thought motherhood was hard. Rare disease motherhood was next-level.

Along the way I learned a lot of things—things I wished I'd known right away. But because this road isn't typical, it takes a while longer to figure them out. Because our children's diseases are rare, finding information is devastatingly difficult. So, unfortunately, we don't discover many of the things we need to know until later on our journey.

But can you imagine how things would be different if you knew them right away? What a difference it could make and what a time-saver it would be? Now, after years of walking this road, I've been exposed to a whole set of rare disease resources and rare moms. They have provided a wealth of valuable information. In talking to other moms, I've realized that although our children's diagnoses are different, the challenges we face and the paths we're on have a lot of similarities. A multitude of things are universal to us.

These universal "rare mama truths" appeared time and time again in my conversations with other rare mamas, and I got to thinking about how it would help if we all knew these truths right away. Our time is so precious, so limited, and we are pulled in so many directions. How could we get this information sooner so our children and families could benefit from it right away? How could we enter the right frame of mind and put on the right armor to tackle all that was in front of us? How could we approach this journey with bravery instead of fear?

If you're a rare mama who's been on this road for a while, I want you to have your feelings affirmed, be reassured you're on the right path, be envigored with renewed strength, and be comforted by a sense of community with other rare mamas.

Out of these thoughts, the idea for this book was born. The idea also came from the thought that in dealing with something so overwhelming, it sure would help to have a friend who had been through it before—someone who could relate, give sound advice, and perhaps even offer a kick in the pants when needed. Some of the most meaningful and useful advice and guidance I've received has come from other moms. They are my heroes, and they inspire me. Moms are better together—helping one another out, cheering one another along, and picking one another up when one falls down.

But the truth is that most of us don't have a best friend who has been through this. Our road isn't typical. Since most of us don't have this type of confidante, we often feel alone and isolated. My guess is that along the way, you'll start to meet other women whose children also have a disability, and some of them may even become your closest friends. But you sure could use that friend right now. You sure could use all of that good advice today.

So for now, I'm happy to be your rare best friend, and this book can act as if you and I went out for coffee (or vodka) to talk about it all. You could cry and vent and scream about how hard this is, and I would listen and touch your arm and say, "I know, friend. I know." Then I would tell you everything I know to help make this a bit easier for you.

Like any good best friend, I would give it to you straight and tell you everything—the good, the bad, the ugly, and maybe even some things you don't want to hear. Then I would look you straight in the eye and tell you, "Yes, this journey is tremendously hard, but you can do it. Did you hear me, friend? You can do this!" or "Friend, you can keep going. Believe me, you can. Here are some ways."

I'm living proof because one day, not too long ago, my son was newly diagnosed, and I was spinning in sadness, confusion, and worry. But I found my way, and so can you.

Now, there is something I should probably tell you right up front. I never wanted to be a writer, and this book shouldn't even exist.

There were a lot of things I was planning to do in my life. Writing a book was not one of them. But then again, I also was not planning on my child having a rare disease. Chances are, neither were you. Yet here we are.

Yes, I worked in advertising and then at a magazine for many years, but I worked on the marketing and research side, not the editorial side. I had to know a thing or two about writing for business but rarely wrote for a purpose outside of work. I'd never had an idea for a book or wanted to be an author, yet I felt compelled to write this one.

Yes, compelled. Going through this journey has tugged on my heart. I kept thinking about all the rare mamas out there going through this alone. I kept thinking about how hard it is to find information, how useful it would be to enter this journey with the right mindset, and how helpful it would be to have a coach who could come alongside and encourage you to keep going. I kept thinking about you all. You've been on my heart for years now. But truth be told, even though I had all of this information that I wanted to share, I didn't have time to write a book. The last thing I had time to do was write. So the fact that this one is written is pretty much beyond my comprehension.

This book woke me up at 4:30 a.m. on countless mornings to write. I'm talking without an alarm clock. No joke. Once I started, I couldn't stop writing. I came off long walks, workouts, prayers, and my son's harrowing procedures and surgeries and added to it. *There's one more thing I need to tell them. Oh yes, they need to know that too.* Could. Not. Stop.

But let me be clear, every word was typed with discernment. Everything was run through the filter of "Will it help these mamas?" Yes? It's in. No? It goes. I know how sacred your time is, and I'm not wasting it on one unnecessary word.

I poured every ounce of my being into this book. I cried, kicked, stomped, grieved, cheered, prayed, danced, and reverberated as I wrote it. It stirred up all the emotions of my own journey, and I took it all out on the keyboard, pounding out words in a fury as sometimes tears rolled down my face.

So here it is. All because you were on my heart, and if I could make this road just a little easier for you, then I sure wanted to try. If I could give you everything I wished I'd known when my son was newly diagnosed, then I sure wanted to try. If I could give you what I thought could save you time along the way, and if I could encourage you when the road was too much to bear, then I sure wanted to try.

My soul spilled out into this book, and it's here to serve *you*! It's my heart on a platter, served up raw. It's my love letter to you. Even though I haven't met you, I already love you, friend. I love you right now, right where you are. Even if you're sitting there in your sweatpants that haven't been washed in weeks. Even if you can barely keep your eyes open long enough to read these words. Even if you have tears streaming down your face. I love you in your mess. I love you because I know that, despite it all, you're still showing up to take care of your child. You are the definition of love. And I love you for that.

Along my journey, I've dealt with the gamut of emotions, obstacles, roadblocks, trials and errors, nos, hurdles, and falls on my face—but sister, I'm still standing. I figured, *What's the use of going through all of this if I can't use it to help someone else?* What if I could prevent you from having to go through some of those things, or at least prepare you for them? Looking back now, I can see there are steps that can be taken to move you from distress to prowess—from exasperated to empowered. But in the beginning, it's hard to know how to get there without having a guide. And even if you've been a rare mama for a while, you'll hit points when you're so dang tired you'll wonder how you will wake up and do it again tomorrow. So it would be my absolute honor to steward you through your journey.

That being said, I'm still on my journey and still learning. So while sometimes I may get it right, sometimes I may get it wrong. It's just the view from where I sit and where I've sat. So let me give you a few insights about the type of friendship/guidance/coaching that I will offer . . .

1. I'm going to keep it real. What you need right now is the type of friend who's going to give it to you straight. The type of friend who, if you ask whether it's obvious you haven't washed your hair in three days, will lovingly hand you some dry shampoo and say, "Yes." I can't truly help you if I don't give you truthful information. Plus, keeping it real is just how I roll. Mama, you don't have a lot of time, and neither do I, so let's use it wisely and get down to business.

2. Hope is my modus operandi, my M.O. I believe you can keep it real and still keep hope in your heart. I approach everything from a place of hope. My hope doesn't come from blind optimism; it comes from a place of expecting and believing in the best *despite* my circumstances. It has helped me immensely, and I believe it will help you too.

3. Humor is one of my best weapons. Though this subject matter is heavy, one thing I told myself I would not do, no

matter what life threw at me, was lose my sense of humor. And believe me, I almost did. But I fight against losing it every day. Why? Because it's one of the best arms in my arsenal. This journey is tough, and you gotta pull out everything you have in your bag of tricks. Humor is in my bag, and I'm pulling it out. So I hope you know when it's being used, it's not to make light of the subject or the hardships; it's a tool used to get through them.

4. I'm a woman of faith. My faith will show up all over this book because it's a huge part, if not the most important part, that got me through in my times of greatest need. I know not everyone shares my faith, and that's okay with me. But it's been an anchor, and just like everything else, I'm sharing it with you too.

5. I believe this book is my purpose. I'm not overly emotional, and I'm rarely mushy. But my heart beats for a few things: my faith, my family, my friends, and my fellow rare mamas. When I write to you, my heart beats so fiery red it feels like it might fly right out of my chest. Life has thrown me some pretty unexpected curve balls, and while being in community with you and writing to you has been completely unexpected, it feels like exactly where I belong. Every fiber of my soul feels like I am meant to be here with you rare mamas, and this has been one of the most fulfilling aspects of my life. It's my heart's song.

Now that you know what you're getting yourself into with this book, let me tell you what I believe you'll get out of it.

What you hold in your hand is the book I wish I could have received when my son was diagnosed with his rare disease, spinal muscular atrophy (SMA). I wish the doctor would have said, "Your child has a rare disease called SMA. I know you're scared. This book may help." I mean, truthfully, I wish the doctor would have said something else entirely! But if there had to be a rare disease diagnosis, I wish it would have come with a manual.

In the rare disease world, we always say, "Rare disease doesn't come with a manual." Well, why not? We desperately need one! And while this book is not the manual for *your child's* rare disease, my hope is that it is a manual for *you*, the mother of a child with a rare disease. Another saying in the rare disease community is "Rare disease doesn't come with a manual. It comes with a mother who never gives up." That's true. And that mother is *you*.

Moms are powerhouses. They can do some pretty remarkable things. I already know you're going to do, or are already doing, things you never in a million years thought you were capable of and things that are just downright awe-inspiring. I know there is a fierce fighter already within you. My goal is to help you channel that fighter so you can blaze your trails.

So this book is . . .

- *A manual*: a reference, a playbook. It's filled with strategies, how-tos, best practices, need-to-knows, and practical tips for rare mamahood.

- *A map*: the lay of the land, directions, a popcorn trail from a mama who's walked this road. I have taken the tour, been around the block, and—like it or not—moved into this rare world, taken up residency, and now I live here every day. As a rare world resident, I'm unfolding the map; pinpointing all the roadblocks, barriers, and detours; and highlighting its gardens, water sources, and lifeblood.

- *A welcome mat*: a bridge, an invitation, a connection to the millions of mothers whose children have a rare disease. We need one another. We need to hear one another's stories. We need to find our place in this world, and I believe we do that through community. You know how we walk this rare road? Together, that's how. We do it together.

But most of all, I want this book to be . . .

- *A match*: a power source, jumper cables, an electrical outlet, fuel, a light when the day is dark. I want it to burn so bright and so hot in your hands that it ignites the fire in your belly. Quite simply, I want it to empower you.

When we're done, I believe you will be filled with information and encouragement and will walk away with your inner fighter awake and ready to attack. It's the kind of encouragement that I think will fuel you to do what you need to do and the type of information that will put you in the right frame of mind to take on what's before you. It's a blend of concrete tactical tools mixed with the mentality and attitude you'll need for this journey. It's the hope that you need to know exists from one mother (who's been where you are) to another.

You may be in the hardest part of your journey, and no one should go it on their own. I want you to know that you're not alone, you can do this, you're a fighter, and—even if you're in the middle of your deepest darkness—you will see the light once again.

PART I

The Rare Mamas Mindset

CHAPTER 1

Awakening Our Inner Animal and Unleashing the Fierce Fighter

"There are places in the heart you don't even
know exist until you love a child."

ANNE LAMOTT

When I was pregnant with my second son, Miles, I made a music playlist for his birth. I filled it with fast tracks that would help me through the birthing and delivery. My playlist was jam-packed with various songs, but when I was in the heat of the moment, the song I wanted to listen to over and over was "Eye of the Tiger" by Survivor. I repeated that song probably thirty times—listen and repeat, listen and repeat. It felt like my war cry. It made me feel strong, brave, and capable, and it inspired me to keep going even though I was hot, exhausted, and in pain. That tune revved me up and fueled me throughout Miles's delivery.

Little did I know then that song would become the theme song for my son's journey. At the age of eighteen months, Miles was diagnosed with spinal muscular atrophy (SMA), a rare, degenerative neuromuscular disease that would slowly rob his muscles of their strength. When he was diagnosed, we were told that SMA was the number-one cause of genetic death in infants, there was no treatment and no cure, and the progression of the disease was inevitable.

Since that earth-shattering diagnosis, our family has been in the boxing ring, fighting for Miles's health and consequently his life. Despite the circumstances, Miles has a brave, determined, and tenacious spirit. He's a fighter in every sense of the word, and if he is the tiger, then his journey has certainly awoken the tigress within me.

When you become a mother, there's something so natural, so innate, so instinctual about protecting your child. All those phrases—mama bear, dragon mother, etc.—hold some truth. We have an animal-like instinct to protect our children. But what happens when we can't protect them from the grips of a disease, disability, or disorder? What then?

That instinct to protect is still there, but what happens when the enemy we're facing feels unknown, uncommon, and insurmountable? For me, the commission was great, the stakes were high, and the emotions were extreme.

I wasn't prepared, I didn't feel equipped, and I knew nothing about raising a child with a disability. My son's diagnosis was the most devastating thing I've ever had to deal with in my life. The prognosis was cruel, and I was left in the shambles of my own emotions—yet my child needed so much that there was no time to waste.

Would I, and could I, rise to the challenge? My son certainly needed me to. He was eighteen months old, helpless, and living with a severe disease. But how would I do that?

There was only one way to find out: show up, willing to try.

That's what I had to do when Miles was diagnosed, and it's what I still do every single day. Though I am weary, I rise anyway to protect my child and give him the best life I am able, despite the circumstances we have been dealt. This journey threw me into a wild jungle I never expected and had never been in before. My inner tigress was awakened. My fierce fighter was summoned.

I believe that, like me, you have an animal, or fighter, within you, though you may not know it yet. Maybe you just received your earth-shattering diagnosis, and maybe you don't even feel like a person, let alone like a brave fighter or unintimidated animal.

I see you, friend. And I see a fighter within you. Believe me, she's in you.

You know what else I see within you? Love.

To become a mother is to answer a call to love.

It all starts with love.

From love. Because of love. For love.

When love calls, a mother answers. Love is what is calling you to rise up to do something that is bigger than yourself. Love is why you are reading this book.

Love is fuel. Love is power. Love is the most commanding, potent, moving, persuasive, forceful thing there is.

So, you already hold in your heart one of the greatest of all things to help your child—love! This love will allow you to do things you never thought you could do. When you question how you will do it, it's love that is the answer. When you wonder how you will rise again after another dark night, it's love that will get you out of bed in the morning.

We do it for love. And that, my friend, is everything.

There is something visceral and instinctual about this love, similar to that of a mother animal protecting her young. When you find out your child has an illness, there is a wild animal–like fury that unleashes within you, an inner primal passion that screams, "I must save my child!"

When my inner tigress was unleashed, she was filled with fiery fervor. I wanted to run up to the closest mountaintop and roar—roar for the devastation of my son's disease, for the desperation of our situation, for all that was being taken from him, for all the injustice I saw for all rare disease patients, and to let the whole jungle know that I was here and I just wouldn't stand for it.

When human beings are faced with something so unexpectedly life-changing and life-threatening as a rare disease, we also experience an element of sheer survival that kicks in. It happened to me one day. Somewhere, there in my desperation, the human will to survive kicked in. Somewhere in the middle of the sadness, confusion, and angst, something in me welled up: the fight in me. I could lie down, or I could stand up. I could let my son's diagnosis send me into a coma, or I could fight my way out of it. I still had two beautiful kids, an amazing husband, and a life to live. I needed to fight for Miles, who couldn't fight for himself. I needed to give my older son, Mason, a childhood despite our circumstances. I needed to enjoy my life with the man I loved.

You know what else happened? I got pissed off. The reality of SMA, which I was told upon diagnosis, was that it would rob my son of the strength his body needed. Other seasoned SMA moms also told me it would rob us of our time, our finances, our relationships, and on and on. But I decided right then and there that it wouldn't rob us of everything. Enough is enough, SMA! I would fight against it robbing my older son of his childhood. I would fight against it robbing my husband and me of our love for each other. I would fight against it robbing us of our dreams, our joy, our sense of humor, our faith, and our hope. This was still our child. This was still our family. This was still our life.

And this is still your life too.

Mama, you've been thrown into this unfair fight, and I know you're heartbroken, overwhelmed, and confused. The rare mama plight can spring forth all kinds of emotions within us and without our say—rage, devastation, confusion, numbness, shock, angst, anxiety, fear, frenzy. And it all stems from that deep love that's underneath it all. These emotions are either going to be our fuel or our foe. So, we are going to tap into them and channel them for good. They are going to be our power source. That inner animal/fighter that is unleashed can be our biggest ally if we channel her effectively.

> We're going to use all of that passion and fire, and transform it into meaningful action for our children.

So, you know what we're going to do? We're going to use all of that passion and fire, and transform it into meaningful action for our children. We're going to take all that sadness, confusion, angst, anxiety, worry, and fear, and put it all into our tanks as fuel to become the mightiest fighters there are for our kids.

That's right. And I'm going to show you how.

But first, before we start, I think it's important that we just go ahead and call this what it is right from the outset. I promised you I would keep it real and tell you the truth, and the truth, as I see it, is that we just may be in the fight of our lives. This might be the greatest fight we've ever had to fight or will ever have to fight.

There, I said it. And why am I saying it? Because when you're thrown into this fight, I don't think anyone truly prepares you for what's ahead. There might come a point when you start asking yourself, *Why is this so hard? Am I doing this wrong? Is this even possible?* But maybe if someone just came right out and told you, "Listen, this is the fight of your life!," you would think, *Oh, okay, that explains it!*

You could at least wrap your head around it and know what you're up against. There's a saying in the mental health world: "If you can name it, you can tame it." So, I'm naming it right out of the gate so maybe we can start to tame it. I'm labeling it not to scare you but to prepare you. We need a framework for our minds to understand the task that is ahead. Let me break down why this might be the fight of our lives.

1. **We have been thrown into a ring we didn't ask to be in.** We didn't ask to be in this fight. We had no say in it. Many of us didn't see a rare disease diagnosis coming. We were expecting something else entirely. Many aspects of rare disease feel completely out of our control.

2. **We haven't been trained.** We haven't been given the right gear. We aren't conditioned. We don't know the moves and the techniques. Most of us have no idea what we're doing, and the learning curve is steep.

3. **It's an unfair matchup.** We are dealing with health, which is one of the most important aspects of life. The stakes are at the highest levels. Many of us are looking at scary statistics and facing unimaginable possibilities. Many of our children are dealing with life-threatening illnesses. We are standing in front of a significant opponent. As mothers, our mission is to protect our child, and yet we can't protect them from a rare disease diagnosis.

4. **The opponent threw the first punch.** The punch we don't see coming is the one that usually hurts us the most. Rare disease can come on strong and fast, leaving us little time to get our footing, block, and evade before we are forced to react, make decisions, and pursue life-saving counterpunches.

5. **It's hitting below the belt.** This is personal. These are our children. They are our hearts. They are the very things that we hoped for, prayed for, and dreamed about. This is our family. This is our future. If we don't step up and advocate for them, who will? There is an enormous amount of weight that comes with making decisions on behalf of someone else, especially when we so earnestly want to do our best for them.

So, here we are.

Up against the most daunting of opponents in a fight we never wanted to be in.

And now the question becomes: What are we going to do about it?

The answer, of course, is that we are going to fight. We love our kids, so there is no other choice. The *only* choice

> The *only* choice we have is to fall down, grieve, wrestle around with this diagnosis, accept it, rise up, and fight.

we have is to fall down, grieve, wrestle around with this diagnosis, accept it, rise up, and fight. Yes, the commission is great, the challenge is unfair, and the opponent is hitting below the belt. And yes, this fight is going to ask things of us that just aren't right. Period. But we're going to dig deep within ourselves and do it anyway.

My guess is that because you're reading this book, you're ready to get busy fighting. But one of the huge hurdles about this fight that we rare mamas face is that before we've even had time to process all the emotions surrounding *being in* this fight or to prepare for it, we are off to fight the fight. Rare diseases, by their very nature, throw us into crisis, chaos, and confusion. We're often forced into a very reactionary fighting mode because health concerns afford us no time to waste. So out of love for our child, we start fighting with all our hearts. Now, as I said, fighting with heart and passion is one of the most important tools of a fighter. It's the fuel that comes from deep within, and it's powerful. All great fighters fight with heart.

But it's not the *only* tool that's needed for a successful fight. In fact, fighting with just our heart will only fuel us for so long before our bodies can't keep up. If we come out swinging just with all heart, we are going to run out of stamina, and we are going to feel the effects mentally, physically, and emotionally.

Like any good fighter, we need training, we need to learn some skills, and we need a game plan. That's where this book comes in.

Great fighters possess skills such as speed, power, agility, accuracy, and endurance. In addition to those skills are mental qualities like intelligence, confidence, courage, and guts. And don't forget about flexibility, adaptability, and resilience. We're going to work on all of these.

First, we're going to explore the mindset that's needed for the fight of our lives. Fighting is often called a mental game. We must master our minds and be aware of our emotions so we can *use* them productively.

Next, we're going to figure out our strategy. We need to spend a little time planning and plotting our attack. Rare diseases unleash chaos on life. We need to take back some semblance of control (even if it's just the illusion of it) by figuring out a game plan for how to move forward.

Then we are going to learn the moves and master the skills. There is a lot to learn in the world of rare disease. I'm going to show you all the things we rare mamas have learned along the way, things you can often only learn from living in this rare world. I want to level the playing field and arm you with everything I can so that you go into this fight informed. You can read this book from start to finish, skip around if needed, or read only the parts you need right now and pick it back up when you need another part. However you decide to use this book, I'm going to show you all the moves.

Last, we are going to muster up every last bit of moxie and grit and show 'em what Mama's made of.

Welcome to the training ground for the fight of your life. Will this be hard? Yes. Will it be worth it? Also yes.

Friend, I have so much to tell you. But one thing I can say with absolute truth right now is that though distress is where you may start, prowess is where you'll end up.

Prowess is:

- Skill or expertise in a particular activity or field
- Bravery in battle[1]

Though powerless is how you may feel at the beginning, empowered is what you'll become.

Empowered is:

- Having the knowledge, confidence, means, or ability to do things
- Making (someone) stronger and more confident, especially in controlling their life[2]

Believe it, mama. You are going to become the expert of your child, you're going to become confident and capable, and you're going to show bravery in battle.

Are you ready to awaken your inner animal and unleash your fierce fighter? Are you ready to train for the fight of your life?

Lace up your gloves and meet me at the ring.

Rare Mama Truth

We're mostly all love and light unless
you mess with our children—then we're
all kinds of scary and savage.

CHAPTER 2

Acknowledging Distress

"We must embrace pain and
burn it as fuel for our journey."

KENJI MIYAZAWA

Before we can go forward with our fight, it's essential to know where we are and where we've been. Before we can get to prowess, we must examine our distress. And while this may not be easy or pretty, it's a critical step in the training ground. Distress is another emotion we will use to fuel our fight. So let's just talk about the complicated subject of distress for a moment, shall we?

Getting a confirmed diagnosis that delivers the type of news you never wanted to hear is one of the hardest things to go through in life. No one is prepared. Getting the news that something is wrong with your child comes with an entire life shift. You start out with all these hopes and dreams of the life you will give your child, only to have those dreams disrupted by something completely beyond your control.

The most stressful life events, according to the Holmes and Rahe Stress Scale, are 1) death of a spouse or child, 2) divorce, 3) marital separation, 4) detention in jail or prison, 5) death of a close family member, 6) a major illness or injury, and 7) marriage.[1]

So there it is. A major illness is one of the top stressors of life. When that illness is deemed *rare* or complex, another layer of stress and anxiety is bolted on top of it. *Rare*, by its very definition, can bring up feelings of aloneness and isolation. That doesn't mean we would feel any less grief about a diagnosis that is more well known or that a more well-known diagnosis would be any less challenging to manage. It's just that when we're delivered alarming news and don't fully understand what that news means, the uncertainty and fear are exacerbated. Many of us didn't even know our child's disease existed, let alone anything about it, until they were diagnosed.

Like me, you've probably had your own heartbreak and experience with distress over your child's rare disease diagnosis. I don't know exactly where you are on your journey, but I'll share what catapulted me into being a rare mama and my experience with distress in order to give you some perspective of my road.

OUR STORY

After I married my soulmate, Tony, we enjoyed our married years together, traveling and working, and waited five years to have our first child. Mason was born healthy and happy. When Mason was almost two years old, we had our second son, Miles. Miles hit all his milestones until it came time to stand and walk; that's when we realized he wasn't able to bear weight on his legs to pull up to stand and take steps. After six long, hard months of testing, Miles was diagnosed with spinal muscle atrophy (SMA). SMA affects the motor nerve cells in the spinal cord and robs people of physical strength, taking away the ability to walk, eat, and even breathe. At the time, it was the number-one genetic cause of death for infants under the age of two.

At the time of Miles's diagnosis, we learned that not only was there no treatment or cure, but also that Miles would inevitably get weaker over time. In addition, the disease often caused respiratory complications that proved fatal for some children. One in fifteen thousand babies have SMA, and one in fifty people are carriers.[2] The fact that SMA is a genetic disease came as a shock to us, as it does to most families whose children are diagnosed with it; no one in our family had ever been affected by it, nor had we even heard of it. Through testing, my husband and I were both confirmed to be carriers, and two carriers conceiving have a one-in-four chance of the child having SMA. Mason wasn't affected, and we later discovered that he isn't even a carrier. But Miles was confirmed to have SMA type II.

Although the weakness affects Miles's entire body, it is more pronounced in his trunk and lower body. Because of this, he wears leg braces, and his main form of mobility is a wheelchair. At the age of two, Miles began to regress and started to lose muscle strength. After much research, we got him involved in a clinical trial for a drug treatment that was showing promise. He started this at two and a half years old, and after receiving the drug, he began to regain some of the strength he had lost.

In December 2016, the drug Spinraza was approved by the FDA and became the first-ever approved SMA treatment. Miles continues treatment with it today, and although the long-term effects are not yet known, it has been keeping the progression of the disease at bay. We don't know what the future holds, but we're taking it day by day and moving forward with hope.

So that's our story. But it's not the whole story. It leaves out the gritty details. I'll be downright honest: Writing about when my son was diagnosed, even years later, is still difficult for me. Bringing up all the emotions of "that" moment feels like a cumbersome, heavy lift. As hard as it is, I know it's important to recall this part of my journey because it's where I came from, it's what I worked hard to get through, and it was part of my path to healing. Sometimes we must acknowledge and honor our grief in order to move forward. So here's a look inside the grief that accompanied my son's rare disease diagnosis.

I still remember that day vividly. Six months into testing, the doctor did yet another test, but instead of coming back normal, this one came back abnormal. All my worst fears were confirmed in the blink of an eye. Yes, something was definitely "wrong." Then, we had to walk to another floor of the hospital to get a genetic blood test that would eventually confirm the doctor's suspicions of SMA. Time stood still. There was silence. Complete silence, except for the sound of my breathing and my footsteps walking down those halls to the lab.

As we approached the lab doors, my body's flight response made me want to run to the corner, coil up into a ball, and let tears explode from my eyeballs. It was just too much to bear. But that wasn't an option. I didn't want my son to see the fear in my eyes. I had to steady my gait, focus my gaze, take my child in hand, hold his arm down, and comfort him while he cried during the blood draw, all the while knowing that if the suspicions were true, this blood draw would be the least harrowing thing we'd be up against.

We waited three wretched weeks for the blood test to come back and confirm what I already knew in my heart. Of course, I had looked up the suspected disease, and everything about it rang true for my son. Learning that it shortened lifespan was the most horrifying thing I have ever read. Then came the bloodwork results and a confirmed answer of SMA. No treatment. No cure. Progression inevitable. I'd have to watch Miles slowly lose his strength. How cruel and unbearable could this be?

As the shock wore off, the pain set in. Grief washed over me like an all-out flood. I'm talking me on my hands and knees, on the cold bathroom floor, wailing. This period was truly the definition of *distress*. I felt it in every bone of my body and with every beat of my heart.

I grieved . . . for months. I would wake up and remember that my son was diagnosed with SMA, start crying, and fall back into bed. How would I live in a cruel world where this was true? Day after day, the same thing. Wake up, cry, and repeat, my husband and I holding each other as we wept. The pain was beyond anything I had experienced or imagined. And I couldn't change it.

I was shaken to my core. There was a crater-sized hole where my heart used to be. I went inside myself. I lived there in that fog for several months. Perhaps you wouldn't have known it if you saw me then, because I was busy making calls to get my son in to see all the specialists that he needed to see. And I was getting up and making breakfast because my kids still needed to eat. Paying bills, loading the dishwasher, cleaning out the cat litter box, and all the things, because life kept right on moving. But looking back now, *I* know. I was a shell of a person—grief-stricken, frenzied, in over my head, panicked, and desperate to save my son. Was there even any choice of any other way to be?

I wrestled with that diagnosis for months, flailing and grasping for anything and everything that could help me comprehend my son's disease, straining to come to terms with it, fumbling for anything that could show me what to do, and wading through the emotions of being profoundly sorrow-filled for my son's new reality. All the while, Miles was looking up at me with innocent eyes and a bright smile on his face, an eighteen-month-old so eager for the world. How could his world include a rare disease?

It was the hardest time of my life.

Sound familiar?

I'll be honest: At the time, the only thing I wanted to do was get out of that grief period. I didn't like how it felt. But I learned later that this grieving period was crucial. I realize now that as I grieved, I was looking my son's new reality in the face. I was absorbing all that it meant and all that it entailed. As hard as it was, I was wrapping my head around it.

> This shedding of the life we thought we'd have is the only way we can truly live the life we have been given.

The other thing the grieving process allowed for was letting go. I was letting go of how I thought things would be, the plans I had in my head for my son and our life, and the typical road I'd been counting on. Letting go is a necessary step in the process of acceptance. This shedding of the life we thought we'd have is the only way we can truly live the life we have been given.

When we experience a painful loss, grieving is necessary. It's a crucial step on the path to healing. The grieving period shouldn't be skipped over or it will well up and find us later. We have to deal with our grief directly. We either deal with it or we find ourselves still struggling with emotional pain years down the road.

That's why I thought it was vital for us to take time out to examine grief. According to *Psychology Today*, grief is the acute pain that accompanies loss.[3] It can come in many forms, including anger, denial, guilt, bargaining, and depression. However, recent studies show that most people will not necessarily progress through these stages in a specific order. Grief is now understood to be highly individualized and unpredictable. Grief obeys its own trajectory, and there is no timetable for feelings of pain after loss.

For some people, grief is a short-term phenomenon, also known as acute grief, although the pain may return unexpectedly at a later time. However, other individuals may experience prolonged grief, also known as complicated grief, lasting months or years.

It is not possible to avoid suffering altogether. In fact, attempts to suppress or deny grief are just as likely to prolong the process while also demanding additional emotional effort. If you haven't already, give yourself the time to truly grieve. Release your grief so your heart can begin to heal.

Mama, can I tell you something else? Be kind to yourself during this time. This is probably one of the most unprecedented times of your life. You may see yourself in a way you've never seen yourself. Personally, it was the first time I had seen myself truly shaken. I had been through difficult life events before, but none that I didn't think was a normal rite of passage or a thing I couldn't ultimately overcome. But this? This felt outside of normal. This felt like I was hit by a truck. For the first time, I had no control over my emotions, which were spinning wildly out of control. I walked like a zombie through those first months.

This, too, is all normal. This is what it looks like when a body, heart, and soul are turned entirely upside down. It looks messy. And that's okay. So give yourself a little grace during this time. It will look a bit different for each of us. There is no "right way" to do this. So let yourself process, feel, grieve, understand, and make your way.

All the feelings of distress you've felt are understood here. Among rare mamas, you're a fellow sister experiencing the piercing, time-stopping, ground-shaking moment of receiving a rare disease diagnosis. Most of us mothers can recall the exact details of the diagnosis day more vividly than we might like.

Although I can still feel the sting of the diagnosis phase in my heart like it was yesterday, I have moved forward since my child's rare disease diagnosis. I've traveled through many stages. What I've come to find is that I've evolved. I want you to hear this, mama. Right

> The way you feel at the beginning is not necessarily how you will feel forever. You will adapt.

now, right where you are, it changes. Your feelings will not remain this way forever. No doubt this is a hard road, but how you deal with it will change as you move along its path. The way you feel at the beginning is not necessarily how you will feel forever. You will adapt. If you're at the beginning of your journey, it may be difficult to believe this, and I understand if you have no idea what I'm talking about or think I'm flat-out crazy. But as I look around at all my rare mama friends, I see how they have evolved and grown since their child was first diagnosed. It's a process that happens over time.

Many of us come to understand that grief can take many forms along this journey—grief over missed milestones, anticipatory grief, and even ambiguous grief. I've learned to recognize its shape, notice what triggers it, and find ways to cope. Just as importantly, I've discovered that grief doesn't cancel out joy. I can mourn one part of my child's story while feeling deep gratitude for another. That truth has been one of the most surprising and healing parts of this path. I hope it is comforting to know up front that grief is important and there is potential for your grief to change over time.

Now that we've examined where we've been—our distress—let's get to where we're going—prowess.

Onward.

Rare Mama Truth

Grief doesn't ask for permission. It shows up unannounced, like on a regular Tuesday in the school pickup line. But I breathe, feel it, and keep going—because pickup waits for no one.

CHAPTER 3

Mastering Mindset

"The thing about being brave is it doesn't
come with the absence of fear or hurt.
Bravery is the ability to look fear and hurt in
the face and say move aside, you are in the way."

MELISSA TUMINO

Because battles are often first won in the mind, the mind is where we must begin. Every action, and every reaction, starts with a thought. It all begins in the mind. Your mindset is a set of beliefs that shape how you make sense of the world and yourself. It influences how you think, feel, and behave in any given situation. Research shows that mindsets play a significant role in determining life's outcomes. By understanding, adapting, and shifting your mindset, you can improve your health, decrease your stress, and become more resilient to life's challenges.[1]

As mentioned earlier, successful fighters prepare not only physically but also mentally. The mental state of a fighter can play a big role in outcomes. A great deal of mental capacity is required in what's ahead, and rare mamas have to be prepared mentally to take on the challenge. It's essential that we make our mental preparations and get our head game strong before we get started. Let's explore the mindsets that can help us in the rare disease fight.

GROWTH MINDSET

After decades of research, world-renowned Stanford University psychologist Carol S. Dweck, PhD, discovered a simple but ground-breaking idea: the power of mindset. In her book *Mindset*, she shows how success in school, work, sports, the arts, and almost every area of human endeavor can be dramatically influenced by how we think about our talents and abilities. People with a *fixed mindset*—those who believe that abilities are fixed—are less likely to flourish than those with a *growth mindset*—those who believe that abilities can be developed.[2]

Dr. Dweck found that people's theories about their own intelligence have a significant impact on their motivation, effort, and approach to challenges. Those who believe their abilities are malleable are more likely to embrace challenges and persist despite failure.[3]

Mama, you are diving into uncharted territories. Most of us don't know how to fight the rare disease fight. We don't know how to be a parent of a child with a rare disease. Most of us don't comprehend the science behind our child's condition. Most of us don't inherently know best care practices. Most of us don't understand medical therapies and interventions. All of these things must be learned.

As we are thrown into this new ring with no training, no gear, and no technique, it is vital that we believe we *can learn* the skills needed to navigate a rare disease. We must be open to growth. We must adopt this growth mindset if we're going to move from feeling powerless to empowered.

This growth mindset tells us that even though we don't understand all these things now, with effort and time, we will. We have the ability to learn what we need to know to help our kids. We have the opportunity to grow our knowledge. We have the capability to learn how to fight the rare disease fight.

> We can learn the skills needed to navigate a rare disease. We must be open to growth.

If you adopt a growth mindset, in a sense you'll be saying, "There is a big obstacle in front of me, and though I don't understand everything about it yet, I'm confident I can learn all I need to know and ultimately help my child." Perseverance and resilience are produced by the growth mindset.

When I started out trying to learn about my son's rare disease, much of the information I was gathering was way beyond my competency. I certainly didn't understand biology, anatomy, genetics, and all the other specialties that come with a rare disease. But with time and effort, I learned. I studied information until I had a true understanding of my child's disease—or at least enough of an understanding to allow me to care for him. The more knowledge I gained, the more my belief that I would be able to take care of my son grew. This growth mindset helped me increase not only my knowledge but also my confidence.

One of the first things you're going to need to do to help your child is to learn all you can about their disease. But first, you must believe you can. And, mama, trust me, you can and you will. Believe it or not, after a while you'll know more about your child's disease than many healthcare providers—no joke. But it all starts here with the growth mindset and believing you have the ability and are capable.

COURAGE MINDSET

Next, you'll need to adopt a courage mindset. A courage mindset is taking action even when you're afraid. Action generates courage; courage is not a prerequisite for action. The way you move from fear to bravery is through action.

Fear is often out of our control. It's a biochemical response to a presented situation. But choosing action? This is most definitely in our control. Action is the antidote to fear.

Listen, let's just acknowledge something up front. Rare diseases come with many fear-inducing circumstances and situations. However, fear itself is not the enemy. Fear is a valid human reaction to the situation we're in. Being fearful doesn't make us weak; it makes us human. So it's not about whether or not to acknowledge that you feel afraid. It's about acknowledging the fear and then choosing what you're going to do with it. You can either be motivated by it or debilitated by it. It can fuel you or freeze you.

Now, let's talk about the opposite of fear. Let's talk about courage for a minute. The very definition of courage is the ability to do something that frightens you. The definition is not to be fearless or without fear. The definition suggests that yes, you are human, and yes, you feel frightened, but you do the frightening thing anyway.

Courageous people aren't superhumans whose superpower is the ability to not feel fear. They are not wired differently. They have simply made the choice to respond to fear with action. Every single one of us can make this choice.

Most strong and courageous leaders will tell you that when faced with a difficult situation, it wasn't that they didn't feel fear. It's that they didn't let fear stop them. They did the hard thing anyway. They did it scared. That's the difference between someone who is courageous and someone who is not. The courageous person did the thing they were afraid of despite being afraid.

Courage is like a muscle that needs to be used and stretched in order to grow bigger. Courage comes from pushing ourselves outside our comfort zone and outside the unknowns. Courage comes from "doing."

This entire rare disease journey is filled with unknowns. In fact, most of what we're facing is new and unknown. And our comfort zone? Sayonara, sister! We definitely left that a long way back. To face these things that have been put before us, we're going to need to exercise our courage muscle. We are going to need to take action.

This is how it works. If you don't have courage now, believe me, you eventually will. How? Because that's what happens along the way when you're getting stuff done. Stuff's gotta get done. Who's gonna do it? You are. And somewhere along the way, there you are doing it. There you are being strong without even thinking about it. Because you're doing what needs to be done.

You're taking your kid to undergo anesthesia for a test or a treatment. Standing up to educators who tell you they're not going to provide what your child needs at school. Appealing insurance denials for necessary treatment or equipment. Why? Not necessarily because you're feeling strong or courageous, but mostly just because you want your child to have what they need. You're doing hard stuff because it needs to get done. Then you've done it, and you feel a little stronger and more courageous because you know you did it, and that means you can do it again.

By choosing action and doing the hard things anyway, you will be cultivating courage. Your courage will grow with every action you choose.

If you choose this courage mindset over and over again, before too long, some of your fears will subside. Over time and over the years, you may face scary situations again and again, but I bet you start to feel less afraid of them. It's not that the situation you're facing doesn't warrant fear; it's that you'll start to know deep inside that even though it's scary, you can do it anyway. You've done it before, so you'll do it again.

The fearful situations may not cease altogether, but you'll be better prepared for them. You'll know from experience that you can get through them. One day you'll look up and your courage will surprise you. You'll realize you have become a brave person, evidenced by all the hard and courageous things you've done. It will come from the actions you've taken.

> One day you'll look up and your courage will surprise you. You'll realize you have become a brave person.

Don't wait until you stop feeling afraid to start the thing, whatever the thing is. Do not wait. Start anyway. Take action.

You know what else? Your well-being depends on it.

Around every corner of this journey, there may be something new to figure out or some obstacle to overcome. What will you do? Will you keep growing? Will you let them push you forward?

This is a choice you must make. If you choose to let those obstacles push you forward to take action and be brave, you are in a sense choosing not to be a victim. A victim mentality rests on a couple of key beliefs, including that bad things happen and will keep happening and any efforts to create change will fail, so there's no point in trying. This type of mentality can negatively affect your entire physical and mental well-being.

What if by choosing action, what you are really choosing is possibilities? What if your actions and steps are opening up doors for new outcomes and possibilities for your child's disease? What if doing the very hard thing makes life easier and better in the long run?

Instead of being immobilized by fear, what if that fear catapults you into new possibilities? What if you let it push you into new territories that yield new results?

Take all your heartache and all your angst and put it into action. See where that action leads. See what you can set into motion. See what doors you can open.

When you feel too fearful to take a step, remember your *why*. Your *why* is the reason you're doing the hard thing. You're taking hard steps forward to help your child. I know your heart aches that your child has to go through this. I know you'd do anything to help them. I know so much of this journey feels out of your control. But this is the part you *can* control. You can decide right here and now that your fear is not more important than what needs to get done for your child. Tell your fear to take a back seat. Your child's needs are *way* more important.

I'm sure you've heard about powerful things mothers have done in order to help their child. We all know the story of the mother lifting up a car to save her baby. When it comes to our children, don't mess with mama! So when fears start creeping in, or when you're doing a scary thing, remember you're doing it for your child and for the sake of their health.

I cannot believe how many things I have done while rattled with fear. I have sat with Miles through painful procedures and surgeries. I have asked big, hard questions. I have stood up to experts and authorities. It's actually quite surprising when I think about it, but it was what my child needed, so I did it. I did it scared.

And all the while I felt the physiological responses to fear. I felt my heart pounding. I felt my palms sweat. I felt my stomach tie in knots. I felt weak in the knees. I have also experienced the emotional symptoms of fear. I have felt my mind racing and unable to focus. I have felt scattered and have forgotten important things. I have felt unnerved, short, and fatigued.

But I did it anyway. Because I didn't want my son to go without something he needed because I was too scared to ask for it, or fight for it, or to do whatever hard and scary thing was required to obtain it.

It wasn't easy, but I am so glad I chose action over fear. I'm telling you without a shred of doubt that it often set in motion things that directly benefited my child's health. Believe me, I am not taking credit for all the amazing things that have come from his exceptional team of doctors and therapists and from the researchers and companies that worked on treatments for his disease. But I am saying that as his parent, choosing action was a contributing factor in helping him.

Besides our child's physical health, you know what else depends on this? Their emotional health. True character is often determined not when life is easy but when it's hard. Adversity is most certainly an opportunity for growth, and it's often a teaching opportunity.

Our children are watching. They are looking to us to see how we will handle hard circumstances. We are modeling behavior. When faced with a situation, children often look to us parents to know how to respond. If they feel scared, they will look to us to see if we are scared. If they are upset, they look to us to see if we are upset. They are picking up cues from us all the time. They are watching. They are taking it in. They are learning. This is an opportunity to teach courage. This is our chance to let them know, "Yes, Mommy feels a little scared inside, but I am going to go do the hard thing anyway."

Do you wonder how your child will handle all that is before them? Do you fret about how they will deal with medical procedures, being different from other kids, being dependent on help during their life? This is the time to *show* them! Use these opportunities to show them how to face these obstacles. Use these situations to admit feeling fearful and model being courageous and strong in the face of fear.

Miles has to face scary medical procedures often. It's a part of his regular life. His disease requires continual medical interventions that include pokes, prods, surgeries, injections, and on and on. In addition to all the medical aspects of his disease, there are also many emotional aspects that require him to be brave too. He is one of only a few children in his entire school of more than sixteen hundred children who is in a wheelchair. He has to do things differently than his classmates. He has to face obstacles and challenges every single day.

The reality is that throughout his life, he's going to need to be brave and courageous to meet all that is in front of him. I pray that he learns this important virtue. But the best way I can teach him is by showing him. The best way for him to learn bravery is by seeing Mom admitting to being afraid but then choosing to be brave in my actions. More than any words I can say to him, modeling the behavior I want him to learn is what will make the biggest impact. I think to myself, *What do I want him to learn from me? How do I want him to face his fears?* Often, I choose to be brave and show courage in the face of my fear so that one day he will make this choice too.

A very smart writer I admire said, "Brave moms raise brave kids." I absolutely love this. And I absolutely believe it to be true. What will you teach your child? What will you teach your family? What will you teach yourself?

And can I just add my own two cents to that quote? "Brave kids raise brave moms."

I now see my son being brave in many, many situations. When I see him being brave, he gives me courage. It's a powerful circle.

We teach each other.

Winston Churchill said, "Fear is a reaction. Courage is a decision."[4]

Don't let fear win out. Don't let it delay you, slow you, or stop you altogether.

Adopt a courage mindset.

HOPE MINDSET

Hope. It's not just a word. It's a mantra. It's my family's mantra. This mantra has seen me through my darkest days. It's given me the will to hold on. It's let me see possibilities when there supposedly weren't any.

What are your hopes? Hold on to them. Let them guide you. I still hope there will be a cure for my son's disease. It'll either come true or it won't, but that hope wakes me up in the morning and nudges me to march on. Maybe I'm a dreamer. Maybe I'm a fool. But so what? Those hopes have helped my family, and they have helped Miles.

And you know what else? Decades ago, some parents put their hopes in motion and started an organization for SMA that funded critical research for treatment, and now years later, my son is on one of those FDA-approved treatments. This treatment may not have helped their own child in time, but they kept on hoping and fighting, and I thank God for them and their hopes. They made change happen, and our family is being blessed by it years later.

Nothing extraordinary was ever achieved with small hopes.

About a year after Miles was diagnosed, I had a conversation with one of his providers. He was telling me the direness of Miles's diagnosis—all the things that Miles wouldn't be able to do and all the difficult things that would happen. He applied this approach to the care he was providing as well, expecting the worst. Though we were new to the diagnosis, I had to lay some ground rules right then and there.

I told him that I had met with the geneticist and the neurologist and had been to the conference for my son's disease, so I knew the harsh realities we would face. I had researched the disease, so I knew the numbers, the statistics, and the long-term prognosis. I lived, ate, and breathed it. But despite all that, we had decided to approach our life with hope. Hope—not from a standpoint of ignorance, naivete, or blindness to the situation before us—but hope despite our situation. A hope that left room for possibilities. I told him I wanted our future conversations to have that hopeful outlook because that's how our family needed to approach life in order to thrive and not just survive. I drew a line in the sand that day.

We never had that type of dismal conversation again. It's not that we ignored the realities; it's that we still explored the possibilities rather than dismissing them as being pointless. This provider watched as a new SMA treatment came on the market and my son defied the odds time and time again. The outcome played out very differently than the foregone conclusion that was expected. The beautiful thing is that I think watching this unfold gave this man hope too.

I guess what I'm trying to share with you right now is that science and specialists can be wrong. Now that I'm immersed in this rare mama world and have spent time and heard countless rare mama stories, I know how many times parents were given no reason to hope. And I am thankful that parents and mamas are stubborn and didn't pay attention and decided to hope anyway. Because I've heard story upon story about providers being wrong. Listen, it's their job to tell us the harsh realities, facts, statistics, knowns, prognoses, and often the worst-case scenarios. It's part of the job. But that's not always how it unfolds.

I've heard thousands of stories about different outcomes. My son's story is one of them. So it's important that even though you may have conversations that leave you without hope, you choose it anyway. I tell you this not to give you false hope, because I do want you to understand the realities and be grounded in facts and information, but I tell you this so that you can stay open to new possibilities and to pursuing new options. This is part of your job as the parent of your child. As mamas, we need to stay open and hopeful for our children so we can chase down new leads and be open-minded to alternative approaches.

The dictionary's definition of *hope* is

1. a feeling of expectation and desire for a certain thing to happen

2. a feeling of trust[5]

Someone once asked our family for our definition of *hope*. My definition of hope is "putting on your sunscreen even though the forecast calls for rain."

Our forecast called for rain. Our forecast called for gray, dark, damp, wet, uncomfortable days when we didn't want to get out of bed. Our forecast called for puddles and mud and muck.

And yet the sun has shone. Some days, it shines so brightly that we put on our sunglasses and swimsuits and go to the beach.

Hope is a beautiful thing that allows for miracles, possibilities, options, opportunities, chances, and the unexpected. And really, isn't that what we all need right now?

Maybe you're afraid to get your hopes up too high and have them knocked down. I can appreciate that. We all feel the need to protect our hearts, as they have already been broken by a rare disease diagnosis. But, mama, one of the most important things I can advise to you is to keep hope alive. It's another choice among many you will face about how to live your life despite your circumstances, despite the inevitabilities, despite the facts and the statistics.

> If we have hope, our responses look much different than if we don't. Hope shifts our choices and actions.

When we look at our current circumstances, perhaps we have reason to feel hopeless and weary. But just because there may be reasons to forego hope doesn't mean we should. Hope may not transform our present situation immediately, but it will change our response to it. Hope isn't about being unrealistic. It's about opening ourselves up. Having hope will allow us to respond with creativity and openness. This has the potential to shape outcomes. If we have hope, our responses look much different than if we don't. Hope shifts our choices and actions. It's a mindset that embraces the possibility of positive change.

Another thing hope can change? Us. We may not be able to change our circumstances, but we can change ourselves. Hope is the response to difficult situations that can make things better because it can make us better. Darkness and difficulties test us to no end. If we choose hope over despair, it can be the catalyst for the highest good. Hope is energizing. Hope believes in what it cannot yet see. Hope believes in something higher, something more. It can help us reach our highest self.

Yes, your heart is aching, and yes, you have every right to feel bitter and burned. You may have more than enough reasons to feel despair instead of hope, but let me tell you, friend, hope is exactly what you need. It is the antidote to fear, despair, and defeat. Against all odds, keep hope in your heart, choose it as a mindset, and you may be surprised by the light that it shines for the journey ahead.

Growth, courage, and hope is the mindset mix I'm recommending for rare mamas. A three-pronged mental mélange through which you will filter all your moves.

Now that we've mastered our mindset, it's on to fill our minds with knowledge. One of mama's best powers is her brain power!

Rare Mama Truth

My mindset? Setting my mind
on not losing my mind.

PART II

Strategies for the Rare Fight

CHAPTER 4

Acquiring and Tracking Information

"Knowledge is love and light and vision."

HELEN KELLER

Part of the terrifying nature of rare diseases is that they're unknown. And what's the best way to battle the fear of the unknown? Make it known. The obvious first step is to learn everything you can about your child's disease. Go out and get the information you need to understand, and make it your mission to fill up with as much information as you can.

Once we've adopted a growth mindset, we believe that we can and will become experts on our child's rare disease. The way to become an expert is to start learning, researching, observing, looking for clues, tracking information, sharing information, and connecting with various providers. This will allow you to have informed conversations with your child's care team, build your confidence, and help secure your place as your child's best advocate. But the first step is to learn all you can. Information is your friend, and knowledge is power.

In truth, what *should* happen (and frankly, it makes me foam-at-the-mouth mad that it doesn't) is that when you're given your child's rare disease diagnosis, you're also handed every resource available that exists for rare diseases: the expert specialists, tertiary care centers, research organizations, foundations, patient advocacy groups, nonprofits, support groups—EVERYTHING! I mean, this is already ridiculously hard, so give a mama some help! Don't even get me started. This must be done better. But I digress. The point is unfortunately this is not how it plays out. We leave these excruciating "D-day" appointments with our jaws on the ground and our hearts right there with them, and we're usually not handed many leads. Fortunately, my son's brilliant neurologist handed us information on the organization for his disease, Cure SMA, upon diagnosis, and I am thankful she did. It was the exact lifeline we needed. But many families don't receive this type of assistance. They're left on their own.

Some of us are facing down ultra-rare diagnoses where only a handful of cases have been found worldwide, and therefore such organizations and foundations don't exist yet. This is the point where patients and their families could be introduced to the larger rare disease community. There are millions of us out here, and we are willing to help, as are phenomenal rare disease organizations created for this very reason. But they can't help if a family doesn't know they exist.

So, since we are dealing with rare diseases and information that isn't readily available, you're going to need to do a boatload of research. Yes, that just got piled onto your plate too. I know, mama, it's just not right. But what I'm trying to tell you is that, when you leave that appointment, no matter what is said about what exists or doesn't exist, it's up to you to look for resources anyway. Sadly, whoever is handing you the diagnosis may or may not be as informed or up to date as one would hope. So, instead of just taking their word for it, or relying on what resources they know or don't know about, it's up to you as your child's parent to go and track down whatever information you can find to inform you and guide you forward.

Does that make sense? What I'm saying is that no matter what is said at that appointment—"There's nothing you can do," "There are only a couple cases that we know about," "We just don't know enough about it," or "I wish I had more answers for you"—you're not going to take it at face value. You're going to say thank you, and then you're going to go home and research the hell out of it yourself. Every doctor, specialist, and geneticist will give you the best of their ability, no doubt. But when we're dealing with more than ten thousand existing rare diseases, it's just not possible for every healthcare provider to know the ins and outs of all of them.

That's where you come in. As the parent, and as the soon-to-be expert, you can make it your mission to know everything you can about your child's rare disease. You were made for this. This is what mamas do. Mamas who don't know a dang thing about lacrosse learn everything they can when their child tells them they want to try out for the lacrosse team. They learn everything they can about whooping cough when their child comes down with it. They sit and learn complex algebra when their child needs homework help in that subject. Mamas have been doing this since the dawn of time, and it's exactly what you're going to do right now.

> **Fill in the holes. Find the resources. Find the connections. Find others.**

So, no matter what you're told and given, go and do your own research. Fill in the holes. Find the resources. Find the connections. Find others.

If you start looking, you'll realize there are more rare disease resources available to you than you once thought. But at the beginning, it's going to feel like there's so much to learn and so much to do, and it all feels life-threateningly important. While this may in fact be true, the learning and the researching you're doing is going to serve you for years to come. It's a stepping stone to not only helping your kid, but also building your own confidence. Even more than that, it's going to allow you to feel less helpless over this situation. As you learn, you'll feel like you're taking an active, positive, forward step. Pace yourself, one step at a time, learning, growing, and developing into the expert that I'm certain you're going to be.

Here are a few thoughts on gathering information.

LOOK IN UNEXPECTED PLACES

Your sources of information might come from unexpected places. One rare mama I know explained to me how she found information about her daughter's ultra-rare, only-one-hundred-cases-worldwide disease, in a research paper published online about that specific syndrome. After reading the paper, she looked up all the researchers on the paper and figured out how to get in contact with them. It turned out her geneticist knew one of the researchers, and this helped her navigate what to do next for her daughter's disease. She formed a relationship with that researcher and now swears by looking at research papers and recommends reaching out to researchers when you can.

Other parents have turned to posting online about their child's disease so that they can find other parents out there whose child has the same condition even if they're in another country. Many entities are now recognizing the need for robust databases to house patient registries for those with rare diseases to help congregate information, foster patient networking, and establish protocols. But in the meantime, until these databases are robust and comprehensive, you, as a parent, can essentially start building your own database and making your own connections. In fact, this is often how disease organizations and foundations are built. They start as grassroots efforts by patients and families of patients who want to connect and support one another, and they have a shared mission of finding treatment options.

BECOME A DETECTIVE AND GET SCRAPPY

In the face of little information, you'll have to put on your detective hat and do some digging to find what you need. One thing you'll learn on this journey is resourcefulness. There's just no way around it in the rare disease game. Sometimes the best you're going to get is a clue here and a clue there. You'll need to string all of these clues together to make some sort of sense of it all. If you don't get an answer in one place, look somewhere else. Don't give up. Chase down every lead. Keep digging, searching, and seeking.

Sometimes while you're digging and researching, you're going to hit dead ends and come up empty. Don't let that deter you. You may have to get a bit scrappy. You may have to figure out other creative ways to get information and get things done. Getting scrappy means having a strong, determined character that's willing to argue or fight for what you want, not taking no for an answer. Be resolute.

ASK QUESTIONS

You'll need to get comfortable with asking questions. Lots of questions—until you understand everything you need to understand. Ask those questions even when you think they may be ignorant or repetitive or annoying. And if you get an answer you don't under-stand, ask more questions until you do understand.

You're going to have many, many questions at the beginning of your journey. That's okay. It's your job—and your right—to ask questions and get them answered. You are your child's voice. Speak up, raise that hand, and learn to ask away. You'll do this at every step of the way, even years into your journey. Because as we all know, just when you think you've got things figured out, something will change. This is true for all parenting. We are going to become lifelong learners, question askers, and students of our children.

The year Miles was diagnosed, my husband and I attended a large SMA conference by Cure SMA. It was filled with information, and I learned more about my son's disease in two days than I had in the entire nine months before. But I also made it my mission. My husband and I showed up on time for every session, sat in the front row, and took notes. I was that annoying chick who raised her hand to ask questions at every break and every opportunity. I figured I was there to get information and I wasn't leaving that conference with any more questions in my head.

Become an incessant question asker.

It worked. When I left, I felt armed with knowledge. While there was still so much I needed to do, at least I knew *what* to do and how to get there. Having that knowledge lessened my anxiety. It allowed me to spring into action. The more answers I got and the more things I was able to get done, the more my anxiety subsided.

Become an incessant question asker.

LEVERAGE CONTACTS

Leverage your contacts. Who do you know? Do you have any friends or family members who are in the medical field or who know someone in the medical field? Do you have any friends or family members who know any physical or occupational therapists? Do you have any friends or family members who know a parent of a child with a disability, illness, or diagnosis?

When Miles was first diagnosed, even though his disease is rare, my mom knew a man at her church who had a daughter with the same disease. A friend of mine was friends with an occupational therapist in another city who worked with a child with SMA. The nurse at my OB/GYN's office knew a couple whose child had SMA. Yes, I was dealing with a rare disease, but once I put it out there, all these connections started to form, and I then had three mothers of SMA children I was able to speak to within the first few months of Miles's diagnosis. Those connections were a lifeline to me at one of the most difficult times—when it was all new. So ask around and see whether you can find any connections through people you know.

LEARN TO SPEAK THE LANGUAGE

I don't know about you, but I don't speak medical-ese. It's a whole new language to learn. You don't know how many times I sat in appointments saying things like "Um, slow down. Can you repeat that, and what exactly is that? What does that acronym stand for?" And all the while I'm thinking, *What are you even saying? Is this even English?* Mama, this learning curve is STEEP! Yikes! It can feel intimidating, overwhelming, and frustrating. And none of us like to be made to feel like a fool. If you can immerse yourself in this foreign language a little ahead of time on your own, it can certainly give you a leg up. When you dig around online and research to find information for your child's disease, use another tab to open an online dictionary where you can look up medical terms and jargon; that way you can absorb it in your own time until it makes sense.

This will allow for informed conversations with your child's team.

If you go into these meetings and appointments with somewhat of a basic understanding, it's going to allow you to take an active role in the conversation, ask important questions, and show the person across the table that you are involved. In turn, they will open up and give you more information. So all the time and effort you put in is going to yield even more information.

EMBRACE SOME UNKNOWNS

Even with as much research as you do and as much of a willing learner you are, there will still be unknowns. For a planner like me, that was one of the scariest things about the rare disease world. It still is. There are so many unknowns on this road that living with them has had to become a way of life. My son's diagnosis has no exact, set way the symptoms unfold; it's different for every person, so no one can tell me exactly what's going to happen or when.

Planning used to be what helped ease my nerves. I thought the better prepared I was, the less that could go wrong. But in the rare disease world, I've learned that I must live with uncertainty. You, too, will have to embrace that there's no way you can know it all. Just when you think you might know as much as you can, something will change. That's the way of the rare disease jungle. Unknowns surround us all the time. We're going to have to train our brains to live with them and forbid our minds to go what-iffing into those unknowns too deep or we'll just drive ourselves mad. Know as much as you can and understand that there will still be uncertainty.

BE KIND TO YOURSELF

Learning is hard and humbling. Can we just decide right now to grant ourselves some grace in this department? We're going to have endless information coming at us from every which way, it's all going to feel crucially important, and a lot of it is going to be emotionally heavy. So be kind to yourself as you learn. This will get easier, I promise. But at the beginning your brain will be on overload, and rightly so! Remember to allow yourself time to absorb. Little by little. Step by step, as you can. As you're able. With time and grace as you learn.

One day not too far down the road, you're going to be in awe of the knowledge you've amassed and grateful for the reassurance it's provided and the path it's widened. All this knowledge is going to be part of your power. Oh, how powerful you're going to become!

Here are some places to look for resources. For additional resources, visit raremamas.com.

- American Association of People with Disabilities
- Americans with Disabilities Act
- The ARC (advocacy for individuals with disabilities)
- Centers for Medicare & Medicaid Services (CMS)
- Children's Health Insurance Program (CHIP)
- Consortium for Citizens with Disabilities
- Council for Exceptional Children
- Developmental Disabilities Council
- Disability.gov
- Disability Rights Group
- Every Life Foundation for Rare Diseases
- Family Voices
- Federation for Children with Special Needs
- Genetic and Rare Diseases (GARD) Information Center

- Global Genes
- Medicaid
- The National Center on Birth Defects and Developmental Disabilities (NCBDDD)
- National Disability Rights Network
- National Dissemination Center for Children with Disabilities
- National Institutes of Health (NIH)
- National Organization for Rare Disorders (NORD)
- Patient Advocate Foundation
- Rare Disease Legislative Advocates (RDLA)
- U.S. Department of Education, Office of Special Education Programs (OSEP)
- U.S. Department of Health and Human Services
- Your children's hospital's social work services
- Your state's resources for children with disabilities

TRACK DATA

In addition to finding information, you're going to start recording information about your child. You'll become an observer, a collector, and a recorder of everything about your kid. Countless rare mamas I know say that this is useful for many reasons, including:

- It gives you a baseline.
- It helps you track changes over time that perhaps you can't see when you're too close or when you're looking every day.
- It provides hard data you can share with your providers to have informed conversations.

- Your child's healthcare team cannot be with your child day in and day out, and this allows them a glimpse of the daily impact of a disease.

- Sometimes nuances or cause/effect is only noticed when tracked over time and correlations can be made.

- Your child's symptoms will, of course, never present themselves on the day you have an appointment with the specialist.

- When you're in an appointment and can't remember an answer, you can refer to your notes.

- It's part of a proactive approach to learning about your child and becoming an expert.

- Because every child is unique, even if your child's disease is one of the more well-known diseases, the way your child presents can still be unique.

Listen, part of it might just be to help us feel less helpless about the situation, and really, that's okay with me too. I'll grab on to anything that helps in that department. Some mothers track daily, some weekly, and some as situations arise. Find what works best and feels right for you. This is another step to becoming an informed and educated parent. It will open some doors for you if you're able to come to an appointment armed with this information and it's not necessarily emotion but just observed facts.

You're going to track all your child's procedures, interventions, treatments, medications, therapies, equipment, etc. A few examples:

- On this date my child had a fever of this temperature.

- On this date my child had a seizure that lasted this long.

- After this procedure, my child experienced XYZ.

In a sense, you're compiling your own medical history for your child. You're offering important and relevant information that can help inform decisions and next steps.

In addition to sharing this information with your child's health team, you also can share and compare this information with other parents whose children have the same disease. If everyone is engaged in information-gathering and information-sharing, this helps the community to learn, test, and refine. Imagine if another parent was able to share with you what worked for their child with the same disease and you had the possibility of pursuing this as an option or vice versa. This is the power of information. Moreover, this is the power of parents with information.

You didn't know you were going to become a researcher and detective too now, did you?

Mama does what she needs to do!

Rare Mama Truth

Raising a rare kid turns you into a detective so relentless, even Sherlock would be like, "Whoa, chill."

CHAPTER 5

Creating an Organizational System

"With organization comes empowerment."

LYNDA PETERSON

O nce you've started gathering boatloads of information from researching, data tracking, and every appointment you've been to, you'll probably have paperwork piled up to the ceiling. Girl, it's time to get yourself a system. Now, why am I mentioning organizing to rare disease mamas who have no time? Because I know it will help you. I promised to offer practical tips for everyday life that would help you in rare disease parenting, and this is truly one of them.

Because there is so much information being thrown at you daily and so much paperwork that comes with everything you do, you need a system for organization. Without one, the feelings of over-whelm that many of us experience will be magnified. Establishing an organizational system may take a little time up front, but trust me, it's going to help you in the long run. Organization is your friend.

My family would laugh if they read this, because I love to organize. I love to make lists. I love to make binders. Give me a binder and a three-hole punch, and I'm in heaven. The truth is, it also comes out of a huge need for me. I have a terrible memory. When I read something, I can absorb it, but when it's delivered orally, I have a hard time with retention. So I always need to write it down.

I've also found it's hard for me to focus when everything feels scattered. Rare disease life can feel like one big scatter. As a defense against falling into the gaping hole of overwhelm, organizing helps me feel like there is some sort of system and order. Maybe it's just a control thing. Whatever, it helps me cope. Don't judge. I swear I have other more interesting outlets.

Here's the thing. Often, when you're sitting in doctors' offices, they're shooting out so much information, and it's all in a language you don't understand or haven't heard before. It all sounds foreign, and you're going to need to write it down so you can look it up later.

Here's another thing. The information you're receiving may be troubling. So instead of just listening and absorbing it, your body is having an emotional reaction as you're receiving it. When that happens, your mind starts to wander to unwanted places, and you don't hear much of what's being said. You're going to need to capture all this important information, and you're going to need to rely on something other than your memory to do it.

Also, during this time, your brain is going to be on overload. So many doctors, therapists, and specialists will be talking to you that it'll be almost impossible for your brain to hold and retain all those conversations and all that information.

One day after my son's diagnosis when I started getting busy "doing the do," as one amazing rare mama I know calls it, I had so much on my brain that I almost forgot to pick up Mason from school. I literally almost forgot (swear you'll never tell him this!). That's when I realized I was on overload. Literally. So much was floating around in my head that I almost forgot something so routine, obvious, and automatic in my day. That's when I said to myself, "Girrrl, you need to get it together!" I needed to pull it together before the whole dang thing came unraveled. So out came the binders, lists, notebooks, and spreadsheets.

But let's be honest, not everyone shares my love for organization. Here's the good news. Even if you're a complete disorganized mess (gasp!), there's still hope for you. It's really not that hard, and it makes a world of difference. Listen, sister, eight hundred little yellow sticky notes all over your house aren't going to cut it here. Here are some tips to help you level up your organization game:

GET A SYSTEM FOR CONVERSATIONS

Whether it's a notebook, a laptop, a recording device (make sure you get this one cleared first), or an app—get a system for recording information you receive during appointments. Record everything that is said. Remember, your memory can play tricks on you when you're being told information that causes an emotional reaction. Don't rely on your memory. Do yourself a favor and get it notated. Whatever you use will be the place that holds all the conversations so you can then refer back to them, and they're all in one place.

GET A SYSTEM FOR PAPERWORK

Paperwork piles, people! You will have paperwork piles for days. Every specialist and every doctor you see will give you copies of consents, discharge papers, visit notes, etc. Before you become buried under mounds of paper (just the thought of it makes me quiver), get yourself a system. Whether it's putting the papers in a binder, scanning them and digitizing them, or using an app that you upload to—you choose. Organize all the information according to the various categories or entities that interact with your child, including specialists, therapists, equipment, insurance, in-home health programs, school, and on and on.

GET A SYSTEM FOR YOUR CALENDAR

I'm sure you know by now that you're going to have a multitude of appointments. Our whole world must operate around all these appointments. We rare mamas laugh (or maybe scream) about how we live by our calendars. So you're going to need a calendar system.

I prefer a digital calendar that allows me to digitally invite my husband to the appointments and also allows me to schedule follow-up appointments when I'm out at an appointment. This

> Help yourself with the clutter and the scatter by having a system.

is what works for me. Use whatever you find most helpful for you.

The point of it all is to give your spinning mind a rest, get all the information out of your head and store it somewhere, and help yourself with the clutter and the scatter by having a system so you can easily find information and refer to it when needed. You actually, dare I say, may even like it! At the very least, it will save you from running around the house raving mad because you can't find that one flipping piece of paper that you put in an important place. It's one less thing to be stressed about, and at this time, that's exactly what you need.

Mama, get yourself a system.

Rare Mama Truth

When you see me coming, medical binder,
calendar, checklist, and highlighter in hand—
make way. Mama means business.

CHAPTER 6

Developing a Plan

"It takes as much energy to wish as it does to plan."

ELEANOR ROOSEVELT

Similar to organizing, I'm going to help you contain some of the chaos by planning. Planning is one of those things you either love or hate. You either think of yourself as spontaneous or as a planner. If you're spontaneous, maybe you worry that planning will take the fun out of being spontaneous. Mama, I hear you. But having navigated the rare disease road, let me tell you, friend, it's time to leave spontaneity to dinner plans and Saturday outings. Planning may not be sexy, but it will save your busy butt. When it comes to walking through this rare disease world, it's time to strap on your planning boots.

When you're thrown into the rare world and your to-do list is miles long, you're going to need a roadmap on how to get from A to Z. Coming up with a plan and a breakdown for how to get what you need done just may be your saving grace. I've heard countless rare mamas talk about this. At first their minds were running rampant wondering what to do, or maybe what to do *first*. Once they laid it out into a plan, they felt much better. It didn't change the harsh reality of all they had to do, but having a plan helped them feel empowered.

Formulating your plan of attack will help guide your steps, maximize your time, allow you to work more efficiently, keep you on track when your mind is in a fog, help you manage everything that is constantly being thrown at you, and keep your whole family on the same page about where you're headed.

You might be thinking, *I have no idea what I would even put in a plan right now. I still don't know what I'm supposed to do.* That's okay. My hope is that by the end of this book, you'll have some next steps and ideas for what you're going to go and tackle. The point I want to make is that a plan is going to equip you and empower you—at the beginning of your journey and all along its way.

> **A plan is going to equip you and empower you.**

If you've already got your plan in place, good for you! If you're a planner type of person and don't mind operating this way, then you've most likely already laid your groundwork and are chipping away. You can probably skip the rest of this chapter and head to the next. If you're not the planner type or don't have your plan in place yet, read on for a little coaching on why planning can help you on the rare disease road and how to become a planner.

The good news is that even though you may have never been a planner, it's a skill you can learn and acquire. I'm definitely the planner type. My former career even had it in my job title. I became accustomed to planning, and I relied on it as a way to get work done and manage stressful deadlines and projects. However, when I was hurled into the rare disease world, I didn't realize what an invaluable skill it would be in allowing me to navigate all that was before me. It has helped so tremendously that I want to share it with you and offer rare disease planning as a necessary tool for helping you navigate daily life.

Having a child with a rare disease comes with a list of specialists to manage. Those specialists come with numerous appointments, evaluations, paperwork, and follow-ups. Our children may also have therapies and equipment that need to be managed, as well as insurance and state programs to oversee. All of this may come on top of managing schooling and regular activities. Let's be honest, for children with a rare disease, even "regular" activities require more thought, considerations, and inevitably more time. Things take longer for families like ours. We need to build in more time for even the everyday and most normal of activities. With all the additional to-dos for rare disease parents and the extra time needed for regular activities, there doesn't seem to be enough time in the day to do it all.

Enter your plan.

To be able to complete whichever tasks you're trying to tackle and still be able to take care of the everyday necessities, you'll have to get *real* specific about how long regular activities take you and how much time the task you're trying to accomplish will require. Confucius once said, "A man who does not plan long ahead will find trouble at his door."[1] Girl, I don't want any trouble showing up at your door. Mama has enough to deal with. You want to know the key to staving off trouble at your door? Planning ahead!

You've probably also heard "If you don't have a plan, you plan to fail." I believe the more time you spend planning up front, the less overwhelmed you will be, the less burned out you will feel, and, ultimately, the more successfully you will accomplish the task you set out to do. Let's plan to succeed.

So how do you plan ahead?

1. Get it out of your head and down on paper.
2. Anticipate needs.
3. Ask what-if questions and consider worst-case scenarios.
4. Prioritize actions.
5. Schedule it on your calendar.
6. Build in a time cushion.
7. Review and adjust.

I'd like to illustrate this planning method with a real-world example to show you how this might unfold. Let's use the example of something many of us have to do: taking our children to many medical appointments and having healthcare insurance in place. Getting healthcare in place comes with many steps and can feel overwhelming. Many of us don't know where to start, and a lot of us don't have deep knowledge about the inner workings of insurance. So how do you tackle this task?

1. GET IT DOWN ON PAPER.

First, get everything that is running around in circles in your mind down on paper. If I can illustrate the inside of my head during times when I'm trying to figure something out, I would compare it to a circus. There are dogs barking and jumping through hoops; acrobats flying through the air; clowns walking by doing pratfalls and rolls, honking horns, and squirting water; and motorcycles doing death jumps in the Ring of Fear. All of this equals noise, noise, and more noise. It's complete chaos, and it needs to be wrangled before the contents under that circus tent blow the lid right off!

If your head is anything like mine, you're going to need to grab a pen and paper and write it down. Get the dogs out, the acrobats accounted for, and the clowns cornered. Once you've got that circus sequestered on paper instead of running rampant in your head, you'll free up space and your overworked mind might just be able to think again. This is a critical first step in rare disease planning.

For the example of seeking out healthcare for my child, some of the steps I need to take might include:

- Calling my employer or my spouse's employer and getting benefits information.

- Asking my social worker at my child's hospital or doctor's office about Medicaid.

- Going on my state's Medicaid website.

- Talking to that other woman in my town whose child has a disability.

- Looking at my state's website for children with disabilities and calling my county's healthcare office.

Write all these ideas and steps down so you don't forget them as they pop in and out of your mind. You're starting to make a working list of the items you will tackle.

2. ANTICIPATE NEEDS.

The next step in planning is to anticipate needs. Think about the activity or event on your plan. What needs will you have that day? What needs will your child have? What are the time elements associated with doing these tasks?

For example, let's say you discover that in order to obtain healthcare for your child, you will need to apply for Medicaid. The

Medicaid application is ten pages long and requires you to locate and include financial information. Realistically, you approximate that it will take you roughly three hours to complete the application (I can't remember how long it took; I'm just pulling this number out for example purposes). Where are those three hours going to come from? What is the deadline by which you must complete the application? What if your schedule doesn't allow you to be away from your child for three hours to complete this task? What then? You need a plan to get this done.

Your plan can look like finding childcare for a three-hour sitting and knocking this out all at once, or maybe it looks like you waking up an hour earlier (before your child wakes up) each day for three days in order to find the time to fill out the paperwork. I don't know exactly what works best for you, but you'll have to consider how you do your best work and then design it around that.

Here's the thing: If you leave it up to chance, you could be setting yourself up for frustration and even failure. Why not set yourself up for success? Why not come up with a specific plan on how to get that application done? This may require a little more work up front, but in the end, it will help you get things done more efficiently.

Make a plan for those three hours and anticipate the needs. The application says it will need household income information, tax return information, and employer information. Make a plan for gathering up all this information so when you have the time to sit down and actually work on the application, you have what you need. Also anticipate your child's needs. For example, what will they need for those three hours if someone else is watching them? Snacks, toys, medication, nap gear, etc.—pack that all up so they have what they need.

3. ASK WHAT-IF QUESTIONS AND ANTICIPATE WORST-CASE SCENARIOS.

Next, ask yourself what-if questions to try to consider things you haven't thought of that could possibly happen. What if the time you've arranged to work on this application is going to interfere with your time to cook dinner? Maybe you need to make dinner ahead of time that day. What if your child will start to feel anxious or start missing you? Maybe you better pack them their favorite lovey or movie. Thinking through the what-ifs will help set you up for success, especially when you're planning for bigger items like medical procedures and surgeries. This will help you be able to follow through with your plan.

Listen, some of these what-ifs may never come to fruition, but if they do, already addressing the questions will help you be prepared and not derail the entire thing you have been planning for and working toward. At the very least, they will help give you peace of mind. And, mama, couldn't we all use a dose of that from time to time?

4. PRIORITIZE ACTIONS.

Now that you've got everything dumped on paper, and you've anticipated needs and thought through all the what-if scenarios, you've probably got a lot of things scribbled all over the place. Filter through them, make some sense out of them, and put them in order. Prioritize your list of action items. Put these in chronological order of what needs to happen first, next, and so on. Put the most important things first. For example, when applying for Medicaid, have a list that includes finding all the financial information, scheduling childcare, making dinner ahead of time, packing your child's things, etc. Figure out what needs to be done first, put this at the top of the list, and make your way down through the tasks. Now you've got a prioritized plan that you can start chipping away at.

5. SCHEDULE IT ON YOUR CALENDAR.

Next, use your calendar and schedule these planning tasks. Take out your calendar and look for days and times you can add these to, and schedule them just like you would schedule an appointment. Now you have a defined time during which to tackle these items. Also, if it helps, you can work backward. If you know you have a deadline that, let's say, is in a month from now, you can look at that date on your calendar, then go back and schedule all the tasks that lead up to that date. If the Medicaid application needs to be turned in one month from now, you can schedule the weekly tasks that need to get done leading up to the application due date.

6. BUILD IN A TIME CUSHION.

Next, build in a little time cushion. We all have the best intentions for getting things done, but guess what? Life happens. I have had life happen to me too many times to count. Seriously, I could fill a book just on this alone. Almost every single time I'm planning for some big event or activity, something comes up at the last minute. I get sick, my child gets sick, my car has an issue, someone cancels, weather interferes, etc. It's almost comical when I look back on it. It's not comical at the time, though. At the time, I want to straight-out lose my mind. Seriously, at those times you would not want to cross paths with me in a dark alley. But what has saved me time and time again is that I was already prepared. I had a time cushion. So build that cushion into your rare disease plan from the get-go. Work ahead. Battle all these unknowns with advance preparation.

Listen, I know that much of life is beyond our control and we won't be able to plan and account for everything. Life is going to throw you things that were not built into your plan. But by preparing what you can, you will be one step ahead. You'll be in a much better place than if you didn't plan at all.

7. REVIEW AND ADJUST.

Last, take inventory. See how things played out and review how your plan worked. Where was it successful? Where did it fail? What did you miss? Take mental notes for next time so you can incorporate some of what you were missing into the next item you have to plan.

Maybe you realize three hours was too long of a time chunk for you to sit at your computer or to be entering data. Maybe you became fatigued and it wasn't as efficient as you had hoped. So maybe you need to remember that and next time break it down into three hourlong chunks. Or maybe doing it at your house was too distracting. Maybe the dog was barking, you could hear your child in the next room, or you kept getting up to deal with the laundry. Maybe next time you need to plan to go somewhere outside your house to work, like a coffee shop or the library. Be an observer, always taking mental notes as to what will make you more efficient the next go-around.

In addition to the big events, having a plan will help you tremendously even for the most ordinary of things. The truth is, for families like ours, even the most commonplace things require extra steps and, in turn, extra time. It's hard for us to be on time and have everything we need accounted for. I now plan for even the most ordinary events, like attending a birthday party.

For Miles, there is extra equipment we always need to take with us, such as leg braces, his wheelchair, hand sanitizer, etc. After way too many times of forgetting something important for him, like the leg braces, or forgetting something for the event we are attending, like the birthday gift, or having all the things I needed but almost forgetting my kid (ha!), I realized we needed to get some type of system in place.

I became tired of arriving forty-five minutes late with everyone in our household completely frazzled and in a bad mood. I got sick of being at the party but not being able to enjoy it because we didn't think of what would happen if it rained. Or if it was flu season and some other kid at the party was snotting on everything, and there was nowhere for my kid to wash his hands easily before dessert. My son has to be extremely cautious about catching even the common cold, so I've learned to anticipate needs.

I anticipate the what-if scenarios. I list all the items we may need and pack them up the night before. I put things like gifts and extra jackets and clothes in the car. It always takes so much longer than I think. I estimate it will take ten minutes to grab all that stuff, but somehow, it actually takes thirty-five. But it's okay because it's the night before, and we aren't trying to rush out the door.

I also look up where the party is and how long it will take to get there, and then I build in an extra ten minutes for us to get out of the car and in the door because Miles is in a wheelchair, and this requires a lot of extra steps. By this time, I've usually decided it may not even be worth going to this stupid party. "Happy birthday! Your gift is in the mail." But going to events like these helps us to feel like we're still participating in the normal events of childhood. So when we have energy, our health is intact, and we have time to prepare for them, we try to attend.

The point is, I've taken these rare disease planning steps and applied them to normal life activities, and it has helped tremendously. You know what I've found? That a little planning ahead allows me to be spontaneous in the moment. I've learned that this pre-planning allows me to be present and able to enjoy myself and have fun when I'm actually at the event I'm there to have fun at.

Feel free to use planning as a way to get you through the biggest of big, scariest, hardest situations, like surgeries and procedures, as well as for even the seemingly ordinary and mundane, which we all know are still real time suckers for families like ours.

Sound exciting? I bet you just can't wait to try this beyond-fun planning activity! Oh, joy!

Like I said, planning may not be sexy, but it will save your busy butt time and time again. Planning has become my jam (I'm nerdy like that). Maybe it will become yours too. Maybe not. At the very least, you'll get your crap done, and then you'll have more time for whatever *is* your jam. Get your planning on!

Rare Mama Truth

Rare Motherhood takes 1) careful planning,
and 2) total flexibility as those carefully
laid plans come undone.

CHAPTER 7

Trusting Your Instincts and Becoming an Expert

"The expert in anything was once a beginner."

HELEN HAYES

Trusting your parenting instincts is a vital part of the rare disease parenting journey, but it doesn't happen overnight. It takes hard work, confidence, and a lot of listening to your intuition. But I wholeheartedly believe that, over time, every rare disease parent can find their path to being able to trust their parenting instincts. Let's dive into how.

I've had so many well-meaning experts tell me things that, by all facts and statistics, were true. The evidence, research, and past findings all showed them to be true. But I've learned there are always exceptions. I've watched my child be an exception. It was my job to decipher the information and decide what to do with it, it was my job to discern what I was going to believe and what I was not, it was my job to decide what I was going to accept and what I was going to question, and it was my job to decide how to live with realities and hope at the same time.

I've had a pediatrician tell me my son was fine and nothing was wrong. I've had an occupational therapist tell me I needed to accept my son's limitations and the bleakness of the future. I've had a geneticist tell me it was inevitable that my child's disease would worsen. Each of these opinions went against my parenting instincts, and if I simply believed what was said and took it at face value, my son and our entire family would be in a very different place right now.

If something doesn't feel right, question it. If something doesn't sound true, challenge it. Seek out answers, second opinions, specialists, and experts, because there are different ways to approach things. Science is changing all the time, and what once didn't exist may become commonplace in the future. Keep seeking information and answers and trust your parenting instincts. These same instincts may have given you inklings that something was going on with your child in the first place. Keep following those as you make your way forward. Around every corner, as your child changes and your circumstances change, follow those parenting instincts. You know your child better than anyone else.

> **If something doesn't feel right, question it. If something doesn't sound true, challenge it.**

You are the expert.

And if you don't believe this now, I bet one day you'll say, "Yep, that's right. I am!" I am the expert of Miles. You are the expert of _____ (insert your child's name). I'm sure one day Miles will grow up and tell me that I am not the expert of him, but for now I get to be the expert of something, and I'm going to revel in that for as long as I can.

Miles's diagnosis came with an entire team of doctors, therapists, equipment specialists, counselors, school aides, educators, etc. Perhaps your child's diagnosis also comes with many different specialists and therapists. Someone will need to manage all those providers, and that someone is you. Sound like a big job? Yes, it is at first, but then you'll find yourself naturally doing it. And there you have it: Soon you'll be the holder of the information.

Since information is power, having all the information and sharing it between the different providers will make you the expert on your child. You'll become a nurse, a counselor, a physician assistant (PA), a physical therapist (PT), an occupational therapist (OT), an orthotist, a psychologist, and so on. You'll learn about whatever you need to learn about to take care of your kid. But doesn't every mom anyway? It's just what moms do.

I love this diagram[1] created by Cristin Lind from Somerville, Massachusetts, for a talk she was asked to give on what it's like to raise a child with complex healthcare needs. She placed her son Gabriel, who has a rare genetic disorder called Coffin-Lowry syndrome, in the center of it all. Then she drew seventy colored ovals, each representing an area of care.

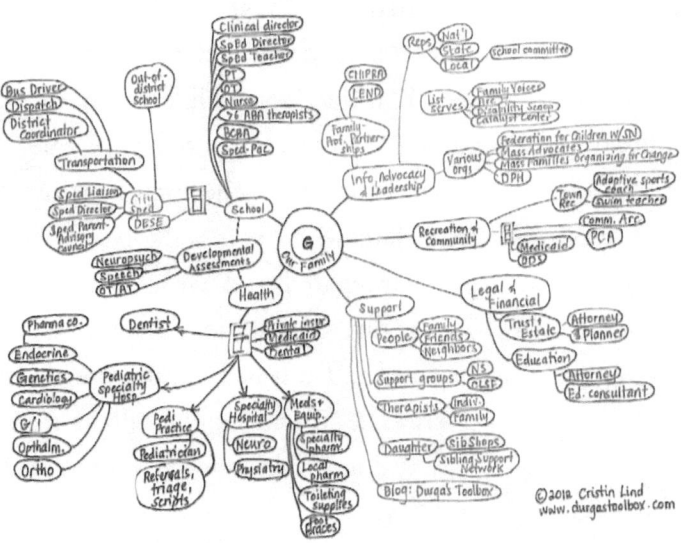

Here's another care map example that illustrates all the different entities that surround another child and family.

These care maps visually illustrate that your child is at the center of care. You'll be working with many different entities to provide the care your child needs, and each one will come with conversations, systems, paperwork, etc. Your job will be to keep tabs on all of them and communicate to each what the others are doing. You are the liaison. You are the project manager. You are the link.

Because you and your child are in the center of all this information and all of these relationships, you will become the expert. Remember the organizational system I suggested you create? This is going to help you look like the expert. Believe me, doctors, therapists, and specialists appreciate when you walk into their office prepared and with information you can share or refer back to as needed. The truth is, even the specialists who are amazing and brilliant sometimes forget things when they're seeing so many patients. It's always good to have

You are an essential member of your child's team, and as such, your input is valid and vital.

the information you need to share with them right at your fingertips. So bring your information and look the part, fellow expert mom. You are an essential member of your child's team, and as such, your input is valid and vital. Walk in like the expert that you are. Own it.

You know what else? You don't have ordinary instincts inside you. You have mama animal instincts, and you just need to believe in yourself enough to trust them, follow them, and pursue them. Leave no stone unturned and rest only when you know that you've looked at something from all angles and considered all opinions and possibilities.

Roar, mama, roar! Don't be afraid to ask questions. Don't be afraid to disagree. Don't be afraid to wake up the whole wide jungle if you have to!

What's the worst that can happen? Let's say you do all this and you land back where you started. But the doing of all this will allow you to feel you've uncovered all there is to know. At the very least, you'll have peace of mind. And peace of mind is golden right now. It will give you comfort during uncertain times.

Another thing that may be helpful to know is that when you're dealing with a rare diagnosis, it can be common to receive conflicting information. Your child may see one specialist who tells you one thing and another specialist who tells you another. This leaves us parents in a very uncomfortable predicament. Often, we trust our healthcare providers to be the final word about which path we should take. We rely on them to help us discern which treatment options, medications, procedures, and interventions to pursue. But when you receive conflicting information, the decisions are put back on you as a parent as to which route to choose. This is where you're going to have to allow some of those parenting instincts to guide you. Again, you know your child best. Use the information you've gathered about your child to guide your decision.

Seek out as much information as possible to make the best decision you can at the time. Gather the information from all the specialists and then, knowing what only you can know about your child, use that to make your decision. Ultimately, you as a parent know more than you think you do when it comes to your child. Use that knowledge and your instincts to guide you on your path.

Also, because you are dealing with a rare disease, it can be common to have unclear paths. Often, there are no set protocols or best care practices in place. This can leave you with uncertainties. Once again, after you've done all the research, seen all the specialists, talked to other parents, and filled yourself with information, it will be up to you as the parent to make the ultimate decision. It will be time to lean into those instincts.

With Miles, I have run up against many "firsts." As new treatments and procedures were initiated with his disease, we had to make decisions that were not yet tried and true. New practices of care were evolving, and we didn't have years of evidence that afforded us the comfort of known outcomes. This felt scary and unsettling. But we wanted our child to benefit from treatments that had the potential to keep his disease at bay. The benefits outweighed the risks, so we took steps forward based on the information we had at the time. This is part of rare disease. We swim in a lot of unknown waters. We are faced time and time again with making decisions without years of hard data to call upon.

A wise physical therapist once told me, as I agonized over a tough medical decision for my son, "Nikki, all you can do is make the best decision you can for right now." She was right. One day I may look back and question myself, but at that moment, I couldn't see the future, and all I could do was go with the best information I had at the time and make the best-educated decision I could. Sometimes that's all you can do.

Mama, I want to encourage you to rise to this task. Instead of shirking in fear from these decisions, lean into your parenting instincts. Trust yourself. Believe that since you have done the work and gathered all the information you possibly could, you are informed to make the best decision you can with the information you have at the time. Trust that since you know your child best, you are the one who should have the final say in how to proceed. There may be more answers inside you than you're giving yourself credit for. Learn to hear that voice inside giving you direction, and use it as a guiding light. This is often the best advice that seasoned rare mamas give to newbie rare mamas.

Trust your parenting instincts. Believe in yourself. You are capable. You are your child's mother. There is no greater authority than that. You were beautifully and wonderfully made specifically and exactly for mothering your unique child.

No one else but you can do what you do.

Rare Mama Truth

Mama knows best. The end.

CHAPTER 8

Advocating Effectively

"I raise up my voice—not so I can shout,
but so that those without a voice can be heard."

MALALA YOUSAFZAI

A dvocating for our children is an important part of parenting. We are our children's voice and representation. While I always knew this to be true, it was reinforced on a level I never imagined when Miles was diagnosed with his rare disease. Advocating on his behalf became a vital necessity to maintaining his health and even saving his life.

Having a child with a disability has required our family to rely on a variety of providers and services, including care from medical specialists, funding from insurance companies, services from our school district, and programs from our state government. If only it could be so easy as to tell these providers what our child needs and then receive it. Sadly, sometimes this isn't the case. It's not uncommon to hit roadblocks. It's not unusual to be faced with lengthy paperwork, appointments, evaluations, and then delays. It's not surprising to receive denials. It's the reality of this jungle.

Now, I try to be a calm and even-keeled person, but these difficulties would trigger an animal-like instinct and response within me. They would well up in a raw, emotional reaction of a mama not getting what she needs for her cub. I would feel my blood pumping, my fangs dripping, and my claws engaged. I felt the injustice of it all. How can they do this?

I had to learn to calm myself down, punch the pillow, go outside and howl at the moon, and then put on my rational, logical, emotion-free advocate hat and get to work.

I had to learn to advocate effectively. Because guess what? No one else was going to, and my child's life was depending on it. I'm not saying that to sound bleak, but it was a wake-up call for me. I thought the system was different. I thought someone else would do it. But the truth is that this one falls on us as parents. I do believe that doctors, experts, school staff, and therapists are all trying their best to advocate for our children, but there are too many patients, students, and clients for the responsibility to fall only on them. We are the parents, and not only is it our job and our right to advocate— it's often downright critical.

So advocate your tail off, girl!

If you think something needs to be looked at again, ask for it. If you think your child's therapist is not a good fit, request another one. If you think your child's medication is incorrect, speak up. If you think your child needs more services at school, tell them. If you think your child's therapy needs to continue, don't let it be discontinued.

Speak up. Ask. Act.

Don't be a wildflower, a bystander, or an observer. Don't be uneducated, unknowing, or unworthy. Don't be too scared, too shy, or too insecure. Instead, for the sake of your child, be bold, be fearless, be relentless. Be involved, be a part of the team, be collaborative. Be educated, be deserving, be expectant.

The best way I can explain how you'll need to advocate is to be assertive but with kindness. I call this "bold and benevolent." Being bold is knowing what you need and not being afraid to ask for it. In order to advocate, first you have to be knowledgeable about what your child needs. Do your homework and know what you're asking for. Next, you need to ask for it—while also being benevolent.

Here's the thing about advocating: It's a balance. If you don't ask, you'll never know if you can get what you need, and therefore you'll never get it. But on the other side, if you just walk around roaring aggressively all the time, you may be discounted as a belligerent adversary. Don't get me wrong, belligerent people get stuff done, and we all need our stuff to get done. But no one wants to help someone who's contentious and biting, and believe me, you're going to need a lot of help along this road. So therein lies the balance that must be found.

If you're shy, you're going to need to find your voice. If you're aggressive, you're going to need to find your diplomacy. I would say I fall on the not-so-shy side of the scale. This road has tested my patience like never before. Oh, mama, I have had to hold my tongue many a time along this road. Numerous times I've wanted to rip into someone for not giving my child what he needed when it was clearly warranted. But in the long run, I didn't think that chewing someone out or telling them they're an incompetent idiot was truly going to help the situation.

Listen, I'm not saying that they weren't an incompetent idiot, but you're going to have to leave your emotions out of it and speak from a place of fact, not emotion. The reason that asking this of us is so difficult is because, let's be honest, this *is* emotional. It's our child. It doesn't get more emotional than this! But getting emotional can get in the way of getting what you need for your child.

So as best as you can, learn to keep your emotion and your temper out of it. Speak from fact. Speak from research. Speak with the goal in mind. Not only will you get better results, but you'll also feel better about it.

At the end of the day, after you unleash wrath on someone (no matter how deserving they may be), you probably won't feel too great about it. After that temporary unleash relief dissipates, you may think, *What have I done?* Especially since you may have to once again face this someone you're relying on to help your child.

I'm not saying you should be insincere; I'm saying choose to be diplomatic and remove the emotion as you seek what you need. We're all humans doing our best, and we have to assume the person on the receiving end is a human doing their best too. Hold your tongue, take a deep breath, and press pause. Now start again. What are the facts? What are the truths? What will help you build your case? What factual evidence will help back up what you need? If you're shy, let this factual information empower you to ask for what you need. If you're aggressive, let this factual information be your mouthpiece. Then, if you need to later, run around and punch the air, scream into your pillow, clean out every last drawer (take that, dust!), or write that scathing letter and then rip it up.

> If you're shy, let this factual information empower you to ask for what you need. If you're aggressive, let this factual information be your mouthpiece.

Mama, hone this skill. You will use it all the time!

At the beginning of this journey, I didn't realize how often and how hard I'd have to advocate for my child. But now I understand that rare disease advocating is a crucial part of taking care of our children. Rare diseases are so intricate and complex. Not every organization, healthcare provider, educator, therapist, and service provider is going to understand these intricacies, and therefore, they may not fully understand your child's needs. This is why you'll turn into the best rare disease advocate your child could ever have. Because you understand your child and their needs so well, you'll be the best person to advocate on their behalf.

You'll find yourself advocating in many different instances, whether it's for medical care, education services, equipment needs, in-home health programs and services, insurance, funding, research, or to build awareness of your child's disease.

One particular mom I met is the most fun-loving, kind-spirited, easygoing soul you could ever meet. Loving and giving, caring and kind, and not one to cause a fuss. And yet I saw her stand tall when her doctor told her there was nothing she could do to help her child's legs that were tightening so much that he was having trouble sitting and walking. He already used a wheelchair and a walker to assist with mobility, but it was becoming more and more difficult to walk.

Her advocating kicked in. I watched her track down a special surgery that only one doctor in the country was doing for this particular condition. I saw how, after she found out that insurance wouldn't cover the surgery, she went on to raise money on GoFundMe to pay for it. I saw how she made all the plans to prepare for the surgery. I saw how she juggled caring for her one-year-old baby and her older daughter, all while taking her son to a different state for the surgery. I watched as she wrestled with all that would need to come after the surgery, including leg bracing, physical therapy, schooling at home, etc. She kept blazing trails and figuring it out in her unassuming, quiet way.

Then one day, I sat in my car and watched as she picked up her son, who had newly returned to school post-surgery. He crossed the street in his walker, striding like a gazelle—big, powerful, confident strides on long, lean legs, strong and able, holding his body upright, making their mark with every step, their footing so sure and comfortable as if they'd been waiting to step like that their entire life. It was hard for me to move my gaze from those beautiful strides, but when I finally looked up, I saw something even more beautiful. It was truly a moment I will always remember. I saw the look on his face. Sheer bliss. The biggest, truest, most beaming smile. Mouth open, cheeks pushed up to the highest points of his face. Joy! And I wept. I wept in my car watching this. I witnessed a miracle.

I finally flung my door open and had to hold myself back with all my might from running over to this boy and picking him up. I mean, I didn't want him to think I was a freak show, and I didn't want my own kid to get wind of this and be embarrassed by his crazy mom who was picking up and hugging his friends. I babbled, jabbered, and spat all my congratulations and support for their triumph.

I marveled at this mother and son. What a victory!

I admire every ounce of this mother's determination, grit, and fight. She helped steward change for her son. This beautiful, kind, loving soul who is made up of an exuberant spirit stood tall and advocated and got it done.

If you would have asked her at the beginning of her journey if she would have thought she'd be doing things like this, she might have laughed and said, "Most certainly not."

This journey will push us to new heights of our personality and to abilities we may not have even known were possible. Mama, let me tell you, I'm pretty sure it's in you.

Advocate. Find the balance. Be bold and benevolent, and I truly believe this will edge you closer to getting your child what they need.

Rare Mama Truth

Advocacy isn't a job—it's a lifestyle. All day, every day.

CHAPTER 9

Sharing Information

"Don't let anyone else define your life.
You hold the pen, and it's your story to write."

UNKNOWN

One of the things you'll have to discern as your child's mother is how to deliver information about your child to friends, family, and your child. This can be a job in and of itself. Information spreads in a wild way, but you can be mindful of the information flow.

How you send out and take in information is something you can consider from the start. You'll have the opportunity to decide what information you expose your child and yourself to. You can also decide what you want to share with others and what things you'll want to protect for the sake of your child's privacy.

At a rare disease conference I attended at the beginning of my son's diagnosis, one of the speakers talked about protecting their child's information. They raised a good point that if you thought your child would one day grow up and be less than enthused with how much personal information you shared about their life, then you might want to consider what you put out there. They were certainly talking about social media and the internet, but this applies to any form of information-sharing.

SHARING YOUR CHILD'S DIAGNOSIS WITH FRIENDS AND FAMILY

When your child first gets diagnosed, one of the hard things you'll have to do is share the news with friends and family. Perhaps these people have been on the journey with you and are waiting with bated breath to hear the results of the latest test. Though you may finally have a confirmed diagnosis, you still may not have all the information that comes with it. This was the case with Miles. We had a diagnosis, but we still had a few weeks until we saw the geneticist and neurologist again to discuss everything in more detail and formulate a health plan. Many looming questions still needed to be answered.

We were sad, we were vulnerable, and we were raw. So many friends and family needed to be told, but we were overwhelmed by the severity of the information to be relayed. We weren't ready to talk about the diagnosis in detail because we were still processing it. Also, until we had our appointments with all the specialists, we wouldn't have a lot of information to give about what the diagnosis meant long term.

After much deliberation, we decided to disseminate the information via email. While this felt a bit impersonal, it just wasn't possible to get around to having personal conversations with everyone in a timely fashion. I don't think we could've handled having that type of conversation over and over again; it was too overwhelming and emotional. Sharing via email was the right route for our family. It allowed us to distribute the information quickly, and we were able to include a website where more information about the disease could be found. It also allowed us to thank them for their concern and support.

Several caring friends and family members, upon receiving the news, reached out to comfort me. As we talked, I could hear the fear and worry in their voices. They began asking questions—hard questions, questions I didn't have answers to. "Will he walk? What is the prognosis? What is his life expectancy?"

With every hard question, I could feel myself retreating. Those conversations made me consider things I wasn't strong enough to think about. The questions I didn't know the answers to made me anxious because I felt ill-equipped. The sheer number of questions made my head spin because I realized how much I needed to learn. It wasn't their fault; they were taking an interest and trying to understand. Bless their hearts, they were also trying to figure out how to help us. What I didn't expect was how affected I would be by those conversations. I realize now that *I* just wasn't ready for a lot of questions or for taking on all their fear and sadness.

The other thing that surprised me was how quickly information spreads. We chose to send that email to our closest inner circle, those we wanted to share the news with right away. However, information spreads like wild in the rare disease jungle. The jungle is wild and free. You may tell one little bird, but that bird tells another bird, and that bird tells an elephant, and that elephant tells the rest of the elephants, and now somehow the lions know. Before you know it, the whole wide jungle is whispering and looking at you with sad faces.

On top of that, it can become like a bad game of telephone, where the information can get transferred, changed, and even become incorrect. You'll get a call or email from someone you barely even know, asking you about information that's not even true. All because someone you chose to tell in confidence decided to share your news for you.

So you might want to be mindful about when, how, and with whom you share the information. Because at the end of the day, it's your child's information, and it's your decision on how to share it. You need to do whatever is best for your child and your family.

SHARING YOUR CHILD'S DIAGNOSIS WITH YOUR CHILD

Since you know your child better than anyone, you can decide how and when to share their diagnosis with them. This is a very personal decision, and the timing will depend on many factors, including your child's age, level of understanding, comprehension, and cognitive abilities. As parents, we want to protect our children, and having this conversation is often difficult for many of us because we are concerned about how this news will affect our child.

On the flipside, withholding information from our child can affect them too. How, when, and what to share is complex. But you don't have to figure this out all on your own. There's information to help you. You can speak to a child psychologist or mental health expert about it. If there is a foundation or organization for your child's condition, they may have tips to offer. You can also tap into the child life or social worker services at the hospital where your child receives care.

I personally remember how much trepidation I had over how and when we would tell Miles about his condition. The question always loomed in my mind. Because he was only eighteen months old when he was diagnosed, my husband and I had to decide on the appropriate age to tell him. We wanted to be mindful of this decision and do it at the best time for him. Again, this was way beyond my competency, but the one thing we knew was that we wanted Miles to hear about it from us, his parents. We wanted to tell him in words that wouldn't scare him, and we wanted to let him know we were with him every step of the way.

So I started digging around for resources and information. On the Muscular Dystrophy Association's website, I found a children's book that explains a muscular dystrophy diagnosis in a way that a child can understand. Then by digging around further, I found a lot of similar resources for other diseases and conditions. This gave me comfort that I didn't need to reinvent the wheel and could find help in this area too.

There's no set right way that works for every child, only the right way for your child based on who they are. Seek resources, enlist help, and trust your heart on this one, mama.

SHARING YOUR CHILD'S DIAGNOSIS WITH OTHER CHILDREN

Kids are curious. They ask a lot of questions. Some diagnoses are easily seen; others are not. Miles is in a wheelchair, so he stands out in a crowd. From a young age, every time he rolled into a new classroom or situation, he was bombarded with questions. "Why are you in a wheelchair? Did you break your leg? Can you walk?"

My husband and I knew we couldn't predict or control what other kids were going to say and do, but we could at least provide them information about Miles's condition. We could also provide their parents with the same information so they'd know what to tell their child when asked. Otherwise, how would parents know? They weren't given a manual on how to handle this either. But we figured we could help them out by giving them the words to use.

My husband and I learned from the amazing Dr. Al Freedman

at a Cure SMA conference that in talking with young children about SMA, it's best to keep the explanation simple. Around that time, Miles's friends and peers were three to five years old, so it was appropriate to say something like, "Miles's muscles work a little differently than ours, and they need a little extra help. He uses leg braces and a wheelchair to help him get around." Usually kids at that age would say, "Oh, okay!" and return to playing.

We provided this information to our friends, neighbors, and the parents of Miles's classmates. We armed them with the information they needed to give their kids. This helped Miles become less overwhelmed with questions and seemed to satisfy other kids' curiosity. I know this won't work in every situation, and as parents, we can't run around policing this information for the rest of our child's life, but I think it did help Miles when he was young and shy and still learning about his condition himself.

Another helpful tool we learned from other parents was to write a letter to the parents of our son's class explaining the situation. We did this every school year for many years, until most of the kids knew Miles. The parents of Miles's classmates seemed to appreciate it, and it opened the doors to conversations so everyone felt comfortable talking to us about his condition. We also provided a letter from Miles to his classmates that the parents could read to their children. It explained in basic, age-appropriate words about Miles. This helped get a lot of questions answered up front, and it was a huge help to Miles and our family.

INFORMATION FLOW

You'll also have to decide how much information you want to provide on a continual basis. I remember a conversation with a close contact a few days before I was taking Miles to get a treatment.

He asked when the next treatment was, and I told him. Then he started asking questions about the treatment. "When did I have to get there? What pretests did they have to do before the procedure? When would I tell my son he was going to have the procedure again? How would I tell him? How would that make him feel? How would the procedure be done? Where in his back would they stick the needle? Does he feel it? Does he cry? Does he remember? How long would the recovery be?"

I mean, was this person going to perform the procedure? I literally had to live out the entire experience right before I had to go and do it. When we finished talking, he had a complete and full understanding of the difficult thing we were about to go and do, but I was now an anxiety-filled wreck. Don't get me wrong, I was very appreciative of his concern and the interest he was taking in my son. I know he was just curious and trying to support us and show us love. But going blow by blow through all of the nitty-gritty details did not serve me at all. I felt exhausted and anxious afterward.

I had forgotten something I realized about myself a long time ago. Before I have to go and do hard things, I need to keep my head straight, my gaze steady, my mind sharp, and my emotions in check. I need to prep and prepare like crazy, but after all the planning and preparing has been done, often I need to *not* think too much about what I have to do and just show up and do it. It's a survival tactic that allows me to do hard things. Afterward, when it's all been said and done, I can talk in detail about what we had to do because it's over and behind us. But not beforehand. It just works me up too much.

On the other hand, for some mamas, talking about it in detail with family and friends ahead of

> **Handle information flow the way that is going to serve you and your family best.**

time may be the exact thing that helps them. Maybe it helps to get them prepared and in the right headspace to do the hard thing. If that works for you, do it.

The bottom line is you have a say in the information flow. You decide what information you want to provide and when. Know thyself. Know what *you* need. Know what helps *you*. Then do that. Handle information flow the way that is going to serve you and your family best.

TAKING INFORMATION IN

Just as you can be mindful of the information you put out, you can also be mindful of the information you take in. I'm deeply affected by images I see. I mean, I can't even watch the preview for a scary movie, let alone the movie itself, so I have to seriously consider what I watch on TV and the media content I consume.

On the other hand, there's a lot of great content that helps motivate and inspire me. Over time, I've learned to decipher what works for me, and you might want to do the same. If looking around on social media at others who have your child's disease and hearing all about what they're going through helps you relate or feel less alone, take it in. On the other hand, if hearing about what they're going through or hearing about their losses is too much for your heart to bear, stop taking it in. Only you know what serves you. Honor that.

The bottom line on information flow is to consider and be mindful of what helps you and what serves you and your family, and choose that—even if it goes against the grain, societal norms, or what others want, need, and expect from you. You are the one walking this road, and you must honor what helps you keep showing up each day with your body, mind, and spirit intact.

Rare Mama Truth

Can someone invent an app for sharing hard news?
Ideally, one with a soothing voice, a "translate
medical jargon into human" setting, and a "repeat as
needed" button. Please and thank you.

PART III

Navigating Rare Systems

CHAPTER 10

Managing Medical Systems

"Doctors diagnose, nurses heal,
and caregivers make sense of it all."

BRETT LEWIS

One of the first things you'll need to do to manage your child's disease is assemble an expert care team. Rare diseases often affect multiple body systems and require various specialists. Getting your team assembled is no small feat. There is often a disparity of knowledge when it comes to rare disease specialists, and knowing that not all specialists can offer you the same skill and experience levels when it comes to rare diseases puts the decision on you as the parent to determine which team members are going to be right for your child. When dealing with a disease that most healthcare providers do not see often, be sure to seek out the best, most-proficient players in the specialty.

Let me hit you with some truths up front.

It's not uncommon for your pediatrician or local doctor to have little information and/or experience with your child's rare condition. It's not unlikely to receive conflicting information or misinformation. It might be necessary for your family to travel to other cities and even states to see an expert. Getting an appointment with an expert or specialist can take months. Parts of the U.S. healthcare system are fragmented and disorganized, and therefore, coordinated care does not always take place. You as the parent are often going to be the one driving the train and promoting effective collaboration. It will be necessary for you to be an involved and vital member of the care team.

Doctors are often taught, "When you hear hoofbeats, think horses, not zebras," emphasizing common diagnoses over rare ones. Yet rare diseases are far more prevalent than previously believed. This is why zebras, with their unique stripes, have emerged as a powerful symbol for rare conditions, highlighting the importance of recognizing their existence and addressing the urgent need for awareness and care.

There are many talented professionals who are passionate about rare diseases, but sometimes the hard part is finding them. You may meet some specialists who become true partners on the rare disease road as you explore and navigate your child's rare disease together. You may meet others who won't. I guess what I'm saying is that your experience finding and assembling a medical care team can unfold a thousand different ways. Often, there isn't a given when it comes to medical care for a rare disease. That being said, what can you do? Here are some tips on finding expert medical providers, ways to work with the care team, and the different types of care providers you may encounter.

FINDING EXPERT MEDICAL PROVIDERS

Perhaps the team you worked with to diagnose your child's rare disease happens to be the best provider/expert in the area of your child's diagnosis. Hallelujah! You're one of the lucky ones. But this also may not be the case. Once you have your child's diagnosis, you'll need to seek out the best care team possible specifically for that area of expertise. The expert may not necessarily be the doctor at your local hospital or the first specialist you see. Getting to the right specialist is most likely going to take a little legwork. You'll want to take an involved and proactive approach to assembling your child's team.

You're seeking the most studied, proficient, and experienced specialist in the medical discipline for your child's disease. Ideally, this is someone who has seen other patients with this diagnosis or similar types of diagnoses, someone who has their finger on the pulse of research, and someone who is actively involved in disease-specific organizations, medical advisory boards, research efforts, etc. You want them to be a true expert on your child's disorder.

If there is a patient advocacy group or organization for your child's disease, contact them to see if they already have a list of medical providers. Check with the rare disease organizations. Get on children's hospitals' websites and research the doctors in the relevant departments. There may be a tertiary center or a center of excellence in that particular area or type of disease. These act as the center of knowledge not only locally but often nationally and even globally, working to establish standards of care and protocols for specific diseases. They are at the forefront of cutting-edge research, treatment, and interventions. Find out if a center exists for your child's particular category of disease.

Also check into research centers. Clinical research centers (CRCs) or general clinical research centers (GCRCs) refer to designated medical facilities used to conduct clinical research, such as at a hospital or medical clinic. They are used to perform clinical trials for various medical procedures and treatments. These research centers provide the infrastructure for investigators who conduct research with patients. Investigations can include studies of cause, progression, and cure of diseases. These research centers work with doctors and healthcare providers to carry out their research studies. You may be led to a doctor immersed in your child's disease by identifying a research center and research studies. This is another place to look for experts in the field.

When Miles was diagnosed with his rare disease, which falls under the category of a neuromuscular disease, we had to decide where to take him for care. There was a children's hospital close to our home, but at the time there had been some changes to the neuromuscular department and some turnover of the care team. Instead of just defaulting to the closest doctor in proximity even though the department wasn't thriving, we decided to seek out the best neuromuscular doctors and centers that were in a bigger radius. It turned out that another hospital two hours away from us was world-renowned for their neuromuscular department, so we decided to drive the extra distance to go to this hospital and be seen by doctors who had vast experience specifically with SMA.

The doctor we saw was the head of the neurology department. Not only did she have many years of experience under her belt, she was also a teaching doctor and a researcher. This meant she was always learning and privy to new information and therapies. We loved the blend of both her years of experience that afforded her wisdom married with her progressive approach that came from being a teaching doctor and having her finger on the pulse of research.

It turned out that even though we had to go through the necessary steps of testing, she suspected SMA from the start. She had seen it and had experience with it. Not only that, as soon as we were given my son's diagnosis, she was able to tell us what to do next. She was in possession of the most current best practices. I now believe so wholeheartedly in this mantra of seeking out the most knowledgeable doctors that we do it for any medical situation within our ability and power.

One more example from my own experience is the first time Miles had to have surgery on his hips. Having this particular type of surgery was new to children with his diagnosis, and there weren't a lot of doctors on the West Coast where we lived who had performed this surgery on an SMA child. It was a common surgery in general, so they had performed it on children with many other types of diseases, but it wasn't routine to perform it on an SMA child.

Therefore, the West Coast team didn't have firsthand outcomes specifically on a child with SMA. They couldn't tell me clinically or anecdotally how SMA patients healed or benefited from the surgery, so we sought out doctors who had. One of the leading doctors who had been performing this surgery on SMA children was on the East Coast. We reached out to him to ask questions, volley scenarios, and learn about patient outcomes. We exchanged emails, and I was able to get many questions answered. Even though we weren't physically anywhere near him, we still received insight from this guru.

Track down the experts any way you can.

Track down the experts any way you can. Leverage your contacts. Who do you know? Do you have friends or family members who are in the medical field or who know someone who is? Ask around to see if you have any connections. Attack this rare disease fight from all angles.

Let me be honest: This takes time. This takes work. This takes a lot of effort from mama. This takes research and phone calls and appointments to vet doctors. This takes digging around to find these contacts and ways to access them. I know this won't work in all cases. Some of us live in areas where we don't have access to top children's hospitals, and we just can't travel to other centers, or we don't have insurance coverage that allows us to access these expert specialists. Some of us have to go to certain doctors because they are within our proximity or within our coverage plan. But it is worth at least making you aware that if you *do* have a choice in your child's care team, seek out the best.

When I started our rare disease fight, I didn't even know to think that way. My go-to for routine medical needs was just to call and make an appointment with the doctor who was closest to where we lived and with whom it was the easiest to get an appointment. Over time I've learned that we have a choice and can choose doctors based on skill and expertise. Therefore, if you have the ability and the time to seek out the expert in your child's disease, it's worth the investment.

> **Invest the needed time to find the right care team for your rare disease fight. It will yield better care.**

This applies to all care providers for your child, including physical therapists, occupational therapists, speech therapists, behavioral therapists, and equipment providers. We now apply this to everything within our ability, and we have been blessed with an amazing care team for our son. We know that we are privy to the most up-to-date information, and we feel confident that he is receiving the best care.

Invest the needed time to find the right care team for your rare disease fight. It will yield better care, better coordination of care, and greater level of access to the latest information and technologies.

WORKING WITH THE TEAM
Act as a Liaison

You are going to become the liaison between all of your child's different providers. Remember that care map I showed you in chapter

7? Your child is in the center of the care map. You will have a whole team that is supplying services, medical interventions, and programs to help your child.

Many children's hospitals will have multidisciplinary teams where your child will attend a clinic, and in one day, they will see all their various providers from the different disciplines. Afterward, they will meet to discuss your child and share information. This is an extremely efficient way for your child as the patient to see specialists all in the same day and for the entire team to weigh in on next steps.

In the absence of a multidisciplinary appointment approach, your specialists may have access to the medical records from the other disciplines they can view and consult as needed. However, if you are seeing providers across different hospitals and systems, this may not be taking place. In the absence of this, you as the parent may have to act as the liaison to make sure information is shared from one discipline to the next. The U.S. healthcare system can be extremely fragmented. This puts the onus back on you as the parent to manage all the various providers and make sure information is relayed between all the team members. But since you have an organizational system for keeping tabs on all the paperwork, procedures, medical history, etc., you're the right woman for the job.

Your goal is to make sure there is coordinated care, sharing of test results and other vital information, and communication and collaboration across disciplines. You also want to make sure providers are not duplicating efforts or missing opportunities.

Be an Essential Member of the Team

Take an active role in every appointment and meeting with your child's care team. You are an important and valuable member of the team. You are essential! You are the hands and feet on the ground helping your child day in and day out. Your family is responsible for getting your child to appointments, carrying out at-home plans, and following up and reporting back on progress. Help the care team help you by showing up with some level of understanding of your child's disease as best you can, eager to participate, with an attitude of collaboration, assertive and ready to advocate when you need to, and appreciative of the team's efforts. The team needs you, and you need them.

Find the Best Fit

Sometimes we will only have so many available options of providers to work with who understand our child's disease. But in cases where you have the choice between providers, find one that is a good fit. It's very important that you find a team you can trust, feel comfortable working with, and is comprised of members who listen to you and your child. You'll need to have a positive working relationship with these individuals in order to give your child the most effective care. If there ever comes a point when you feel the provider is not providing the best, most up-to-date care, or you don't feel comfortable, or the relationship is strained despite your best efforts and not bearing fruit for your kid, consider moving on. Again, some of us might not have the luxury of this because there may only be a few options of providers to work with. But if you have options and you have a choice, choose the best fit for your child and for your family.

Make the Most of Meetings

Bring your notebook, paperwork, and tracked data so you can inform your child's team about progress and have your notes available to refer to as needed. Specialist appointments are hard to come by and often take months to get. We rare mamas always talk about how hard it is to come by these appointments and how far in advance we have to book them. So when you finally have your appointment, come prepared to make the most of it.

Bring a list of questions you need to get answered or a list of observations you want to address. Don't rely on your memory to remember these questions in the moment. Trust me on this one; it's happened to me too many times. Your head might be filled with all the information the doctor is providing you, or your child might be fussy that day and you're trying to distract them while trying to have a conversation, or maybe you're rushing to get to the appointment so you show up all disheveled and forget everything you wanted to ask, etc.

If you're trying to show your specialist something your child is doing, or can't do, or a particular symptom you're noticing, etc., consider recording a video ahead of time. Don't leave it to chance that your child will perform it on cue or that the symptom will be present the day of the appointment. Murphy's law says it won't. I don't want you to waste your chance to show your specialist after you've been waiting two months to see them.

Also, as we discussed, make sure you're taking good notes at your appointments. Bring your system for recording conversations and procedures. Consider taking someone else with you to these appointments, as sometimes two heads are better than one. My husband and I always walk away from appointments with different levels of details, and between the two of us, we can fill in the gaps and make sure we both absorbed everything.

Set yourself up for productive meetings by doing the following:

- Come with prepared questions to ask.
- Take notes, record all conversations, procedures, interventions, next steps, test results, etc.

- Record videos of your child ahead of time and bring them to show at the appointment.

- If you need scripts, ask for them at the appointment so you can leave with them.

- If your child gets tests done, get a copy of the results while you're there, even if it means signing paperwork or paying to have a disk made. It's worth it to have it in your own records so you can cross-share this information as needed and you're not running around trying to get it later.

- Ask for a copy of the appointment visit notes.

- Get a copy of your child's diagnosis in writing.

- Find out if the hospital or clinic has an online charting system you can enroll in and access from home.

- Bring toys, snacks, water, sanitizer, etc.—all the things you need to keep your child distracted while you meet with the provider.

Keep Your Pediatrician in the Know

Often, your child will still have a local pediatrician who they see for regular illnesses and routine check-ups. You'll want to make sure your pediatrician is in the know and up to date with your child's rare disease and medical history. Opt in to have your specialists send all the history of any visits or procedures to your local pediatrician so they can access records.

Find a Point of Contact and Their Best Method of Communication

Specialists are busy, and often it's hard to get in touch with them personally. At some of the initial appointments, ask for their nurse coordinator's or physician assistant's (PA's) contact information. Nurses and PAs will become your best friends. They are often the gatekeepers and/or the coordinators of many of the doctors' follow-ups. They can be the ones to get you answers, scripts, signed forms, etc. My suggestion is to meet them when you can, get their contact information, and ask them for their preferred method of communication. Then use that preferred method so you're more likely to get a response.

I have become really friendly with our specialists' nurse coordinators and PAs. They know Miles by name at this point. We have developed a great working relationship, and I can contact them to ask questions and obtain scripts. Most of them prefer email or the online MyChart system because they spend the day in clinic appointments, away from their desk and not sitting by their phones. They are usually eager to help, and they appreciate the efficiency of being contacted through their preferred method. At the end of the day, your specialist, nurse, PA, coordinator, etc., is a human being doing their job and managing a substantial caseload. So find the most efficient way to work with them.

> You're going to *want* to build a relationship with your child's care team. Things just work together better when you have a healthy, positive relationship.

I have a dear friend whose child has a rare condition, and she herself is a nurse coordinator for a very prominent children's hospital care clinic. Some of her best advice is to build relationships with the nurses. In her experience, care providers earnestly want to help their patients. They pursued the medical field with a deep desire to improve the quality of life for those they care for. But having seen the interworking of a hospital setting, my friend also sees the level of need, the limitations of the systems, and the reality that there just aren't enough hours in the day for the demand of the specialists. That's why her advice is to establish relationships with their team so you can work together to get your child what they need.

Build Relationships

This leads me to building relationships. Mama, this is key! Once you have your care team assembled, you may have them in your life for a long time. We have decades-long relationships with some of our providers at this point. And let me be frank here, mama: You're going to *want* to build a relationship with your child's care team. Things just work together better when you have a healthy, positive relationship. So put some effort into building one. Your child will benefit in the long run.

Be Assertive (Not Adversarial)

Times will come when you'll need to assert yourself. Honestly, mama, there are going to be a lot of these times. But as we've discussed, you're going to strike the balance on being assertive without being adversarial (unless you're at the point where you need to be adversarial; then do what you need to do). Start with an assertive, involved approach from a place of factual information, pushing back when you need to. Use all your research and tracked data to arm you and help you present your case. Pushing back when necessary is your right as your child's parent. You're representing your child, and your goal is to get them what they need.

I went through this in the hospital post-op after one of Miles's surgeries. Over the course of his disease, for various reasons and procedures, my son has undergone anesthesia many, many times. He has always done surprisingly well coming out of anesthesia. But this particular time post-surgery, he didn't. He was sicker than a dog for about twelve hours—nauseated, vomiting, and unable to keep even water down. Not uncommon, but uncommon for him. This wasn't our first surgery rodeo, so I started asking questions about what he was being given, all the meds, the IVs, everything. I identified something different that was being put in his IV. Different for him, as in he'd never had it before.

At this point, there was a resident making the post-op rounds, and when she came through, I talked to her about it and asked her why he was on it. She said it was standard nutrition care for SMA patients post-op. Interesting, since my son had that exact same surgery at the exact same hospital, for the exact same reason, and that post-op nutrition care protocol was not given previously. I asked who ordered it, and she named a different department than her own.

Luckily, I had just attended a seminar about nutrition care for SMA patients and learned about standards of care and protocols. I tried to do my best to diplomatically provide her with the latest and greatest nutrition care protocols that were released by the SMA medical advisory board.

I could tell by her response that she was less than willing to concede and a little power play was going to ensue. I'd been here before. So I took a deep breath and tried to take away all her doubts by rationally and diplomatically stating my case. My son had been on it for twelve hours, so he was sufficiently nourished by this point. Pulling him off of it for an hour or two to see if it allowed him to feel better would be of no harm. But it would allow us to see if he, in fact, started to feel better and could then eat on his own. Which, by the way, was one of the goals he had to meet before he could go home. Again, not my first rodeo.

I also told her I'd be willing to speak directly to the ordering department if she didn't have the authority to make the call. I did this all while trying my best to hide the fact that I was fuming that my baby—who had been under anesthesia tons of times, went through the same surgery, and had always done well—was given this different protocol that I didn't know about and had to endure feeling sick to the point where he couldn't even converse, all while experiencing the pain of recovering from the actual surgery itself.

Twelve hours was enough, and I'd had it! I wasn't going to take no for an answer, but I tried to state my case from a place of fact so it actually made sense and didn't sound like a panicked, frenzied mother who couldn't bear to see her baby in pain. I mean, I was that mama, but this wasn't coming from that place. This was coming from a place of experience of knowing my child and knowing what works for him and what doesn't. So my goal in that moment was to be so rationally convincing that I would get what my son needed.

She agreed to allow him to be taken off it to see if he could come around and eat on his own. Lo and behold, he did. Within an hour or two, he was asking for pizza from the hospital menu. Of course, I was pissed that I didn't make the connection sooner and that Miles had to spend twelve hours feeling like hell. But at least I can offer it to you as an example of a mama knowing her baby and pushing to get him what he needs. Or to get him off what he doesn't need. Take the crap out of the IV already! Okay, I guess I'm still mad about it. Don't mess with mama.

But back to the point, push and advocate and get assertive and pull out all the stops. Maybe I would have had to get adversarial if she had said no. But I started without going there, and it worked. You're going to get very good at learning how to state your case diplomatically and persuasively. Just another set of skills mama's gonna learn!

Show Gratitude

I've talked a lot about how to handle situations that aren't going as you hoped and as you need. But let me tell you, for every unpleasant situation, I have tons more examples of positive experiences and amazing care providers who are passionate about helping—many who have bent over backward to truly change the course of my son's disease.

A great provider is a true gift! As parents, one of the best things we can do is to simply acknowledge their efforts. A quick email, a thank-you note, or a kind word all go a long way in expressing our gratitude for their time and talents. Believe me, it's appreciated. I mean, who doesn't want to be noticed and acknowledged for a job well done? Who doesn't want to know they've made a true difference in the life of a child and of a family?

During that same hospital visit I just told you about, Miles had the most amazing post-surgery care nurses—I mean just stellar. They helped him (and me) more than I can say. I wrote them both thank-you letters afterward because I was so appreciative of their care. I also wrote notes to their supervisors singing their praises. I believe good work needs to be noticed, and I want the next kid (and parent) to receive that level of care.

Since great providers are a true blessing, let's let them know, shall we?

And, since we're on the topic of care providers, let's talk about some of the ones you'll probably meet.

TYPES OF CARE PROVIDERS
Child Life Specialists

According to the American Academy of Pediatrics, child life programs are a vital part of hospital-based pediatric care, addressing the psychosocial challenges of hospitalization and healthcare experiences. Certified Child Life Specialists are child development experts who work to ensure that life remains as normal as possible for children in healthcare settings by promoting coping, normalization, and emotional well-being.[1]

The Association of Child Life Professionals says that Certified Child Life Specialists play a critical role in supporting child health and wellness by providing developmentally appropriate interventions such as therapeutic play, psychological preparation, education, and coping tools. They collaborate with healthcare teams and families to meet the unique needs of each child, offering preparation for medical procedures, support during treatments, and strategies to reduce fear and anxiety.[2]

Working in various settings, including inpatient units, emergency departments, and outpatient areas, child life specialists focus on family-centered care by fostering therapeutic relationships and advocating for the emotional and developmental needs of children. Their services include:

- Educating children and families about health conditions

- Preparing children for medical procedures or treatment using language that children understand

- Introducing coping strategies to help reduce anxiety and enhance cooperation with the healthcare team

- Planning and rehearsing pain-management strategies with patients and families

- Helping children work through feelings about past or impending experiences

- Providing support and distraction during medical procedures

- Offering opportunities for play and expressive activities, to encourage normal development and a sense of fun in spite of challenging circumstances

- Promoting family-centered care by providing information, advocacy, and support to families of pediatric patients

- Partnering with families to establish therapeutic relationships between patients, siblings, and caregivers

One of the primary roles of child life services is to help families prepare for a hospital stay. Since many of our children may face this experience, let's explore some practical tips for getting ready for a hospital stay.

Preparing a Child for Their Hospital Stay

Hospitals can be a confusing place for a child, and preparing children ahead of time for the things they may experience in the hospital will reduce much of their anxiety. It will also help them cope and trust you and the people they meet in the hospital. According to UCLA Health, here are some tips for preparing a child for a hospital stay:

- For younger children (under the age of 5), talk to them a day or two before the experience. Older children should have a few days to a week to get information and ask questions.

- Use age-appropriate words the child will understand.

- Older children and those who can comprehend may need clear answers about what and why things are happening to them and to be included in the discussions about their care with doctors and nurses.

- Encourage the child to discuss feelings and ask questions about the upcoming experience. Their imaginings may be much worse than actually talking about scary or painful things.

- Be careful not to force a discussion if your child does not seem ready.

- Teach various relaxation techniques in advance such as deep breathing and guided imagery to help the child gain control over their fears.

- Have your child pack a suitcase with the things he or she wants in the hospital to have a sense of security—a comfort item, favorite toy, warm socks, something to distract them such as books, videos, music, etc.

- Reassure them that a parent or loved one will be there to support them.

- Ask about pre-hospital preparations provided by the hospital's Child Life program. Often they can prepare surgery tours or consultations to help your child prepare for a procedure.

- Since children's responses to hospitalization and medical procedures will differ, depending on their age, the procedures to be done, and their past experiences, it is not uncommon to see changes in a child's behavior before, during, or after hospitalization.[3]

Preparing Parents for Their Child's Hospital Stay

Children aren't the only ones that can benefit from preparation for a hospital stay. Hospitals providing inpatient procedures for your child will allow parents to stay overnight with their child while they are admitted. In this case, you'll want to make some extra preparations for your overnight stay too. Here are some tips for parents to prepare for their child's hospital stay:

- Speak to other parents. Ask your child's doctor, the social worker at your children's hospital, or your disease organization to put you in contact with other parents whose children have been through the procedure. They will be a wealth of knowledge, and help you learn things you can do pre-procedure or post-procedure to prepare in advance.

- Plan how you will care for yourself while your child is in the hospital. For the two-parent family, perhaps you take turns staying with your child every other night or switch off between day and night shifts. This allows you to maintain your own health and sleep levels as you care for your child's emotional needs. For the single-parent family, ask other family members or friends whom your child knows and trusts to stay with your child so you can have a break from caregiving.

- Pack comfort items. Your child is not the only one who's going to need comfort while away from home. Bring items to make the stay as comfortable as possible for you, such as comfortable clothes, sweats in case it's cold (it always is), slippers, toothbrush and toothpaste, face wash, phone charger, books, magazines, or something else to distract you, and of course your trusty notetaking device to record or track anything needed.

- Prepare for post-care. What are you going to need when your child returns home post-procedure—special equipment, PT/OT, medications, special meals, etc.? Work ahead of time to get all of this in place to take it off your plate post-procedure. That post-procedure time will be busy enough.

- Enlist help. Line up assistance with meals, grocery shopping, care for other children or your pets, etc. This is one of those times to get all hands on deck.

- Block out time for your own recuperation. Surgeries and procedures may require additional physical, mental, and emotional capacity from mama. Block extra time off for you to recuperate from the ordeal. When the procedure is over, your child may need to spend time recovering. This means mama is "on." Your child may be resting, recuperating, and healing, but that doesn't mean you will be. You may be administering medications, helping with physical therapy, preparing special meals, etc. This can be a high-needs time for you. Make sure to build in some downtime and recuperation time for you after your child is healed. After they are past a certain post-op phase, then it's mama's turn to rest. We don't talk about this often enough. We don't get this advice ahead of time. But I'm telling you, mama, you might be wiped when you're on the other side of your child's recovery. So plan for your own recovery too!

Therapists: Physical, Occupational, Speech, Respiratory, and Behavioral

Many of our children will need therapeutic interventions to support and maintain their health. Physical therapy, occupational therapy, speech therapy, respiratory therapy, and behavioral therapy are some of the common therapies that will be recommended.

Physical Therapy (PT)

Physical therapy addresses medical problems or other health-related conditions that affect a child's ability to move and perform functional activities in their daily lives.

Pediatric physical therapists are movement specialists. They use treatment activities and techniques to increase strength, muscle function, coordination, endurance, and mobility. Physical therapists also work with individuals to prevent the loss of mobility and reduce pain. Pediatric physical therapy uses play and fun activities to entice children to work hard and exercise to promote the highest level of independent function.

Occupational Therapy (OT)

Occupational therapy helps patients to safely and independently perform activities of daily living, including bathing and dressing. Using a wide range of interventions, occupational therapists adapt tasks and modify the environment to enhance each patient's ability to function in their physical and social environment. They provide sensory-motor treatments for strength, endurance, range of motion, coordination, and balance, as well as therapeutic activities for memory, orientation, cognitive integration, and daily life skills.

Pediatric occupational therapists work with children and their families to help develop skills in the following areas: play skills, fine motor skills, and personal or self-care skills. They use strategies that may include working on hand/finger/arm strength, trunk strength and stability, specific self-care tasks, and overall sensory processing. Play is used as a way to address desired skills and encourage the child to be an active participant in their therapy sessions.

Speech Therapy (ST)

Speech language pathologists design treatment plans to address communication problems, memory loss, and swallowing dysfunction. These treatment plans can focus on comprehension skills for written and verbal communication as well as cognitive status, which may include memory, orientation, and reasoning skills. For patients with swallowing disorders, speech language pathologists also work to address oral muscle strength and function for speaking and for safe eating and drinking.

Pediatric speech therapy serves children and their families to address typical and atypical communication and feeding skills. Common treatment techniques may include oral motor strengthening and range of motion exercises, reciprocal interaction through modeling and play, training on the use of audiovisual aids, the use of assistive technology, and strategies to facilitate functional communication.

Respiratory Therapy (RT)

Respiratory therapy is for patients with breathing and cardiopulmonary disorders. Treatment plans are designed to support optimal pulmonary function while promoting an understanding of the disease process. This may include a pulmonary medication regimen and education, airway clearance modalities, a ventilator, tracheostomy and oxygen weaning protocols, lung expansion and coughing techniques, and pulmonary muscle training.

Behavioral Therapy

Behavioral therapy for children involves techniques and strategies aimed at modifying undesirable behaviors and promoting positive ones. It focuses on understanding the factors that influence a child's behavior, such as environmental triggers, cognitive processes, and social interactions. Therapists work with children to develop skills such as problem-solving, communication, emotional regulation, and social skills. Techniques commonly used in behavioral therapy for children include positive reinforcement, token economies, modeling, and systematic desensitization. The goal is to help children learn more adaptive behaviors and cope effectively with challenges they may encounter in their daily lives.

Parents of children with rare diseases can participate in behavioral therapy with their children in several ways:

- Education: Parents can learn about their child's rare disease and how it might impact their behavior. Understanding the condition will help parents anticipate challenges and tailor behavioral strategies to their child's specific needs.

- Collaborative goal-setting: Working closely with the therapist, parents can help set goals for their child's behavioral therapy based on their unique circumstances and challenges related to the rare disease.

- Implementing strategies at home: Therapists often provide parents with strategies and techniques to use at home to reinforce the skills learned in therapy sessions. This might include setting up structured routines, using visual aids, or practicing relaxation techniques.

- Providing support and encouragement: Parents play a crucial role in providing emotional support and encouragement to their child throughout the therapy process. Positive reinforcement and praise will help motivate children to practice new behaviors and skills.

- Communication with the therapist: Open communication between parents and the therapist is essential for monitoring progress, addressing concerns, and making adjustments to the treatment plan as needed. Parents can provide valuable insights into their child's behavior and any changes they observe at home.

Overall, parental involvement is integral to the success of behavioral therapy for children with rare diseases, as parents are uniquely positioned to support and reinforce their child's progress both inside and outside of therapy sessions.

Therapists' Roles

Therapists play significant roles in your child's care, and in some instances they see your child on a more routine basis than your specialist. In addition to therapists providing therapy in their specific area of discipline, they will also recommend medical supplies and durable medical equipment, develop and provide training on at-home therapy plans, provide therapy for recovery from surgery and procedures, assist with feeding needs, address daily living and mobility needs, and more. Below are some of the areas therapists will support:

- Developmental activities
- Movement and mobility
- Strengthening
- Motor learning
- Balance and coordination
- Recreation, play, and leisure
- Endurance
- Daily care activities and routines
- Equipment design, fabrication, and fitting
- Tone management
- Assistive technology
- Orthotics
- Positioning during daily routines and activities
- Adapting toys for play
- Expanding mobility options
- Using equipment effectively
- Facilitating safety for the home and community

- Accessing community programs and resources
- Providing information on the child's physical and healthcare needs
- Supporting family caregiving
- Smoothing transitions from early childhood to school and into adult life
- Posture, positioning, and lifting

Therapy as Play

The approach to pediatric therapy differs from that of adult therapy in that therapists will aim to make therapy "playtime" for children. Therapists must demonstrate a high level of patience and compassion, since children might not understand the need for therapy and can have more trouble staying on task than adults would. Patient compliance is a factor in the success of therapy. In order to gain a child's interest, therapists use equipment and activities that look like fun but are actually proven strategies for achieving treatment goals. Each activity is an intervention proven to help pediatric strength, mobility, and balance. They may use therapy balls, platform swings, adaptive bikes, a jungle gym, sports, crafts, or video games.

Sometimes children are scared, and it's hard to keep their attention. In such cases, therapists may invite a parent to act as lead therapist while they provide direction. Parents play a primary role in their child's ongoing development, so this helps educate us as well.

Home Programs

Pediatric therapists work with both children who need treatment and their family members and caregivers. Caregivers play a vital role in successfully enacting a treatment program. Therapists can support families in advancing their children's development progress by offering services such as providing specific information on the patient's needs, offering guidance on using equipment directly, and providing training on home programs.

In fact, a home therapy program is crucial to success. Pediatric therapists will ask about a child's living situation and daily routine and will adapt a treatment plan accordingly. A comprehensive plan of care will help pediatric patients improve their long-term development, confidence, and independence.

Working with Therapists

Many of the same principles and suggestions for working with specialists can be applied to working with therapists. It is essential to form collaborative, productive partnerships with your child's therapists. Parents act as active members of the team, collaborating and strategizing on goals, implementing at-home therapy plans, disseminating information between specialists and therapists, and keeping therapists abreast of their child's daily activities, progress, challenges, changes, etc.

Parents also act as advocates in these relationships, representing their child and making sure their needs are supported and addressed, whether it's advocating for more therapy time, pushing for needed equipment, etc.

Finding the Right Fit

Since therapists will be working with your child regularly in a very hands-on approach, finding the right fit is key. It's important to keep in mind that just like finding doctors and specialists who are a good fit for your child and family, it's instrumental to find therapists who are able to productively work with your child (and you).

With my son's first experience with occupational therapy, Miles started maybe two or three months after diagnosis when we were newbies to all therapy. His occupational therapist was assigned, and we began attending biweekly appointments. I was an eager-beaver newbie rare mama desperate for help, so I was beyond grateful for these appointments. Miles was barely two years old at the time, and we had a lot to learn. We showed up week after week, but I noticed Miles was not warming up to his OT. I chalked it up to the fact that he was young, new to therapy, and not used to some stranger having her hands on him, and I figured that over time he'd adjust.

One month led to two, two became three, and finally, about six months into therapy, I realized that nothing was changing. Miles just wasn't having it. The sessions ended up being unproductive and therefore extremely frustrating. I couldn't understand it, because we weren't having this experience with physical therapy. Miles was forming trust and a bond with his PT (and so was I). But not only was he not warming up to his OT, he was actually quite adverse to the occupational therapy altogether. It got to the point where Miles became quite obstinate in a way I hadn't seen him behave with anyone. He dreaded going to OT (and so did I), and when he got there, he wasn't himself. This wasn't good for anyone.

When it came to his occupational therapist and her therapy style, I couldn't quite put my finger on it, but something just didn't feel right. She misread a lot of Miles's cues, and I'd find myself trying to explain them to help her understand him. Honestly, she did the same with me, and I'd find myself having to explain myself. Don't get me wrong—my son was headstrong and stubborn (hmm, I don't know where he gets that from), and I'm sure I was no cup of tea either. But something just wasn't clicking with this OT. I don't know any other way to say it other than we just weren't a fit.

But what did I know? How would I know what the right fit was when we'd never had any experience with OT? I had nothing to compare it to, so I just assumed it was us and it would eventually get better. But it didn't.

Finally, after much agonizing and trepidation, I built up the nerve to ask for another OT. I didn't want to be ungrateful, because I was beyond thankful for her time and services. I didn't want to throw anyone under the bus either. I mean, I wasn't necessarily pointing out something she did wrong; it just wasn't working, and it just wasn't a fit for my kid. I came up with this whole speech I was going to give the supervisor when I asked for a different therapist and what I was going to say if I was told no. Seriously, I think I wrote it all down and then practiced out loud in front of the mirror.

So finally I asked. Do you know what they said? They said yes. And they said it right away with no questions asked. Guess what I found out later? I wasn't the only one who had requested a different OT than her over the years. It turned out she had been there for many years (too many, in fact). She was close to retirement and had been biding her time until then. Turns out we weren't getting the best of her; we were getting the rest of her.

Miles was assigned a new OT, and she came in eager, excited, and with all kinds of ideas and energy and spunk! Miles took to her right away. She made OT feel like play. She made it fun. He liked her so much that he was eager to please her, and so he did. He did his OT like he was playing a new game, eager for a challenge, competing to do it to the best of his ability, and ready for more. He looked forward to the sessions each week, and so did I. It was night and day. She brought out the best in Miles.

That was my first lesson about finding the right fit and what a difference it can make. Rare mamas who have been around the block will tell you this without batting an eye. If a provider is not a fit for your kid, move on! Seriously, if you have choices, just go ahead and move on.

The truth is that there can be huge disparities in skill levels of providers, personalities, and tactics. Sadly, sometimes there are staffing issues, turnover, burnout, and politics at play. It's worth the energy and effort to find the right fit so your child can make the most of their therapy time.

Taking a Break

When Miles was three years old and starting preschool, we were busy running around to physical therapy, occupational therapy, equine therapy, and swim therapy. Then school started, and three days a week he was going to school half a day. This was a big adjustment. Every day we were running to school or therapy. We both were exhausted. I could tell that all the hustle, bustle, and shuffle was getting to Miles. He wasn't as cooperative in therapy, he was fatigued, and he was cranky (which wasn't like him). And frankly, so was I. We were hitting a wall.

When spring break week came, school was out, but there was still therapy. I had a choice to make. I felt that we needed a break from it all. Even though his therapy seemed so vital, we took the week off. I worried about what our therapists would say—but you know what they said? They said, "We get it." They understood that every now and then kids and parents need a break.

Hallelujah! And that little week off allowed us to breathe, sleep in, not rush out the door early in the morning, not hustle and shuffle. We enjoyed time together and replenished our tank. Then the next week, we got back to business.

Therapy is often essential to our child's care. But as parents, we have to stay attuned to our child's psychological needs and state of mind too. Even though therapy schedules might be ongoing with no recommended breaks, every now and then we might need to make tough calls like allowing our kids to take time out to rest. In our case, the week off of therapy did not put my son's health at risk, and there was a mental health benefit. This is something to keep in mind as you navigate through ongoing therapy.

Mental Health Providers

Obviously we are focused on our child's physical health, but it's important to be aware that rare diseases can affect mental health as well. In fact, statistics say that patients who suffer from a rare disease experience higher levels of anxiety, stress, and depression.[4] That's why many researchers and healthcare organizations that treat and support these patients are turning their attention to mental health. It is important for patients, their families, and the greater medical community to be aware of and understand rare diseases' potential impact on mental health.

Research indicates that children with rare diseases can experience significant mental health challenges, including anxiety, depression, and low self-esteem due to the unique stressors associated with their conditions, such as lack of understanding about their illness, physical limitations, social isolation, and the uncertainty surrounding their treatment options. This research highlights the need for dedicated mental health support tailored to this population.

According to a study titled "Psychosocial Considerations for the Child with Rare Disease," children living with rare diseases experience barriers that impact their quality of life and psychosocial functioning, as demonstrated by higher levels of mental health needs. In a recent cross-sectional study conducted in Western Australia, 43.9 percent of parents of children with rare diseases reported that their child experienced mental health difficulties. Researchers found that parents of children with chronic illnesses were two times more likely to report that their child experienced emotional distress and lower levels of self-confidence.[5]

According to a study published in the *Orphanet Journal of Rare Diseases*, at least 25 percent of children with rare diseases experience psychological difficulties. Issues like anxiety, mood disorders, behavioral problems, and difficulties with emotion regulation are prevalent.[6]

More and more medical professionals are recognizing the need to integrate mental health into the care plan for patients with a rare disease. If you feel your child or your family could benefit from seeing a mental health professional, seek a provider that is experienced in treating patients who are suffering from an illness. Most mental health providers treat a range of conditions, but one with a specialized focus may be more suited to your needs.

To find a mental health provider, you have several options:

- Seek a referral or recommendation from your primary care provider or specialist.

- Check with social workers, case managers, or child life services at your children's hospital who can often offer referrals.

- If you have private insurance for your child, ask the health insurance company for a list of covered providers. Many insurance companies make a list of their providers available online.

- If you have Medicare or Medicaid for your child, contact them to find out what types of mental health services are covered. The Medicare Physician Compare can assist you in finding a physician who is enrolled in Medicare. Your state Medicaid office, whose contact information can be found using the map on the National Association of State Medicaid Directors site, may be able to assist you in finding a provider who accepts Medicaid.

- *Psychology Today* has a robust database allowing you to search for providers by area and learn more about each practitioner. (Many people start searching for a provider by scrolling through their insurance company's list of providers, then cross-referencing those against this database.)

- Contact a local or national mental health organization such as the National Alliance on Mental Illness (NAMI), American Medical Association, the American Psychiatric Association, the American Psychological Association, or the Association for Behavioral and Cognitive Therapies.

- Check with nonprofits, patient advocacy groups, and rare disease organizations.

Just as with other specialists and providers, you'll want to form collaborative relationships with mental health providers. Don't hesitate to ask lots of questions, provide information and background, and find the right fit. Finding the right match is crucial to establishing a good relationship and getting the most out of treatment.

Managing medical care and systems is one of the most crucial parts of your strategy in this fight. It's where you'll spend a lot of time and effort. It's a lot at the beginning, but once you get a care team in place that is working, you'll have laid the groundwork and the foundation your child will benefit from for years to come.

Rare Mama Truth

Rare disease doesn't necessarily come with a specialist. It comes with a mama who scours the earth to find the right one.

CHAPTER 11

Finding Financial Programs and Services

"A 'no' is not the end; it's a comma
in the sentence of your journey."

UNKNOWN

After you've assembled your child's medical team, your next
mission is to obtain programs and services available for
children with disabilities. Medical care, equipment, caregiving, and therapies—all necessities—come with a high-ticket
price. Increased expenses combined with the potential loss of income
due to time spent caregiving can create immense financial pressure.
One of the best things I can advise is to take the time up front to
find alternative sources of funding and obtain programs and services
to help cover these new expenses. They can be a lifeline.

Most programs and services vary by state, but there are some
universal guidelines and tips I can share with you. I'd like you to hit

the ground running and make progress toward getting the financial help you need right now. Let's dive into what programs and services exist, how to find them, and tips for navigating them.

FEDERAL PROGRAMS

The United States has programs at both the federal and state levels to help children with disabilities. These programs can help fund insurance, therapies, medications, equipment, nursing care, and more.

At the federal level are Supplemental Security Income (SSI) and Medicaid. These programs allow your child to receive healthcare and equipment at no cost or with a share of cost.

Supplemental Security Income (SSI)

SSI is available to families whose children have a disability and have income below a set amount. To learn more and see if your child qualifies, visit www.ssa.gov/benefits/disability/apply-child.html.

Medicaid

Medicaid is another federal program designed to provide health insurance for low-income adults, children, pregnant women, elderly adults, and people with disabilities. Because private insurance does not cover many services children with disabilities require, or children with disabilities cannot get insurance, Medicaid allows another pathway to access healthcare coverage.

Medicaid provides funds directly to the states to use as they decide, and it is administered by states according to federal requirements. Each state determines what programs they will fund with their Medicaid dollars, and they dictate the eligibility requirements for their various programs. If your household income meets the set requirements, you may qualify for Medicaid. Eligibility is reevaluated every year. To learn more about this program, you can visit the following websites, but ultimately, you'll want to search for your specific state's Medicaid program:

- www.ssa.gov/disability
- www.hhs.gov/answers/medicare-and-medicaid/who-is-eligible-for-medicaid/index.html
- www.medicaid.gov
- www.healthcare.gov
- www.cms.gov/about-cms/contact/database

Medicaid Waiver

If your family's income is above the set requirements for Medicaid, then you'll have to dig a little harder to see if your state has a Medicaid Waiver. Medicaid typically counts the entire family's income when determining eligibility, until a child turns eighteen. The Medicaid Waiver program waives the household income and only counts the child's income. Since the child has no income and has a disability, they qualify for the program. This waiver allows individuals who may not normally qualify for Medicaid due to their household income being higher than the set limit to qualify to receive services.

The purpose of this program is to help children receive care in their home. At one time, children with severe illnesses were "institutionalized," which means they were placed in an institution for care because their communities and families did not have the funding or resources to keep them in the home. Since then, evidence has proven that in most cases, children are better off living at home and being cared for by their loved ones, and in fact, it costs less for children to live at home than in an institution.

To that end, the Medicaid Waiver program was put into place to permit "institutional deeming," which allows children to stay in their home and receive services they would otherwise receive in an institution or medical facility. Instead of the state paying an institution to care for the child, this government program essentially pays the family to care for the child at home.

The waiver may also offer additional services such as in-home health, PT, OT, speech, respite, or training programs.

Though the Medicaid Waiver is a federal program, it's managed by each state, and the name and type of program varies by state. According to Kidswaivers.org,[1] there are four basic types of Medicaid waivers and programs.

Tax Equity & Fiscal Responsibility Act (TEFRA)/ Katie Beckett Programs

This provision of the Tax Equity and Fiscal Responsibility Act (TEFRA) of 1982, often called the Katie Beckett or TEFRA option, gives states the option to extend Medicaid to children with severe disabilities by only counting the income of the child with a disability and not the income of the parents.

Under the TEFRA option, children must meet certain criteria to qualify. They need to have a disability that meets Social Security Administration standards and requires care in a hospital, nursing facility, or intermediate care facility. This program is available to children from birth to age eighteen and is intended to include children with various disabilities. However, some states primarily focus on children with physical disabilities or complex medical needs requiring specialized technology.

One key benefit of TEFRA is that states offering it must serve all eligible children who apply, without implementing a waiting list. Eligibility is determined solely based on the child's income and resources, excluding parental income.

However, there are drawbacks to the program. TEFRA only provides access to standard Medicaid services and does not include additional benefits like respite care or home and vehicle modifications. Furthermore, participation in the TEFRA option is voluntary for states, and many opt not to offer it due to the financial burden of covering all eligible children.

1915(c) Home and Community-Based Services (HCBS) Waivers

The 1915(c) Home and Community-Based Services (HCBS) waivers are among the most commonly used waivers, representing collaborative programs between federal and state governments. These waivers are tailored to serve specific groups of individuals with disabilities and offer Medicaid coverage along with additional services to support community living. Since each state designs its own programs, there is significant variation, making it difficult to provide a one-size-fits-all description.

Populations typically served by 1915(c) and HCBS waivers include older adults, individuals with physical or medical disabilities, medically fragile or technology-dependent individuals, those with brain or spinal cord injuries, people with HIV/AIDS, and individuals with autism, developmental disabilities, intellectual disabilities, or serious emotional or mental health conditions. States may address these populations differently; for example, a child with autism might qualify under an autism-specific waiver in one state, a developmental disabilities waiver in another, or an intellectual disabilities waiver elsewhere. Similarly, a child with cerebral palsy or epilepsy might qualify under waivers for physical disabilities, medically fragile populations, or developmental disabilities, depending on the state.

Some waivers consider only the child's income for eligibility, while others factor in parental income.

1915(c) and HCBS waivers are tied to specific levels of care: hospital, nursing facility (NF), or intermediate care facility (ICF). The level of care determines the scope of services a person can receive, capped at what their care would cost in a comparable institution. For instance, children requiring ventilators or those with severe mental illness may qualify for hospital-level care, while those with physical disabilities might be eligible for nursing facility–level care. Children with autism or developmental disabilities are often assessed for intermediate care facility–level care.

One of the key benefits of 1915(c) and HCBS waivers is the provision of services that go beyond standard Medicaid, such as respite care, home or vehicle modifications, personal supports, specialized equipment, training, and behavioral interventions.

However, these waivers are not guaranteed entitlements. As a result, many programs have long waiting lists, sometimes exceeding years, before individuals can begin receiving services. This lack of immediate availability is a significant drawback for families in need.

Each state creates its programs and what it will fund. Since every program is different and varies by state, you will have to check your specific state to see what your state's waiver offers.

1115 Demonstration Waivers

States can opt to develop specialized programs to address the needs of individuals with disabilities or even overhaul their entire Medicaid system through 1115 demonstration waivers. In some states, these programs replace traditional waiver types and serve individuals with disabilities differently. While some 1115 waivers closely resemble

TEFRA or 1915(c) waivers on a smaller scale, others implement broader reforms that reshape the state's entire Medicaid service structure. Because each state's program is uniquely designed, generalizing about 1115 waivers is challenging. Only a limited number of states use this approach to provide home- and community-based services.

A well-designed 1115 waiver offers the advantage of simplifying eligibility processes and combining multiple programs to serve diverse populations more effectively. However, these waivers also allow states to bypass certain Medicaid rules, which can reduce protections for participants. This flexibility means that 1115 waivers might impose restrictions on eligibility or limit available services, creating potential challenges for those relying on them.

State-Based, 1915(i), 1915(j), and 1915(k) Programs

Some states have established their own programs designed to resemble the TEFRA option. These programs vary widely—some broaden eligibility, while others impose more restrictions. Similarly, some offer full Medicaid coverage, while others limit the services available. These state-specific programs are relatively rare, with Pennsylvania's PH-95 program being the largest example. A few other states have also implemented similar TEFRA-inspired programs.

Additionally, some states use other Medicaid waiver authorities to provide home- and community-based services through their regular Medicaid plans for children already enrolled. These include:

- **1915(i):** This waiver allows states to offer a wide range of home- and community-based services, including respite care, home or vehicle modifications, and in-home supports, to individuals who qualify and are already enrolled in Medicaid. While states can target specific age groups or diagnoses, they cannot implement waiting lists. For instance, Idaho's 1915(i) program supports children enrolled in Medicaid through a Katie Beckett/TEFRA program and provides them with additional services under the state plan.

- **1915(j):** This option permits Medicaid recipients to self-direct their personal care services. It also allows states to compensate parents of minors for providing these services. California's In-Home Supportive Services (IHSS) program is an example of a 1915(j) waiver in action.

- **1915(k):** This waiver enables states to deliver personal assistance and in-home support through the regular state Medicaid plan to eligible individuals without waiting lists. Many states have adopted this option to enhance accessibility for those in need.

How to Find Your State's Medicaid Waiver Program

Each state manages these programs individually. Both the state programs and the federal programs that are administered have their own set of names, rules, and requirements. Therefore, it's best to look into your specific state's programs for children with disabilities. Since the name of this waiver varies from state to state, you'll have to research the Medicaid Waiver program in your specific state. Here are a few ways to find that information:

- Search "Medicaid Waiver Program [Insert state name]" and see if the links come up to take you to the Medicaid Waiver program for your state.

- Visit your state's Medicaid website and dig around.

- Call the Department of Human Services or visit them at www.hhs.gov.

- Check out www.kidswaivers.org.

- Ask your hospital's social worker or care team.

- Contact the Continuity of Care Department at your state's children's and university hospitals.

- Ask other moms in your state whose children have a diagnosis.

- Contact The ARC, a national group that advocates on behalf of people with intellectual and developmental disabilities. Visit their website (www.thearc.org) to find information about government programs including SSI, Medicare, and Medicaid waivers.

How to Apply for the Medicaid Waiver Program

The first step you must take is applying for Medicaid. Each state is different, and you will need to check the eligibility factors for your household at the state level. Be prepared to provide information about your income, personal assets, family size, and child's disabilities.

You can apply for Medicaid at any time; you do not need to wait for an open enrollment period. You will create your account through the Health Insurance Marketplace. If you qualify for Medicaid, the Marketplace will forward the information to your state's Medicaid agency. If your income is too high, then your child will qualify with a share of cost. The share of cost will be waived once you have the Medicaid Waiver in place. It's a little chicken and the egg, but you'll need to get your child into the Medicaid system by applying for Medicaid first.

Another option available is to contact and apply directly with your state's Medicaid agency. An agent will guide you through the process of applying for coverage. Once your child is approved for Medicaid, you will need to apply for the Medicaid Waiver through your state's Medicaid office. You'll fill out an application, and then you'll be contacted to set up an intake evaluation. During the evaluation, you'll be asked questions about your child's health and needs. You then will wait to receive an approval.

Once your child is approved for the waiver, they'll receive Medicaid to pay for medical care and equipment. If your child has private insurance or insurance coverage through your or your spouse's employer, Medicaid will act as a secondary insurance. This means that medical care and equipment costs will be billed to your private insurance first. Then the portion that is billed as the patient's responsibility will be covered by Medicaid. As a result, many of your healthcare expenses and equipment may be covered.

STATE PROGRAMS

Another state program funded with Medicaid dollars is the Children's Health Insurance Program (CHIP). Your child may qualify for this program if you don't have health insurance and your income is too high for Medicaid. You can find out more about this program at https://www.healthcare.gov/medicaid-chip/ childrens-health-insurance-program.

As mentioned, if your state offers an HCBS waiver, then once you qualify for Medicaid, you may also qualify for other state-funded programs. These Medicaid-funded programs can also provide home health aides; daycare; respite care; and physical, occupational, and speech therapy. They also will allow the family to hire a childcare worker or family member to help with the daily living needs of a child with a disability.

Since each state manages these programs individually, the names of the programs vary by state and the requirements and processes are different depending on the state you live in. For example, in one state this program is called In-Home Supportive Services (IHSS). In another state, it's called In-Home and Family Support Program

(IH/FSP), and in yet another state it's called the Home Service Program (HSP). So you'll have to do some searching to try and locate these other potential programs.

These state-funded programs are helpful for a multitude of reasons, including that many children's medical needs are so great that the parent can't delegate the care to someone else. In these instances, one parent may stay home full-time to facilitate the therapies, doctors' appointments, and caregiving. The loss of that parent's income, compounded with the increased medical costs and new expenses of equipment and therapy, can create immense financial pressure. For many families, the Medicaid Waiver and the state-funded in-home support programs are the only way they can cover the costs of both healthcare and childcare or nursing care. Some of the in-home support programs allow one parent to act as the caregiver and receive funds that they can use to pay themselves for caregiving.

Navigating Programs and Services

To find these resources to offset increased costs and potential diminished income will require time and research. I know this is time you don't have, but trust me when I tell you to invest the time to get your fiscal plan and affairs in order before you start feeling the financial heat—because, mama, it's already hot in the jungle!

Getting a Medicaid Waiver program in place can be a lengthy, frustrating process. I want you to know this reality up front so that instead of being taken back by it, you can be armed and ready so when you hit a frustrating patch or things are taking longer than expected, you can know in advance that this is just part of the process. You can say to yourself, *Ah, yes, this is what she was talking about.* Then you can take a deep breath and keep pushing forward.

Friends, it took me years—too many years—to figure out the programs and systems that could help our family. I don't want that for you. So let me just point out the roadblocks you may encounter.

One of the challenges is that these programs are not well publicized. It would be helpful if every child who was given a diagnosis was also given a list of their specific state's resources and programs that could help pay for healthcare and equipment needs. Some hospitals have a social worker or department that can inform you of these programs. Others don't. Even if your hospital does have a social worker or system to provide you with information, sometimes they may lack the knowledge about the Medicaid Waiver program or other programs in your state. So there you are at square one, not even knowing if programs exist. I've encountered too many rare mamas who spent years not knowing that programs and services were available in their state. The first step is seeking awareness and educating yourself on what is available to you.

Then, once you finally find the programs, you'll have to find out how to apply for them. They each have their own systems and processes, and they are not easy to understand. You'll have to fill out applications and forms. I'm here to tell you, if you're ever wondering, *Is it me? Do they make these forms and applications impossible to understand?*, no, it isn't you. It's just the lovely gift of one more confusing thing to figure out.

Not only can the paperwork and processes be confusing, but dealing with the offices that manage these programs can be less than pleasant. It's not uncommon to be faced with appointments, evaluations, and then delays. It's not uncommon to receive denials. You may need to provide additional justifications. You may need to appeal. Unfortunately, to get what you need, you'll have to advocate.

Another thing you should know up front is that there is often a waiting list for these waivers and programs. Someone from the state agency handling the waiver or other programs will determine your child's level of need, and this will determine how soon you can receive services. Some states have waiting lists, and sadly, sometimes these waiting lists can be years long.

My advice is to get on the waiting list as soon as possible. Take the time to research the Medicaid Waiver and state-funded programs to figure out how to get your child on them. Definitely make it one of the priorities on your to-do list. These services can be a financial lifesaver, so investing the time will be more than worth it in the long run.

There may be points when you feel like throwing in the towel. Don't. There may be times when you will ask yourself, *Is it worth it?* or *Can I do this?* The answers are *Yes* and *Yes*. It's worth it to take the time up front to get services and programs in place. It will ease the financial burden and stress of medical care, treatment, equipment, respite, etc. Even though it may feel a little daunting, you can definitely do it.

> **Decide in advance that if you are delayed or denied, you will not give up.**

Put on your detective hat and start digging, searching, and clawing to get the answers you need. Talk to other moms who have had to apply for and obtain these services in your state. Often, they'll know the game.

Be assertive. Be persistent. Be determined that you can and will find and obtain these programs and services. Decide in advance that if you are delayed or denied, you will not give up. Understand that this is part of how the game is played. Is it fair? No. But don't be deterred. These programs and services exist for a reason. They are there to benefit your family. Stay the course, and you will gain in the end.

HEALTH INSURANCE

Your child has healthcare needs. You have medical claims. You need equipment. Insurance is another funding source that can help with these expenses. You'll have to go through your state's Medicaid program or through private insurance, or both.

It's not uncommon for insurance companies and their medical reviewers to be unfamiliar with your child's rare disease. Therefore, insurance companies may not understand why your child needs the equipment, treatments, and services you (and even your child's doctors) say they do. Clearly you need them and expect them to be approved, but often they aren't. So the next step is that you and your child's doctor may need to provide more detailed letters of justification or your child's specialist may need to do a peer-to-peer review with the medical reviewer at the insurance company to educate them on the disease and the need. Enlist your child's specialists and their teams to aid you in the justification and appeal process.

Perhaps the insurance company is hoping that you'll get the denial and say, "Okay, never mind. You're right. We don't actually need that piece of life-saving equipment." If you give up, they get out of paying for an expensive piece of equipment. But does a rare mama stop at a *no*? Well, no. No, she doesn't. Your job is to believe that the *no* is temporary and you have to turn it into a *yes*.

You'll have to appeal. You may get denied again. You'll have to appeal again. You may even have to appeal so many times that now you have to take it to the insurance board for your state. I've been through this process many, many times. Girl, my fangs are dripping just writing this.

The first piece of equipment we ever tried to get for Miles was a stander because he couldn't stand independently, and standing is necessary for bone density, preventing bone fractures, preventing constipation, preventing contractures, and the list goes on and on.

This is just straight-up medical science, and you can find it in any medical book. But our insurance denied it, saying it wasn't medically necessary. Oh, mama, was I livid. I was fuming. How could they? That was my baby they just said no to!

I got on my computer and searched like a mad woman for why children with neuromuscular diseases need standers. I searched for sample insurance appeal letters. I researched and researched. I cut and pasted and wrote a letter to build our case. I cited medical journals and articles. I cited doctors and specialists. I didn't know what half the things I was reading meant. I was in way over my head; this was way past my intellectual capacity and my area of expertise. But I did it anyway. We appealed all the way up to the state insurance board.

I was exhausted. It was time I didn't have. I should've been caring for Miles. I should've been playing cars and trucks with Mason, who was a toddler at the time. It sucked energy and time from my family and me. Oh yes, I was mad about it! Then we waited.

It worked. We got a letter in the mail saying that the state insurance board had overturned the decision. My son would get his stander. That made it all so worth it. Victory! Don't tell mama her baby can't have what he needs!

Since then, I've had to do it a couple times more. I have learned to lean into my child's care team to help with the justifications, and it's gotten a little easier each time. I don't get as worked up about it now. Yes, I'm still furious about the time-suck and delays it causes, but I say to myself, *Game on! You messed with the wrong mama!* I mean, yes, I still don't think it's right that we as rare disease moms have to jump through hoops and learn things way beyond our comfort zone, but unfortunately, it's the way the game is played. So if you have to play it, you might as well find the *yes*!

Mama, I know it may feel like there is a lot to do, and these are definitely not easy systems to navigate. But there is no doubt in my mind that you can get the services and programs you need in place. I've watched countless rare mamas do it, and I know you can too!

Be relentless.

Rare Mama Truth

"Hell hath no fury like a woman scorned," or a rare mama whose medical insurance has denied something for her kid.

CHAPTER 12

Obtaining Medical Supplies and Equipment

"A medical device can be the difference between struggle and survival, between fear and freedom."

UNKNOWN

C hildren and young adults with special healthcare needs often require various forms of durable medical equipment (DME) and medical supplies. These include items or services that help children with disabilities improve or keep their ability to function in everyday life, such as strollers, pushchairs, wheelchairs, walkers, gait trainers, standers, positioners, seating systems, lifts, bath supports, commodes, ventilators, suction machines, cough machines, hospital beds, orthotics, prosthetics, assistive technology, and communication devices. There are a few ways you can obtain this equipment.

HEALTH INSURANCE

Obtaining medical equipment and supplies is a process and often can prove to be quite complex and lengthy. First, a script must be written by your child's specialist. The type of equipment will determine which specialist will write the script. For example, a pulmonologist will write the script for breathing equipment, while an orthopedist will write the script for mobility equipment such as wheelchairs and walkers. If the equipment is recommended by your child's doctor/specialist, they may write the script and provide it to you at an appointment or send it directly to the equipment vendor/supplier.

Your child's PT or OT may also recommend equipment, consult on which type of equipment will be most beneficial for your child, and even facilitate a demo of the equipment. Physical therapists may consult on equipment that assists your child's movement and mobility and provides access to their community. Occupational therapists may consult on equipment that assists with daily living needs such as feeding devices, bath equipment, commodes, etc. Speech therapists may consult on equipment that facilitates speech and communication such as assistive technology and communication devices. Often therapists work with suppliers and vendors to stay up to date on the latest technology offered.

If the need for a piece of equipment is recommended by your child's PT, OT, or ST, you will still need to obtain the script from your child's doctor/specialist. This is one of those instances where having the contact info for your specialist's PA or nurse will come in handy. You'll want to reach out to this person to request the script.

Next, your child will see an equipment vendor/supplier who will evaluate your child's needs and recommend the type, make, and model of the equipment. The supplier will also take measurements and customize when necessary. Depending on the type of equipment, your child may be able to try a demo. If insurance will be used to purchase the equipment, the vendor will request medical records and justification from your child's doctor. The script, justification, and medical notes will be sent along with the order to your child's insurance.

If your child has Medicaid or Medicare, it's important to understand that these programs will only cover DME if your doctors and DME suppliers are enrolled in the Medicaid or Medicare program. Doctors and suppliers have to meet strict standards to enroll and stay enrolled in Medicaid and Medicare. It's important to ask a supplier if they participate in the programs before you get DME. If suppliers are participating in these programs, they must accept assignment (which means they can charge you only the coinsurance and Part B deductible for the Medicare approved amount). If suppliers aren't participating and don't accept assignment, there's no limit on the amount they can charge you.

This is the process, and it can be convoluted and complex. Accessing DME through the designated state Medicaid and Medicare programs can be a challenging process for beneficiaries and advocates due to structural complications and complexities in the rules.

Then, every time your child outgrows their equipment and needs a new piece of equipment, the process will start again.

EQUIPMENT POOLS

Many organizations for children's diseases or disorders have equipment pools. If you're looking for a specific piece of equipment or device, and if your child's disease has a foundation or patient advocacy group, check with the organizations to see whether they have an equipment pool that families use to share.

There are also many organizations dedicated specifically to providing equipment for children in need. Research these organizations in your area to see if there might be gently used equipment that can be borrowed and used at no cost.

You can also join online groups for your child's disease and see if any of these families have equipment that their child has outgrown or no longer needs.

CHARITABLE ORGANIZATIONS

Additional resources may be available through charities and organizations that provide assistance for children with disabilities. They may fund therapy, equipment, medications, recreational activities, and more. Some of these include:

- Disabled Children's Fund (www.disabled-child.org)
- Easter Seals (www.easterseals.com)
- Elks Foundation (www.elk.org)
- First Hand Foundation (www.firsthandfoundation.org)
- Giving Angels Foundation (www.givingangelsfoundation.org)
- Gracie's Hope (www.hboinfo.com/hhi/gracies-hope/)
- Kiddo's Clubhouse (www.kiddosclubhousefoundation.org)
- Kiwanis Club (www.kiwanis.org)
- Lions Club (www.lionsclubs.org)
- Maggie Welby Foundation (www.maggiewelby.org)
- My Gym Foundation (www.mygymfoundation.org)
- Parker's Purpose (www.parkerspurpose.net)
- Shriner's Hospital for Children (www.shrinerschildrens.org)
- Sunshine Foundation (www.sunshinefoundation.org)
- United Healthcare Children's Foundation (www.uhccf.org)

- Variety the Children's Foundation (www.usvariety.org)
- Wheel to Walk Foundation (www.wheeltowalk.com)
- Wheelchairs 4 Kids (www.wheelchairs4kids.org)

INDIVIDUAL FUNDRAISING

Another way to raise funds for a personal cause such as a piece of equipment, a surgery, or any other need is to set up your own online fundraising account, called crowdfunding. A variety of websites make it easy and effective to do this. The list of sites is evolving every day, so do an online search for medical crowdfunding to review the site that may be the best fit for your needs.

> Equipment and medical supplies can be life-giving and open up doors to mobility.

Obtaining and refreshing your child's equipment as they grow and their needs change will be a necessary and ongoing part of your journey. This is another area where you may be met with delays and denials, and you will have to be an advocate, justifying why your child needs the DME, following up on orders and deliveries, and keeping tabs on when equipment needs to be repaired or replaced. Since these pieces of equipment and medical supplies can be life-giving and open up doors to mobility, it will be worth it to stay on top of pursuing and obtaining these items.

Rare Mama Truth

Hi, me again. Thought I'd check on that equipment for my child one more time in case you forgot to call, or you called, and I missed it, and you didn't leave a message, or you lost my number, or my email, or my name, or your phone. Call me! Thanks; bye.

CHAPTER 13

Understanding Educational Systems

"Education is the key to unlock the
golden door of freedom for every child,
irrespective of their unique abilities."

MAYA ANGELOU

L ike everything else in the rare disease world, helping our children access their education can feel like an overwhelming and daunting endeavor. It can require us as parents to learn a whole new system—the education system, or more accurately, the special education system. I want to encourage you that while it can feel overwhelming and require many steps initially, it does get easier as you put things in place. All the time spent up front educating yourself can lay the foundation for a successful future of learning, in whatever way, shape, and form that may look like for your child's unique needs.

First I'd like to lay out some basics about special education for any parents starting out navigating the system. Then I'll offer some tips to help you advocate effectively and set your child up for success in the school years ahead.

SPECIAL EDUCATION

Special education is instruction that is specifically designed to meet the unique needs of children with disabilities. Special education and related services are provided in public schools at no cost to parents and can include special instruction in the classroom, at home, in hospitals, in institutions, or in other settings.

A child who is found eligible for special education may receive a variety of services, including speech and language therapy, psychological services, physical and occupational therapy, counseling services, adaptive recess, assistive technology, transportation, and other supports needed to access and benefit from their education.

In general, all school-age children who are individuals with disabilities in the United States are entitled to a Free Appropriate Personalized Education (FAPE). The FAPE outlines various governing guidelines, including the following:

- Education services must meet individual needs.

- Students with disabilities must be educated with nondisabled students.

- Evaluation and placement decisions must be made in accordance with appropriate procedures.

- Recipients must have due process procedures for the review of identification, evaluation, and placement decisions.

Three federal laws guarantee the rights of students with disabilities, including the Americans with Disabilities Act (ADA), the

Individuals with Disabilities Education Act (IDEA), and Section 504 of the Rehabilitation Act (504 Plan). Let's talk about these in brief so you have some basic knowledge of these laws.

The ADA was enacted to establish that physical and mental disabilities in no way diminish a person's right to fully participate in all aspects of society. ADA provides clear, strong, consistent, enforceable standards addressing discrimination against individuals with disabilities. It also ensures that the federal government plays a central role in enforcing the standards established in the act on behalf of individuals with disabilities.

The IDEA is the federal law that defines and regulates special education. It requires public schools to provide special education services to children ages three to twenty-one who meet certain criteria. The act exists to ensure that all children with disabilities have available to them a FAPE that emphasizes special education and related services designed to meet their unique needs and prepare them for further education, employment, and independent living.

Students who qualify under IDEA receive an Individualized Education Plan (IEP). To qualify, a student must:

- have a documented disability in one of the thirteen categories covered by IDEA, including autism, deaf-blindness, deafness, emotional disturbance, hearing impairment, intellectual disability, multiple disabilities, orthopedic impairment, other health impairment, specific learning disability, speech or language impairment, traumatic brain injury, or visual impairment (including blindness)

AND

- need special education in order to access the general education curriculum (*access* is a term used in education meaning finding ways to remove barriers to learning for children with disabilities)

Children with physical or mental impairments that substantially limit a major life function but who do not meet the requirements to qualify for an IEP receive a 504 plan. This plan is governed by Section 504 of the Rehabilitation Act of 1973. A 504 plan is a plan for how a child with a disability or impairment will be provided with a FAPE to ensure the child has the same access to the learning environment as their non-impaired peers. To get a 504 plan:

- A child must have a disability or impairment (including learning or attention issues).

- The disability must impair major life activity that may interfere with the child's ability to learn/perform in a general education classroom.

Evaluation Process

To determine whether your child qualifies for special education services and which type of services they will receive, an assessment process must take place. This is an evaluation that usually involves tests, interviews, and observations designed to identify your child's strengths and evaluate specific issues related to school performance. The assessment results may also identify the types of special education services your child needs.

A parent, teacher, or other service provider, such as a school psychologist or even your family physician, can request an assessment (called a "referral for assessment"). This must be in writing and should be addressed to the local educational agency (LEA), usually your local school district.

A letter requesting an assessment should state:

- your child's full name

- your child's date of birth

- your name, address, and phone number

- whether your child is currently enrolled in school and, if so, the name of the school

- whether your child has ever received special education services

- that your child is having learning problems that you think might require special education services and that you want an evaluation

Deliver the request for assessment to your child's teacher or school principal. If your child is not enrolled in school, address it to your school district's director of special education. If you do not find anything called "Special Education" on your school district's website, look for something like "Programs for Exceptional Children" or "Student Services," which is often what special education departments are called. Be sure to keep a copy of your referral letter with the date of delivery to the school district.

Once the school district receives the request for assessment, it must give you a proposed assessment plan. The plan must specify the types of assessments to be conducted, and must also state that no special education services will result from the assessment without your consent in writing. Once you receive the school's proposed assessment plan, you may review it to decide whether to consent to the plan. If you agree to the plan, you must sign and return it to the school district within a set number of days. Once the school receives the signed assessment plan, it has a set number of days to conduct the assessment and hold a meeting to discuss the results of the testing.

After you have agreed to an assessment plan, the school district should begin the assessment and schedule a meeting with you to discuss the results. As a parent, you may be asked to participate in testing by answering additional questions about your child's functioning at home and at school. You have the right to request a copy of the assessment results in your native language. You also may request that the written results be given to you before the meeting, to give you time to review them and prepare any questions. At the meeting, the evaluators and professionals who work with your child will present the results of the testing and will give their opinion on whether your child should be considered eligible for special education. As a parent and member of the team, you should also be asked to give your opinion. The final decision as to whether your child is eligible for special education is a team decision.

All the laws and rules governing these processes are set and enforced by each individual state's educational laws. You can learn more about these specific laws and processes by visiting your state's education department website and familiarizing yourself with your specific state's policies and procedures.

IEP versus 504 Plan

Determining whether your child should qualify for an IEP or a 504 plan is often a confusing part of the process. In the world of rare diseases, where our children's diagnoses are often not known and understood, there may be confusion as to which plan your child should receive. Children with rare diseases often have complex medical needs that impact multiple body systems, and these can have implications on your child's physical, mental, emotional, and social well-being, causing difficulties in accessing their education.

Often, special education teams are not experienced with rare diseases and therefore may not understand a disease's impact on the whole child. An IEP may not be recommended due to their lack of understanding and knowledge, even though many children with rare diseases may qualify for an IEP. For this reason, we will take a closer look at the difference between these two plans and will spend time discussing how the parent can play a collaborative role in working with the assessment team to ensure the right plan is recommended and implemented.[1]

IEPs	504s
IEPs are developed under the IDEA, a federal law specific to the education of students with disabilities.	Section 504 plans are authorized under Section 504 of the Rehabilitation Act, a federal civil rights law that protects all people with a qualifying disability from discrimination based on their disability.
IEPs are used when a student requires specialized instruction.	504 plans are used when a student needs accommodations or modifications to programs and facilities.
The student must fit one of the fourteen disability eligibility categories.	Section 504 has a broader definition of *disability*.
The IDEA grants specific procedural safeguards that must be upheld.	Section 504 contains some limited due process rights.
Parents are part of the IEP team.	No parental input is required to develop or implement a 504 plan.
IEPs follow a specific format including evaluation timelines, goals, and objectives.	504 plans are usually written documents but do not have to follow a specific format.
IEPs require documenting measurable growth.	504 plans ensure that a student will have equal access to public education and services.
Generally, IEPs apply to public schools. IEPs may apply to non-public schools under certain circumstances.	Generally, 504 plans apply to all schools that accept federal funding (public, private, religious).
The Office of Special Education and Rehabilitative Services (OSERS) at the Department of Education administers the IDEA and IEPs.	The Office of Civil Rights at the Department of Education administers Section 504 of the Rehabilitation Act and 504 plans.

In summary, if your child has been diagnosed with one or more of the categories named in an IDEA, *and* that disability impacts your child's ability to make meaningful academic progress, an IEP would make the most sense.

If your child does not meet the criteria to have an IEP but has a disability that substantially impairs any major life activity (including but not limited to their ability to care for themself, walk, see, hear, speak, breathe, learn, work, eat, sleep, stand, bend, read, concentrate/think, or communicate), then your child should qualify for a 504 plan.

The Parents' Role

First, I think it's important to understand that we as parents are essential members of our child's education team. We are our child's first and best advocate, and we know our child the best, so we have valuable insights to contribute.

> **We are our child's first and best advocate.**

Our role is to represent our child and speak on their behalf, knowing what only we as parents can know. The good news is that school districts *want* us to be involved members of the team. We need to go in knowing that we are a welcomed, instrumental, and essential part of our child's educational team.

Educating Ourselves

We can be valuable team members by educating ourselves as best we can about our child's condition and needs. The truth is that most often, we as parents don't understand all the ins and outs of special education. We may not understand all the terms, procedures, laws, and never-ending list of confusing acronyms. Special education is most likely not our area of expertise. But we are the experts when it comes to our child. That's what we can bring to the table.

We can learn as much as possible about our child's condition and how that condition impacts their ability to access their education. That's the piece we can offer as a team member, and it's a vital piece.

Because we are dealing with rare diseases, it's common to find that the school district may not be familiar with our child's diagnosis and how it impacts their learning. Therefore, it's our job as parents and advocates to inform and educate as best we can. Instead of assuming that the school district understands our child's condition and needs or that through the assessment process they will be able to glean all they need to know, we will make no assumptions and instead proactively provide them with the required information.

If it's at all possible, I recommend doing up-front research on the types of accommodations, modifications, and services most often recommended for children with your child's type of disease. Now, I recognize that this puts more legwork on you as a parent. I also know it comes with a significant learning curve, just like most aspects of rare disease, and that's difficult because you have so little time as it is, but I assure you that this will be worth your time.

Gaining this type of knowledge will help prepare you for meetings and conversations with the school district, and it's going to help ensure that your child has what they need. We parents have to do some research up front so we go into IEP and 504 meetings armed with information. So, where can we find this information?

- If there is a patient advocacy group or an organization for your child's disease, see what they recommend for school accommodations, modifications, and related services.

- If you know other parents whose children have the same condition, see what types of accommodations and modifications they have in their plans, including what's working and what they recommend.

- In cases where your child's diagnosis is ultra-rare, or there isn't a foundation or organization to provide resources, or you don't know other parents whose children have the same diagnosis, you can research the symptoms. For example, if your child's condition causes fatigue, you can research the types of modifications and accommodations made for students with fatigue, whether it's assistive technology devices, permitting extra time on assignments and exams, alternative PE, and so on.

Gaining this knowledge is going to help you build your confidence in this area and allow you to have informed conversations and dialogues with the education team. The more educated you can be stepping into these meetings, the better outcomes you'll have coming out of them. Do your homework and figure out what plans and services may be helpful for your child. This will be a great foundation for starting these conversations.

Educating the Team

Now that you've educated yourself, you can educate your child's team. Your job is twofold: to make the school administration understand your child's condition and how it affects their ability to access their education, and to effectively state and build a rationale for the services your child needs. Okay, let's unpack this.

As mentioned, the school will do a full assessment on your child, and based on the findings of that assessment, they'll recommend plans and services. In reality, it may be challenging to get the complete picture of a child in an evaluation, so there may be some information gaps. We as parents can help fill in those gaps.

You may need to help the school administration understand your child's condition and how it affects their ability to access their education. Perhaps this is the first time your school administration has come across your child's diagnosis. Or maybe your diagnosis is understood but can present itself in various ways. Make no assumptions. Take the time to lay out precisely what your child is dealing with and how it specifically affects their education, their school day, and their ability to keep pace with learning. Point out how the diagnosis specifically affects their ability to learn from a mental, physical, and emotional standpoint.

Request letters from your child's doctors, specialists, and therapists outlining their disease, how it may affect their learning, and the types of modifications and accommodations for learning that may need to be made. It's going to be extremely valuable for your school district to have access to this information, and coming from professionals and experts in these areas can often make a big difference.

In addition, you can put together a summary—an "All About Me" document— that helps your education team see the full picture of your child. This document can outline your child's condition, how their condition impacts learning, its implications on navigating the school environment, social and emotional issues, the type of equipment your child uses, if any, etc.

Since you're the expert on your child and have been gathering intel and insights long before the school, it's a great opportunity to share what you know. Every child is different and has unique nuances, and this document can allow your child's uniqueness to come to life off the pages of an assessment, help the administration gain a more complete picture of your child, and assist in identifying areas of need. Putting all of this information in a summarized, written format is an efficient way to allow administrators to spend time with the information and refer back to it as needed.

Here are some suggestions for what to include in this "All About Me" type of document:

- Overview of the condition
- How the condition specifically affects your child

- How it specifically affects learning or accessing education
- Tools and equipment used by your child
- Curriculum accommodations and modifications needed

With Miles's diagnosis of SMA, there is often confusion as to what type of plan children with this diagnosis should have. To eliminate confusion, I did my research and put together one mother lode of an information packet stating what a child with SMA and what Miles specifically would need to attend school. The packet contained letters from medical specialists, OTs, and PTs, as well as school best practices from the nonprofit organization for SMA, and the types of services provided to children with the same diagnosis. It was my arsenal to help inform and collaborate.

In short, you'll want to use these tools to help give the school insight into your child. Any factual information you can provide will give your team the ammunition they need to substantiate services. Help them help you.

Collaboration

After providing your administration with all that valuable information, the school will do a full assessment of your child. Then, based on the findings of that evaluation, they'll recommend services.

You'll want to make sure their findings line up with what you believe your child needs. Of course, you don't want to offend your evaluation team by trying to do their job for them; instead, you'll act as an informed member of the team by coming to the table and stating what you feel your child needs based on knowing your child best and having done your research.

The IEP or 504 meetings where you discuss findings, placements, goals, and services should be a collaborative endeavor with all parties working toward the same goal of making sure all your child's needs are addressed.

Effective Communication and Advocacy

If we truly want to be a collaborative member of the team and advocate effectively, then we need to be mindful of the way we communicate with our school district. We have to keep in mind that this team will be responsible for implementing services and facilitating our child's education. We don't want to make them our adversaries; we want to make them our allies and partners in our child's education.

We're going to be in continual communication with our school district. So if we truly want to serve our children, we have to communicate effectively with their education team to have successful outcomes. This is another time when we'll have to be assertive but diplomatic. Sometimes we may disagree with assessment findings or the recommended services, or we may need to ask for more services or speak up because the services and plans that have been put in place aren't working.

I believe it is our job as parents to advocate in these instances. But often, these situations can cause all sorts of emotions within us to well up. Because we care so deeply about our child and so desperately want them to have what they need, it is upsetting when we feel they aren't getting it. But we're going to have to take those emotions out of our advocacy and speak and act from a place of fact, not emotion. Let all that emotion fuel you forward, but have the knowledge you've gained be your mouthpiece.

Enlisting an Advocate

Another route you can go is enlisting the help of an advocate. If you find yourself in over your head, an advocate can attend meetings with you, decipher the information, speak on your behalf, and so on. Ask around and find out if there's a good special education advocate in your area. They can represent you and help you get what you need.

You'll want to ensure that your advocate is familiar with your state's special education policies since the state governs special ed laws. It's also extremely beneficial if your advocate has a good working relationship with key people in the local school districts, including principals, teachers, and special education coordinators.

Here are some places to find an advocate:

- Other parents, families, friends, and specialists who work with your child
- Your state's Parent Training and Information Center
- Your state's Department of Education
- Your school district's Special Education PTA or Parent Advisory Committee
- Council of Parent Attorneys and Advocates (COPAA)

When You Disagree

If you disagree with the school district's assessment, you have the right to request an independent assessment from qualified specialists at public expense. This request should be made in writing and directed to the school district.

In the span of years from kindergarten to college, there may be times when the school system is not adhering to the law regarding your child's special needs rights. If school administrators are denying services to your child, being negligent, or challenging the law, it helps to know what you can do to address the problem.

The IDEA requires that parents have access to due process complaint and mediation. Section 504 requires that schools offer an impartial hearing to parents who have complaints but leaves it to the school district to design and implement the hearing process.

More information about these dispute resolution processes can be found through your state Department of Education. To learn more about your hearing rights and the hearing process, including the option for mediation, visit the website of the Special Education Division of the Office of Administrative Hearings in your state. Parents can also make complaints to the Office of Human Rights or the Department of Education Office of Civil Rights (OCR).

If you've done these productive and effective things to work with the entities above and you still aren't able to attain what you think is fair and necessary for your child, you can contact the disability rights agency in your state. To do this, visit the National Disability Rights Network's listing by state at www.ndrn.org/about/ndrn-member-agencies/.

In closing this chapter, I want to encourage you that although this may feel like a lot to tackle, it will be worth the investment of your time. When I was going through the process of getting education services in place for Miles, I was pushed way out of my comfort zone again and again. I'm not an educator, and I didn't know much about the education system, let alone the special education system. I didn't understand the process or the jargon or special education law. I had to find my way through it, and several amazing fellow SMA moms helped me along the way. They had to do the same thing before me. One of them got so adept at special education law that you'd think she was a lawyer herself. What a force she is—and how amazing that she helped me better understand special education law and gave me the right terminology and verbiage to include in my letters to the school district.

Look for other parents in your local area who have navigated the special education maze and see if they may be able to lend you a hand. Their child doesn't necessarily need to have a rare condition; just their knowledge of the local school district and the players will be extremely helpful.

Your advocacy in this aspect of your child's life can lead to a positive experience with learning and years of enjoying their education.

You got this, mama!

Rare Mama Truth

Special education acronyms: because parenting
a rare kid wasn't challenging enough already.

PART IV

Building
Rare Supports

CHAPTER 14

Developing Your Village

"A support system isn't just about having
people to lean on. It's about having people who
remind you of your strength when you forget."

UNKNOWN

They say it takes a village to raise a child. Well then, it might take more like the whole land to raise a child with a rare disease. So let's talk about the significance of our village and how we assemble it.

Relationships are integral in life, and sometimes we don't realize how much so until we're put into difficult times. *Community* is named as one of the very important things we need to "do life." But I never understood this as fully as when I was in the beginning stages of my son's diagnosis.

As we've discussed, isolation is often one of the harsh aspects of living life with a rare disease. It can happen as an unwanted side effect, or it can even happen subconsciously as we pull away from those we feel cannot understand the life we're living. But instead of isolation, let's talk about building relationships that can support and surround us as we navigate this life. We need a village that includes people who can help us emotionally, mentally, and physically. This village will be paramount.

What's interesting is that your village may look different from how you expect it to look. It may consist of people who were once acquaintances or doctors and therapists who've turned into close friends. It may be missing family members or friends you always expected to be within your village. It forms in its own way and at its own time, and it may surprise you in how it takes shape. But make no mistake, your village will be one of the most important parts of support on this journey.

Your village is the group of people who get you, whose hearts are with you, and who are cheering you on and lifting you up. They are people who will surround you and allow you to lean into them when you need to—and there will be plenty of times when you do. Your support system can surround you in many different ways, and this is ideal because the people in your life have different gifts, capacities, and capabilities. Some people may be great at doing things like bringing a meal or running errands; others may be skilled at emotional support, able to sit and listen as you work through difficult emotions; and still others may be adept at tracking down information and resources.

If friends and family are offering help and you need it, take the help that's offered in whatever way works for you. Asking for and accepting help when you need it is another lesson learned on the rare disease road. We just can't do it all on our own.

I know for some of you, it may not be possible to have people help directly with your child because they're medically fragile or the caretaking requires specific training. But can you allow them to help with something else, such as meals, errand running, taking care of your other children, or carpooling? What are the other ways these people can help free up your time? What are they good at? Take into consideration what your friends and family members like to do and what they are skilled at, then see if they can help in that capacity if it's something you need.

My husband and I have experienced this type of compassionate support. We've had our amazing family and friends show up for us in all different ways with all sorts of things. They have been with us through every step of every up and down and every tear. They have done everything from helping us get equipment, to standing by us at our SMA events, to just loving on our kids.

My parents have been my emotional rocks since I fell apart in their arms that first day I shared the diagnosis, and every day since. They have been my steadfast companions through every storm and every crisis, offering ears to listen, arms to comfort, and hands to help. My mother has been a guiding light in motherhood, a shining example of strength, sacrifice, dedication, and love.

When we shared the diagnosis with our neighbors, they all showed up on our doorstep with meals and flowers. They ran errands for us, picked up Mason from school when I was running late after taking Miles to an appointment, made neighborhood events more accessible—you name it. They rallied around us and become close friends.

I remember one friend offering to do my older son's school supply shopping for me while they were doing theirs. How amazing is that? Miles was little, and it freed me from having to drag him around with me to all the stores to search for the supplies we needed.

We've had a friend use their professional fundraising talents to help us raise funding for research for Cure SMA. Another friend used their media skills to help raise awareness of SMA and our story, and yet another used their professional strategy skills to support our Cure SMA events.

Though our friends had different capabilities and capacities, and some were local and some were not, we were able to lean into them in different ways and at different times through our journey. They wanted to help, they had specific talents and skills that could help us, and they were a huge blessing to our family.

Maybe you're a person who isn't used to accepting help. Maybe you've never really needed it. Or maybe you feel bad accepting it because you don't want to put the other person out. Your caring friends and family who are offering most likely want to do this for you. Often, it's hard for them to see you in such distress, and they want to help, but they feel helpless. Let your village surround and support you by giving them very specific ways they can help.

> Let your village surround and support you by giving them very specific ways they can help.

In addition to giving you ideas on how to build and allow your village to support you, I also want to give you some information that perhaps can only come from someone who's walked this road and lived this rare life. In the name of preparation, I'd like to outline some unexpected losses and additions to your rare village.

UNEXPECTED LOSSES

One of the losses you don't expect to mourn through this journey is the loss of relationships with family and friends. I pray you don't. But unfortunately, after meeting so many mothers of children with medical conditions, I've heard the stories of many that do. Let's talk about this difficult subject in the name of preparation; this is fair warning about a subject I wish I didn't have to broach.

Rare caregiving requires a lot of your time, which often means you have less time to spend with your friends, family, and spouse. This can affect your relationships. High-stakes situations also can bring out the best or the worst in people. Getting a major diagnosis can bring people together or tear them apart. You'll find that people have all different types of reactions to your situation. Some are so genuinely caring that it brings you to tears. Unfortunately, you'll also see some reactions you didn't expect and for which you probably weren't prepared.

The Muscular Dystrophy Association has an entire section devoted to this topic in their *Learning to Live with Neuromuscular Disease* handbook for parents.[1] They talk about how to handle the loss of relationships. This is real, people. Rare disease families deal with this often.

Though I wish it weren't so, I think one of the best things I can do is to make you aware of this situation so if it happens to you, you know you're not alone. It would be nice to know this up front so it doesn't come as such a shock and deliver such a sting. It's salt in the wound, this type of loss. You're dealing with the diagnosis as well as the fears, exhaustion, loss of energy, loss of the life you thought you'd live, and loss of the childhood you thought your child would have. Yet never did you expect to lose family and friends too. These are the people you expect to lean on during difficult times, but unfortunately that doesn't always happen.

Your child's diagnosis may come as a shock to those around you. They may not understand what the diagnosis means or the implications it has on your entire life. Remember, we didn't initially know either, and it's not like there are examples of rare disease life everywhere around us for people to learn from and gain better understanding and perspective. You'll have to forgive those around you and try to provide them with information to help them understand the diagnosis, what comes with it, your new normal, your time commitments, etc.

There will be family and friends who don't understand that having a medically complex child is extremely time-consuming and that it's a real challenge to balance all the new needs with everyday life. You may have to explain that while you still want to do everything you always have and be the type of family member or friend you've always been, your time may be limited now, and what you've done before may not be possible.

When my friend whose child was battling a rare cancer was in the thick of the weeds taking care of her son, who was in and out of the hospital and in therapies, etc., it wasn't easy for her to talk on the phone or stay in contact. She was so buried with what she had to do that even taking time to make a call or send a text would be taking her away from her son or her sleep, which she desperately needed. We all thought we understood. But my understanding grew tenfold when I was in my own battle.

It's not as if we are given more hours in the day along with all of the additional things that need to get done. A chronic illness means that this is ongoing. And when the rare disease patient is a child who cannot do for themselves, you better believe it's the parents' time that's impacted. To the parent, there is no greater priority than this. Period. Most things fall second to a condition that affects a child's health. We don't need to feel guilty because of this. It's just the way it is.

And let's be honest: Sometimes taking care of our child is really *all* we can do. I mean, it already feels like so much *more* than we can do. Sometimes we can barely get by just taking care of our child, plus our other children if we have them, let alone ourselves. If we barely have time to take care of our immediate family and ourselves, how are we supposed to keep up with anything else?

Rare mamas talk about the pressure to keep up with life that continues to throw at them typical commitments and obligations, and plenty of things they want to do too—trying to remember birthdays, attend parties and events, prepare for holidays, handle school and work, and remember everyone's everything—but they just can't. Our brains are filled with so many things, and a lot of them are serious. Something has to give.

The feedback I hear from rare mamas is that while often their friends and family may initially be understanding surrounding the diagnosis, over time some people expect them to pick back up and keep up with life as they always have. They don't understand that when you receive a chronic illness diagnosis, there is no such thing as picking back up and returning to the way of life pre-diagnosis. Everything has changed and shifted. And most likely, you will change and shift along with it. This type of change is so monumental and life-altering that there's no other way to step up and live it except to change. It's almost a requirement to live your new normal. You can't be expected to do everything the same way you did it before. It's not realistic, and it really shouldn't be asked of you.

Some family and friends will understand and will be there for you high tide and low tide. Some people, even though they haven't been through a rare disease, somehow empathize, grant you extra grace, forgive you when you forget things, love you despite how they never get to see you or your child, and keep calling to check on you even though you haven't been able to call them back in months. God bless these people for their hearts and their understanding. They're in it with you even though you can't be what you always were to them.

Others won't feel this way. They'll be upset that they haven't heard from you. They'll be upset that you haven't given them the same amount of time you always have. They may even have thoughts on how you should or should not be handling your child's disease and may be upset with you if they think you're doing it differently than they think you should. Forgive them; they know not what they do. How could they? They don't know because they haven't lived through it.

The truth is we all think we know how we'll handle situations . . . until we're actually in them. Handling them in theory is much different from handling them in reality. People don't understand because they haven't been where we are. They don't know that you just found out that your child is going blind in one eye, or can't hold down their food and isn't getting proper nutrients, or is seizing all day long. They don't realize that the insurance company just denied a piece of equipment your child desperately needs, or the cost of the medical bills is more than you have in savings. They're not aware that you probably just want to throw your hands up and scream, "I'm doing the best I can just trying to save my kid's life here! Can you cut me some slack?" They just don't know.

A rare condition can also impact your child's ability to participate in certain types of activities and may change the way they're able to interact with others. This can change the dynamics of your child's relationships. Some won't understand why they can't take your kid to the zoo, the pool, or on a trip. Forgive them; they're mourning the loss too. They had all this excitement and all these ideas for all the things they thought they were going to do with your child and the relationship bond they were going to form. The diagnosis has changed those dreams too, and it's hard for them to come to terms with it, just as it was hard for you.

This adjustment is tough on relationships, and unfortunately, some people around you simply won't be able to give you what you need for whatever reason. Either they don't have the emotional capacity, it's too overwhelming for them, it's too much of a burden, they want to go back to the way life was before the diagnosis when everything was okay, it's not about them, it's changing the family dynamic, you can't be there for them the same way that you always have, they don't have the time, they don't have the energy, they don't want to be bothered, they are embarrassed, it hurts too much, or they have their own problems or health issues. There are hundreds of reasons, and we may never be able to truly understand them all.

A rare disease isn't for the faint of heart, and some people just can't deal. You'll come across those who will want to talk to you about the weather or their favorite sports team instead of the major surgery your child needs or just had. That may be because they don't have the capability or the capacity to talk about something so heavy. Perhaps it helps them not having to talk about it, but of course it's not necessarily what helps you. You may be looking for emotional support and a sounding board, and some people just might not want to be that person or have the ability to be that person. You'll wonder how they can ignore the major elephant in the room and avoid talking to you about the biggest thing happening in your life. Perhaps it's because they don't want to talk about it. So then, is that really the type of person you want to talk about it with? Is that the type of person who can offer you the emotional support you need? Perhaps not, and so you'll have to consider who you can talk to instead.

Sadly, this changes relationship dynamics. When you can't talk about the biggest, most important things happening in your life, it may start to feel like a surface-level or one-way relationship. Over time, you'll have to decide what type of role this relationship plays in your life.

Listen, mama, I know. It's gut-wrenchingly hard, even devastating. But what are you going to do? You can't make people be there for you in the way you need them to be if they don't want to, or aren't willing, or aren't capable. You can't control the reactions of other people; you can only control your own. You can control with whom you reveal your hurt, to whom you look for emotional support, and with whom you share your heart.

I'm no therapist, but experts say to approach these situations with love and honesty. Explain the diagnosis and the implications to the important people in your life. Tell them that, even though you may not be able to talk to them or see them as often as you once did, you still love them and they're still important to you. Try to help them understand all the ways this diagnosis will affect your child's life and your life, and tell them you're trying to work through it the best you can.

Experts also say to give others time to learn and understand. They have to adjust and make changes too. This may not happen overnight. It may take time for family and friends to fully understand what this new normal looks like. Give space and allow time for others to understand and process.

Unfortunately, you may find that some people fall away. They may start to pull away and you'll be left wondering where they are, where they went, and what happened to the relationship.

If you've tried working through things to no avail, learn to accept. If you're not met with love and a willingness to try and adapt, then accept it, forgive, and leave the door open in case there's an opportunity for change. There doesn't have to be a big battle, a heated debate, or terrible words exchanged—just acceptance, understanding, forgiveness, and letting go.

There are only so many battles you can fight, and this type of battle is emotionally draining and exhausting. You only have so much energy, and you need to preserve it. Your kid needs you whole and emotionally available for the other battles to come. Some battles you can't win, and you need to be wise enough to know the difference.

Sometimes you may need to let go of a relationship because of another person's inability to be understanding or compassionate or if their reactions are insensitive or hurtful. Rare life is filled with so much trauma and stress that you may find your bandwidth stretched and depleted. When your life is filled with so many difficulties, you may not want to add to that by being around people who add drama, bring confrontation, or just don't give a crap about what you're going through. You want your relationships to be places of solace and reinvigoration, and you will no longer be drawn toward relationships that don't offer this.

In the face of having so little time, you'll discern with whom you want to spend it. Because time with your child and your family is such a precious gift, you are no longer willing to sacrifice it for time spent with other relationships that don't add love or joy to your life.

The truth of the matter is that you'll change. You'll change in ways you never expected. Your perspective will shift. How can it not when you're facing a complex illness that affects your child's life? With those changes and shifts comes a sharpening of your needs and desires. You may start to crave relationships that are authentic, conversations about things that matter, and loving exchanges that leave you supported, encouraged, and seen. Some of your current relationships will offer the understanding, compassion, and mutual respect you crave. Others won't.

If you're going through losses or changes in relationships, or have gone through them, my heart aches for you because I know it's heartbreaking. If it's any consolation at all, along this journey you'll also gain unexpected additions to your village.

UNEXPECTED ADDITIONS

One of the beautiful things that will happen along the way is you will meet people who you don't know well, who you don't know at all, or who are even strangers that will come into your life and give you a lift just when you need it most. I like to think of them as angels who touch our lives in profound ways.

You're going to meet many people who may start out as acquaintances but over time turn into so much more and become part of your mighty village. Many of them you'll meet because of your child's disease. I've heard hundreds of beautiful stories like this from my rare mama community—whether it's other rare mama friends who connected through their child's disease, their child's teacher or independence facilitator, a therapist, a doctor, or a volunteer at a center, etc. You may have no familial ties to this person and no history with them, yet over time you build a deep relationship that was unexpected.

Our family has experienced this firsthand. We've met many people who started out as acquaintances or as providers in some form, but who turned into so much more than that. They have become part of our support system. We've built deep relationships that have become part of our foundation. So many people have shown us such love and compassion along our journey.

An equipment provider, who was in a wheelchair himself, taught Miles how to pop wheelies and play wheelchair hockey. Miles's aide at school treated my child like her own and became Miles's "school mom." Our physical therapist has been an unwavering mentor and has even answered my texts during her vacation, to get me the information I needed. A friend of a friend used her expertise and skills to help us fundraise for SMA research and then became a close friend to me. Specialists have gone the extra mile to provide me with the research I needed to make a tough medical decision. The staff at Cure SMA have bent over backward to help us and mentor us. Researchers have continued to work tirelessly to find a treatment for Miles's disease, but even more than that, have become dear friends, uplifting us and supporting us.

You know what else I've experienced and heard about from countless rare mamas? The kindness of strangers, acts of good from unknown sources. A kind hostess gave Miles a special window seat at a restaurant when the place was packed with reservations. A little boy shared his candy with Miles at the Easter egg hunt in the park because Miles couldn't get through the grass easily in his wheelchair. An older couple at a restaurant had a special dessert sent over for the kids. A baseball pro gave Miles a signed baseball card. I could go on.

These acts of kindness have caught me off guard, touched my heart, and filled me up in a way that's hard to explain. We've had many a hard day turned around by these simple deeds, and they have truly allowed me to see the beauty of humanity.

I thought it would be encouraging for you to know that while you may encounter relational losses along the way, you may also witness your relationships grow and expand in unexpected and unforeseen ways. Our rare villages form in ways we may not expect, but they may provide us with exactly what we need.

Rare Mama Truth

Building a rare village is like assembling an
Avengers team, except everyone's armed with
a plethora of patience, endless empathy,
and a secret stash of snacks.

CHAPTER 15

Fostering Spouse/Partner Relationships

"Love is not shelter from the storm;
it is the courage to walk through it together."

UNKNOWN

I f you're married or in a relationship, learning that a rare disease diagnosis can affect your relationship with your spouse or partner can feel like yet another hit on the list of implications of a rare disease. But being made aware of this from the get-go and acknowledging the potential strain on your relationship is a critical first step.

The truth is, the business of life—household chores, kid carpools, work deadlines, taxes, budgets, bills, routines, repairs, commitments, and countless obligations—affects every marriage and relationship. Add in the relentless pressure of rare life—continual appointments, anxiety-filled procedures, and unnerving news about your child's health—and the stressors and schedules leave little energy or time for connection, sometimes making couples feel more like business partners than lovers.

My husband and I have a saying we share whenever we find a moment to reconnect, laugh together, or spend time alone doing something that feels truly "us." One of us will turn to the other with a smile of recognition and say, "Oh, it's you! Hey you, I remember you. I like you!" It's our way of reminding each other that, beneath the chaos and layers of daily stuff, the essence of who we are remains unchanged, and we are still the people we fell in love with— something so easy to forget amidst the demands of everyday life.

As rare parents, our children's needs are intense, and we're facing health that is often at life-threatening stakes. So much of our time and energy is dedicated to our children, and rightly so. High-stakes situations can bring spouse/partner relationships closer together or drive them apart. On one hand, upholding relationships can be extremely challenging. Even if you're married to the love of your life, the stress of a rare disease will test your marriage, and that's the harsh reality. On the other hand, your spouse is the one other person in the world who may be able to truly understand what you're going through. That level of understanding and trust is what true love stories are made of. There's also potential for your love to be deepened in a profound way.

I remember about six or seven years into our son's diagnosis, my husband and I had a very rare overnight away from the kids for our anniversary. We spent the day having fun together, and we came back to the hotel room to relax before it was time to get ready for dinner. We began reminiscing about our wedding day and remembering our vows that were so special to us. I commented on how I had always thought of the "in sickness and in health" line of the vows as applying if one of us got sick—but it had never occurred to me that the sickness could be our child's. The conversation led us to talk about how, never in a million years, could we have known back then what was coming our way with our son's diagnosis. I began to open up about how deeply saddened I was by all that Miles had endured and all that we, as his parents, had endured. Before I knew it, the tears began to fall as I expressed how painful it was to witness his struggles and how overwhelming everything felt. In return, my husband opened up too, revealing the heaviness of his heart. We both wept, sharing the gut-wrenching parts of our journey—the trauma, the constant stress, the relentless pressures. We apologized for the times we let the strain come between us.

We sat there, letting it all out, crying and talking about the brokenness we felt—about how the most brutal truth was the realization that things might not get easier, that this path we were on might remain difficult. We cried together, not trying to be strong for each other but letting each other see our rawest, most vulnerable selves. We shared our deepest fears, our disappointments, and the ways this journey had changed us—sometimes in ways we didn't love. We spoke about the fear of losing each other in the chaos of it all, and we just sat and held each other in that shared sadness for a long time.

And because we had let all the walls fall down, we weren't afraid to ask the hard questions—if this road wasn't going to get easier, how would we keep walking it? How would we journey together? We spoke about the dreams we still held for our children, family, and life together. We acknowledged that life had turned out differently than we imagined but committed, with all our hearts, to making it meaningful.

> Love is about choosing each other in the hardest moments.

And in that most vulnerable, raw, and tender moment, I think we found each other again.

I'll never forget that night because it illuminated a few important things for me. Love is revealing fragility. Love is looking over after a break in the storm and seeing the other still there. Love is about choosing each other in the hardest moments—in the dark of disillusionment, when the path is uncertain, or when we are encumbered by the weight.

Love is finding each other again and again. And again.

Let's delve deeper into strategies and insights from the experts on how to prioritize the relationship with our spouse or partner and navigate the challenging, rare parenting journey together.

ALLOW SPACE FOR DIFFERENCES

Each person reacts differently to a diagnosis and handles stress in a different way. Each person grieves differently and heals differently. There is no wrong or right way to grieve or come to terms with a rare disease. Embrace the diversity of reactions and recognize that each person copes uniquely. Some may need time for solitary reflection, while others may seek immediate support. Allow each other space for coming to terms with the diagnosis in their own way and in their own time. Allow space for your partner to do it differently. Creating an environment that respects these differences allows for individual healing.

COLLABORATE ON A PLAN TOGETHER

Work together on a plan for how you will approach and navigate your child's rare disease so you can walk down this road as a decision-making team and a united force. Discuss how you'll approach uncertainties and challenges, as well as the outlook you'll carry forward. Talk through it all to bounce ideas and approaches off each other so you can come to an agreement on how you'll make sure you're on the same page. Add a regular check-in to your schedule so you can meet and update each other on all the happenings, and work through obstacles and challenges together. Regularly revisit and revise your plan to adapt to the evolving circumstances of a rare disease.

DEDICATE TIME TO YOUR RELATIONSHIP

Amid the demands of caregiving, intentionally set aside moments for each other. Dedicate time to focus on your marriage, because it is one of the foundations of your family. It will be important to spend time alone together and take breaks with your spouse. This can be difficult when you have a child with high needs, but you'll need breaks from rare disease caregiving together. You'll need moments when you don't focus on your situation at all, but instead laugh and have fun together. This may not be possible at first, but when you get to a point in your journey when you and your spouse can take a break from caregiving, make sure you do. Create a support network to provide respite, allowing both of you to recharge and invest in your relationship.

GRANT EACH OTHER GRACE

You are two people who love each other but are going through unimaginable circumstances and an undue amount of stress. Understand that from the outset so you can discern when you or your partner are being affected by the stress of the situation and circumstances; this allows you to be empathetic rather than taking things personally. Realize that stress manifests differently. Be attuned to signs of strain, both in yourself and your partner. There will be times when you're not at your best and times when your loved one is not at their best. That's just the truth. Try to take a step back and ask yourself whether it's the relationship or the stress of the circumstances that is getting to you.

COMMUNICATE OPENLY

Foster a culture of open communication. Share your fears, hopes, and frustrations with each other. Regularly check in on each other's emotional well-being. This transparency strengthens your emotional connection and ensures that you're navigating the challenges as a united team. By leaning into each other instead of pulling away, you can strengthen your bond on an even deeper level.

CELEBRATE MILESTONES

Acknowledge and celebrate milestones—or inchstones, as one rare mama I know likes to say. These victories serve as reminders of your collective strength and resilience. Use these moments to reflect on the positive aspects of your relationship, reinforcing the foundation you've built together.

SEEK SUPPORT

Consider seeking professional counseling to develop coping mechanisms that strengthen your relationship. Seek out a marriage counselor with whom you can talk about the stress and demands of rare disease parenting and caregiving. Get third-party advice, tips, and insights on how to move forward together as a team. Work through issues and obstacles with the support of an expert who can shed light on the situation.

FIGHT FOR YOUR RELATIONSHIP

Fight to keep your foundation strong. Fight for your love! Your love is a powerful force in the rare disease fight. Use it to stand together through the storm and move mountains as a team. Then see how strong your relationship can become. Hold each other tight.

In the face of a rare disease, your relationship has the potential to evolve and deepen. By actively implementing these insights, you can not only weather the storm but also emerge stronger, more connected, and more resilient as a couple.

Rare Mama Truth

Some couples argue about where to eat.
We argue about whose turn it is to pretend to be a
calm human being while speaking to the specialist.

CHAPTER 16

Supporting Siblings

"Love begins by taking care of the
closest ones—the ones at home."

MOTHER TERESA

One of the things I was most worried about when I received Miles's diagnosis, in addition to how it would affect Miles, was how it would affect my other son, Mason. My heart also ached for Mason. He was only three and a half at the time of Miles's diagnosis, and instead of me playing blocks and cars with him, we were running around to doctors' appointments. It didn't seem fair; he still deserved the time, energy, and attention of his parents.

When you have a medically fragile child in the home, your attention is pulled to all the medical needs. In the beginning, I didn't know how we would do it all. I wanted to make sure Mason got enough attention and also protect him from feeling any resentment. I wanted him to have a normal childhood despite our circumstances, and I questioned if we could give him what he needed as well as stability and calm in the midst of our storm.

I agonized over this. It was always on my mind, always tugging at my heart. I wanted Mason to have a childhood filled with bike rides and kite flying and beach trips. But how could I do that when I had another child who couldn't walk and was medically fragile? I wanted Mason to feel important and self-confident despite the constant focus on Miles's medical needs.

Thinking about this was overwhelming. I had no control over these circumstances or the fact that this disease would undoubtedly also affect Mason. But how would I handle these situations? I prayed a lot about it, asking God to guide us, and the answer I received was simply to make Mason feel loved. It was simple and all we had at the time, so we began there.

Mama, you are not alone in your concerns and worries. In talking with so many rare moms, this is one of the topics most often mentioned. It's still always on my mind, too.

Over the years, I've spent time learning more about siblings of children with a chronic illness, rare disease, or disability. I've read articles, spoken to therapists, and attended seminars and webinars. I've been learning and gathering as much information as I can on this topic, and I'd like to pass along what I've learned.

What I've found is that most of the recommendations and tips offered by professionals are consistent. Here's a roundup of the research, advice, and tips I've gathered from child life professionals, child psychologists, and other experts, condensed into key takeaways on the subject of siblings.

COMMUNICATE OPENLY AND HONESTLY

Siblings, like us, want information about their brother's or sister's health and condition. They want to know what's going on. Knowing eases their anxiety about the situation. Sometimes, if we don't give them factual information, their imagination can run wild and make things worse than they are. It's our job to provide them with age-appropriate facts. To do this, be proactive. Seek out trusted sources of information and give siblings the knowledge they need. Allow them to ask questions and express their feelings about it. Acknowledge their concerns when they share them with you and offer reassurance when possible. Leave room for continual communication as the situation changes and as they grow and mature and can understand and process more.

TAILOR YOUR APPROACH TO THE INDIVIDUAL

All kids are different. Like all parenting, you will have to tailor the information and the way you approach discussions on this topic to your unique child. There is no one-size-fits-all. You are your child's parent, and since you know them best, use that information to determine how and when you will deliver information about their sibling to them. Tailor the messaging and how you approach the subject based on their individual emotional needs. Do what you feel will serve them best.

PROVIDE SUPPORT

Whether it's speaking to a counselor or joining a sibling group, provide emotional and mental supports for the sibling to work through their feelings. Whether it's online or in-person, a good support group will help assure siblings that they're not alone in their feelings, experiences, and concerns. Make it a priority to give siblings ample support. Siblings may not voice their need for it. They may not even know they need support in this way. Therefore, you as their parent may be the one who initiates seeking out and providing it.

MODEL BEHAVIOR

Siblings will take cues from us as parents on how we handle their brother's or sister's diagnosis or disability. If we approach it with resilience and positivity, so will they. If we approach it with doom and despair, so will they. If we talk openly and honestly about our feelings, it opens the door for them to do the same. If we vulnerably share the parts that are difficult for us, they will too. Model the behavior you want to see. Show them.

SPEND TIME WITH EACH CHILD

Because so much time and attention will be devoted to your child with the rare disease, dedicate some one-on-one time to your other children. This will allow them to have their special time with you when they don't need to share your attention. This will also let you do activities or outings you may not normally do because of the capabilities of your child with a rare disease. Use this as your time to bond and nurture the relationship.

TRY TO TREAT CHILDREN THE SAME

Set equal expectations for all siblings as best you can concerning behaviors and values and celebrate all your children's accomplishments equally. Stay consistent so all siblings feel equal. Having similar expectations for children with and without disabilities will not only foster independence for all kids but can also lessen the resentment siblings may feel when there are "two different sets of rules" in place for them and their brothers or sisters.

MODERATE RESPONSIBILITIES

Let the sibling be a child; don't put too much caretaking on their plate. Many siblings are told early on that they will be expected to care for their brother or sister when their parents are no longer able to do so. This puts enormous pressure on them. As a parent, make sure you're not asking too much of your child. Make certain responsibilities a choice. Encourage your child to be a kid for as long as possible. Be sure you don't expect too much when it comes to chores, schoolwork, or extracurricular activities. Typically developing children sometimes feel extra pressure to be perfect so their parents don't have to worry about them.

ELEVATE THE POSITIVE

Researchers have found that siblings of kids with disabilities often develop flexibility, adaptability, empathy, tolerance, and resilience due to the family dynamic.[1] Focus on these positives. Use your circumstances as an opportunity for your children and your family to cultivate parts of their character you're proud of. Elevate and grow from the positive aspects of this experience.

CULTIVATE RESILIENCY

One of the most important things we all need to approach life is resiliency. Resiliency is even more critical on the rare disease road. Resiliency is the quality that needs to be cultivated because it's the skill that will help your family survive and thrive. The ultimate goal is to build internal strengths and coping skills in your child with a rare disease and all of your family members.

CREATE FAMILY LIFE OUTSIDE OF RARE DISEASE

Have a family life that revolves around something other than the diagnosis. Whether it's a shared activity like music or art, or an organization, or faith community, have something in which the whole family can participate.

In one of the webinars I attended on the topic of siblings of children with rare diseases, the child psychologist said that in preparation for the session, he did a lot of research to find studies showing and proving the negative impacts on children who have siblings with a rare disease. After much digging, he said he didn't find any research that proved this. I was so encouraged to hear that.

Every child and family are different, and many siblings may struggle as they deal and cope, but this doesn't necessarily mean that when they grow up, their entire life will have some negative stain on it. Having a sibling with a rare disease does not equal that the sibling's life will somehow be "less than" the life of someone who didn't have a sibling with a severe diagnosis.

Yes, as families affected by a rare disease, we will struggle through feelings of fear and despair. Yes, we will be time-starved, sleep-deprived, and overwhelmed. Yes, the list could go on about all the hard aspects of life with a rare disease. But what about the other ways it shapes character? Researchers have found that families raising a child with a chronic illness develop creativity and closeness or cohesiveness that helps the children with and without chronic health problems and the rest of the family manage and cope together with the many stressors that develop over time. They say that often, as a result of these experiences, adults and children learn about their strengths and limitations, talk more openly, and learn new ways to solve problems, which fosters mastery and pride.[2]

I wish there was more talk about these aspects. I think it would truly help us as mothers concerned about our children who are rare siblings. I wish this was more easily known and understood, so I want to shed light on this. There are many sacrifices that siblings make and many hard parts of rare family life, but there is also potential for a lot of positive qualities to form. Sometimes we're so worried about the negative impacts that we forget to consider the positive ones.

> There are many sacrifices that siblings make and many hard parts of rare family life, but there is also potential for a lot of positive qualities to form.

Believe me, I'm going in with eyes wide open trying to manage and care for the rare sibling in our family. But I'm also learning to keep my eyes wide open to the positive characteristics and qualities that are developing because of our situation. This is the perspective time has given. After so much time worrying and stressing over the potential negative impacts, I'm also looking for and seeing the potential for positive character building and life skills.

I've learned that a sibling's feelings will ebb and flow and grow and change through the various stages and ages of child development. There will be new questions, topics to tackle, and issues that may arise at every new phase. It will constantly evolve. This information has helped me know the conversation will continue through the years to come.

Over time, our family continues to feel our way through every stage, trying to give Mason everything he needs and deserves. We're mindful of this at every new phase, being cognizant of emotions and feelings. Since no expert can be with us in our every-day routine to tell us definitively what to do as things come up, we take each day as it comes. We have to trust that as our children's parents who know them best, we will respond and guide them in the best way possible.

The guiding light is love. I could turn all my hair gray right now just worrying about it all. But we'll cross each bridge as we come to it. For now, each day, we'll just keep on learning and loving.

Rare Mama Truth

The only one who rivals a rare parent's advocacy game? A rare sibling—fully certified in "protecting their own," no classes necessary.

CHAPTER 17

Plugging into the Rare Community

"We don't heal in isolation but in community."

S. KELLEY HARRELL

The rare disease community is *powerful*! I'm writing this chapter purposefully after returning from a rare disease conference. I spent three days surrounded by people connected to rare disease in some way, shape, or form. I feel energized, fueled, and charged by being around our community. This community doesn't take rare disease sitting down. They don't accept being told, "Take your child home and love them. There's nothing more you can do." They get out and find what else they can do. You want to feel hope? You want to feel as if there are new possibilities? You want a roadmap for what to do next? Plug into this community and its power. It's one of the most important recommendations I can make to you. Let me tell you all the reasons why.

There are more than 300 million people worldwide living with a rare disease. So while each individual rare disease subset may be small, when we band together, there is strength in our numbers. Here are a few of the highlights you'll find when you plug into the rare disease community.

INVALUABLE RESOURCES

You're going to find numerous resources tailored specifically to rare patients and caregivers. Many of the organizations enlist experts who can inform you on a slew of topics to better equip you for caregiving. You're going to learn from both the experts and other patients or caregivers who have gone before you. There are actually more resources than expected when we look not only at our child's specific disease, but at the larger rare disease community. Pooling our knowledge and resources is how we navigate a rare disease.

> Plug into this community and its power.

ACCESS TO PLAYERS

Legislators, policymakers, advocates, researchers, doctors, foundation starters, organization leaders, and pharma directors can all be found here. You're going to meet trailblazers and changemakers in the world of rare disease. If you're looking to learn which organizations are working on research, you'll find them here. You want to find out who's developing software and technology to make caregiving easier? You'll find them here. You want to find the expert doctor who is performing a surgery specifically for your child's disease?

You'll find them here. The connections in this space are numerous, and they are approachable. You can track down a name and contact information, and if you reach out to that person, you're most likely going to get a response.

INSPIRATION

Many rare disease advocates started out just like you and me. They had a connection to the world of rare disease, and they plugged in and got busy learning how to advocate and change things that they didn't like, or form support groups that didn't exist, or fundraise for treatments and cures. When you hear their stories, it will be hard not to be inspired. We can all use sources of inspiration and positivity. We need to hear examples of overcoming obstacles, of treatments being developed, of better care solutions, and more. You will get inspiration tenfold in the rare disease community.

WILLING HEARTS AND HELPING HANDS

While none of us asked to be in this rare disease world, those who are here are some of the most brilliantly smart, wickedly funny, and tenaciously savvy people I've ever met. They are the people I would choose to be around even if I wasn't in this jungle. They are loving, caring, and compassionate, and their hearts are so big you can almost hear them beating. Their passion is on fire.

Some years back, I helped with a fundraiser to raise money for SMA research. One of these fellow rare mamas helped me out. She had a daughter with a disease completely different from my son's, yet there she was volunteering her time to help with my son's disease. She showed up at all our fundraising planning meetings, and on the day of the event, she was organizing and making things happen behind the scenes. She was so good at it too! The girl had a gift—and she used it to help my child and me. It still blows me away.

I met a couple of other moms at my son's school. We saw each other at school pickup because we all parked in the accessible spots. Dressed in sweatpants, hair in buns, we lugged kids, backpacks, wheelchairs, and walkers. If one of us showed up with makeup on and hair done, we all took notice. We *oohed* and *ahhed* and complimented how nice they looked, so envious but proud of them that they got to wash their hair. The way we fawned over this mom, you'd think she just returned from a luxury vacation.

These girls "got it." They inherently know the struggle. Though I had only known them a few years, I could call on any one of them in a time of need. When I had to have a second knee surgery and the surgery date was unexpected and came on so fast that I didn't even have a chance to tell anyone about it, these girls noticed when I wasn't at pickup. Lo and behold, I got a text from each one, checking on me and offering help if I needed anything. They all had their hands full with their own kids, but there they were offering to help me in my time of need.

Seriously, these women are warriors! So trust me when I say that if you need help, other rare mamas will take you by the hand and show you the way. Let them. One day, believe it or not, you, too, will be that type of woman. It's in you and you'll find it over time through your journey.

Meeting and being in community with people going through something similar is going to fuel you. Some people think of this as their second family—a family rich with people who make it their mission to help others.

The rare disease community has surprised me in so many beautiful ways. It's hard to think back now and realize there was a time when I didn't know this community existed. Many of the people

I've met have become dear friends. There is just something about meeting someone who truly understands. You don't have to spend months and years slowly teaching them about the complexities of your world. You don't have to guard your heart or your thoughts for fear of being misunderstood. You don't have to calculate your words and examine your semantics for fear of offending. You don't have to worry about oversharing and making them feel uncomfortable. You don't have to consider whether your stories are too heavy and will bring down the room. You don't have to search hard for commonalities or ways to relate.

And you'll notice that once you peel all those "don't have tos" away, you can truly and refreshingly just be yourself. It's freeing. It's easy. It's pure.

Bonds form quickly and run deep. Hearts are connected and bound by shared pain and grief, but also by shared hope and resilience. I never wanted to be in this club, but I would choose these friendships over and over and over again.

At one rare disease awards dinner, the table I sat at reflected this. I went to the event by myself. To my surprise, there were no assigned seats at the tables, and when I entered the ballroom, I could see that most of the tables had already filled up. I had a little moment of junior-high-school-lunch-table panic. Where would I sit? Was there room for me at a table? Would I be an intruder or an outsider if I sandwiched myself in between people already seated? And then a seasoned SMA dad who has been like a mentor to me asked if I wanted to sit with him and his significant other.

We quickly found a table that had room for three, as all the tables were filling up. A family was already sitting there—a mom, a dad, and their son with a rare condition who was seated in his wheelchair. The next thing I knew, three familiar faces from the conference, people who I'd only met virtually over the years, joined us at our table. There we were, an unlikely group from all over the country and even some from another country. Parents of children living with rare diseases. Parents of children who had passed away from rare diseases. A rare disease patient who was also a father and a husband.

As we watched the awards and heard the strides and the discoveries of the researchers and scientists, I was so moved by the work they were doing and by the passion they exuded. I was thankful for the self-proclaimed "science nerd" who accepted his award. I felt hopeful and invigorated to hear of all the breakthroughs and successes.

Then, as I listened to a song by an artist that spoke of a child with a rare disease, I was overcome with grief. Tears streamed down my face. I didn't expect all the emotion that I felt. Many of us at that table were there without our spouses, with no one there to comfort us. But yet throughout the evening, I witnessed a hand on a shoulder, an offered tissue, or a knowing nod. Together we braved the hard. Together we braved the hope.

That's the power of this community.

This community is the answer to loneliness and isolation. I hope you'll become a part of it.

Rare Mama Truth

Behind every rare mama is a boatload
of other badass rare mamas.

PART V

Taking Care of the Rare Mama

CHAPTER 18

Taking Care of Mama

"I have come to believe that caring for myself is not self-indulgent. Caring for myself is an act of survival."

AUDRE LORDE

This subject is so important that I'm dedicating a whole section of the book to it. Why? Because taking care of mama is so essential and yet so ridiculously hard!

If you're experiencing physical strain or consider caregiving to be emotionally stressful, you're not alone. According to the "Rare Disease Caregiving in America" study, 67 percent of caregivers say providing care is emotionally stressful, and 58 percent say it's difficult to take care of their own health.[1]

These are common challenges we are all up against. With the physical strain and emotional stress from caregiving at a high, we need to take care of ourselves more than ever. But self-care is elusive for parents like us for so many reasons. We lack time because parenting a child with a rare disease requires so many extra steps and processes that all require additional time. As well, our children are dependent and need us, so we often put their needs first. And we can't rely on just anyone to watch our children; it's not as easy as just finding any babysitter because some of our children's needs require special training or skills that not everyone has.

We've all seen it. We get a rare disease diagnosis for our kid, and we set off in a wild frenzy to save our child, throwing every inch of ourselves into it, barely eating, sleeping, exercising, processing, seeing friends, or getting any downtime. We think, *I'm okay, I don't need a break, I'll be fine, I'll rest tomorrow,* and *I'll take care of myself when things die down.* Years later we wake up, look in the mirror, and wonder who is looking back at us. Our backs are aching, our heads are foggy, and our nerves are shot.

When my son was newly diagnosed, I attended a conference where I was advised to take care of myself. "Care for the Caregiver," they called it. "You can't pour from an empty cup," and "Put on your oxygen mask first," they said. I'll be honest: Somehow, I thought I was above it. *I'm healthy; I'm not too old; this doesn't apply to me. Plus, my son needs me, and his needs are way more important than mine. I'll catch up later once I've gotten everything in place for him. For now, it's full steam ahead. Breaks are for sissies.*

How invincible I must have thought I was.

Or maybe it wasn't even that. Maybe it was that I was so terrified for my child that I was happy to put him first and sacrifice my own self, my own body, and my own well-being if somehow it meant it could save his.

Or maybe it was because I was naive. I don't think I truly understood what it meant to have a child with a chronic illness. Everything hard I had been through before this was for a moment in time, and I don't think I fully grasped that the effects of a rare disease weren't going anywhere, and I couldn't outrun them.

Honestly, I think it was all of it.

It took back problems, a sprained ankle, and a torn meniscus in my knee for me to realize that I needed to slow down and take care of myself. And those were just the undeniable physical effects. I wasn't able to recognize the mental and emotional effects for years to come.

Do you know how many seasoned rare mamas wish they would have taken care of themselves sooner? All! If the amount of a mother's love and self-sacrifice equated to treatments, cures, and pain-free existences for our children, there would be no more rare diseases.

Yes, perhaps there are instances and situations when giving everything we have to give will get our children through some high-stakes situation like a hospitalization, surgery, a procedure, trip to see a renowned specialist, or getting them into a clinical trial, etc. But running fast and hard is not sustainable for endless amounts of time! We are not machines. We cannot keep this pace without major repercussions. We can't keep running forever.

I know we think to ourselves, *I'll just get through this*, or *This is just for now*. But let me ask the hard questions: What if it's not? What if these rare diseases just keep throwing things at us? What if this is our new way of life?

Our bodies, minds, and souls need time to recover and recoup from any major event. The only way to gear up for what may be coming next is to invest time in recovery.

Over time, I've gotten a little wiser to these realities, not because I'm smart but because they've come up and slapped me in the face. I thought mental strength was my specialty, a quality not of my making but just how I was built and wired. It's the way I've always been, but let me tell you, mama, I can't mind-muscle this. I've tried.

When Miles was first diagnosed, I sent an email to our friends to share the diagnosis news, and I wrote, "SMA just messed with the wrong mama," except I used a choice expletive in place of the word *mama*, and I meant it. Getting ready to fight hard was a gut reaction that didn't take much thought. Even in the fog and the heartbreak of the diagnosis, I was ready to pull out my inner tigress and do battle. And so I did.

I was that fighter I talked about at the very beginning of this book. I came out swinging, all heart and speed and guts. I shooed away any good advice to pace myself and any sage warning to consider my own well-being, and now here I am years later feeling all the effects.

I learned the hard way. And it has only made things . . . well . . . harder.

I share all of this with you so you can be smarter than I was. Maybe you can choose to be savvier and less stubborn than "new-to-rare-mamahood Nikki." These are lessons shared from one rare mama to another who wants a better outcome for you.

Actually, they are the lessons of thousands of rare mamas and therapists, and those far wiser than I am who have shed light on the truths about our well-being, self-love, and self-sacrifice. It's my mission to spread this knowledge because sometimes you can't understand it any other way unless it comes from someone who is actually walking the same road. It was easy to discount these truths when they weren't delivered from an actual mom who had lived this. I still kept thinking, *Yeah, but you don't really get it. You don't have a child with a rare disease.*

Perhaps there was truth to the fact that they couldn't fully understand. But there are also truths about the human mind, body, and spirit of which we aren't exempt just because *we have* a child with a rare disease.

So let me impart some thoughts about taking care of yourself from a mama who's been there. In the next chapters, we'll spend some time learning about the different aspects of well-being and taking care of our whole selves, and then we'll make an individualized self-care plan. But for now, I'll lay down a few truths about self-care from one rare mama to another.

WHAT SELF-CARE IS AND WHAT IT IS NOT

First, let's talk about what self-care is and what it is not. I think we all know that self-care is any activity we do to take care of our physical, mental, or emotional well-being. No-brainer, right? But let's also talk about what self-care is not, because there are some myths about self-care we can sometimes buy into. We have to dispel these myths before we can really embrace this wholeheartedly. Let's do that first. I'll make this quick.

What Self-Care Is Not

Myth 1: Self-care is all or nothing.
Truth: A little bit of self-care is better than none.

Myth 2: Self-care is a luxury.
Truth: Self-care is a necessity.

Myth 3: Self-care is selfish.
Truth: Self-care is self-love and self-preservation.

Myth 4: Self-care is something to be earned.
Truth: Self-care is deserved right now.

Myth 5: Self-care takes up a lot of time.
Truth: Even fifteen-minute breaks are useful.

Myth 6: Self-care is an obligation.
Truth: Self-care can be something you enjoy.

Self-Care Is an Essential Counterpunch

Self-care is essential. Full stop.

Self-care in our situation is vital so we can have the stamina to sustain. Taking care of ourselves is even more critical for caregivers like us. It's critical to our well-being, and it's critical to be able to serve our child. Our needs are important and urgent too, and we need to take care of ourselves now. Our care and our child's care go hand in hand. So instead of buying into the common misconceptions about self-care, we need to shift our mindset to start thinking that taking care of ourselves is critical to fight this fight.

This book outlines all the challenges and obstacles that we're going to face. We're in the utmost of high-stakes situations. Self-care is our counterpunch.

How do we sustain a hit to our emotions? How do we weather the hard news we are bearing? How do we survive all the frightening appointments and procedures we're taking our child to and still have the emotional availability to comfort them? How do we endure the physical strain on our bodies from lifting, transferring, and carrying children who have physical disabilities? How do we carry on when our faith is tested, when we feel numb, or when we feel lost?

> Our own care is not something to be set aside because we are rare mamas. Self-care is something to practice regularly *because* we are rare mamas!

Self-care activities are the very things that can help us weather and endure all the above. They allow us to be more productive. According to the National Institute of Mental Health, self-care has a ton of scientifically proven benefits, including improved focus, pain reduction, blood pressure control, stress and anxiety reduction, improved immunity, and longevity.[2]

Our own care is not something to be set aside because we are rare mamas. Self-care is something to practice regularly *because* we are rare mamas!

THERE'S ALWAYS GOING TO BE SOMETHING TO DO

I never understood the "This is a marathon, not a sprint" saying. I mean, I understood what it meant, but I didn't understand how to live it. There I was, sprinting along and trying desperately to get everything accomplished. Trying to keep my head above water. Trying to check everything off my to-do list.

I kept ticking away at that list, thinking, *If I can just get it all done, then I can rest.* But just as quickly as I checked something off the list, something new landed on it. What the what? I'd toggle and toil away at my list again and again. I'd feel a sense of accomplishment as I got through my list, only to have a cannon gun launch three new things my way. Instead of waiting until everything on my list is done—which by the way may mean waiting until the end of time—I learned I need to rest anyway right now. Right. Now.

So do you.

When Miles was newly diagnosed, we were working hard to get him leg braces, a stander, a wheelchair, and an appointment to see a team of specialists. When I had finally checked all these things off my list, I asked his amazing and wise physical therapist if we were done. She smiled and said in a kind and caring way, "Well, yes, you are done for now, but there will always be something you're working on." I didn't know what she meant at the time. In my head I was like, *Okay, that's great, but we're done, right?*

Now, years later, I see what she meant—there will always be something around the corner to take care of, something your child is working on, or something on your list. I'm not saying this to panic you; I'm saying it so you can wrap your head around it early on and look at the road differently than I did. I'm saying it so you can come to terms with this reality. Instead of letting all of the to-dos make you frantic, learn to gently accept them and work through them as you can, when you can.

Children themselves are always changing and entering new phases and stages. Parents of typically developing children talk about this all the time. They are continually trying to keep up with the ever-changing child-rearing demands as their children grow, change, and develop. It's the same with raising a child with a rare condition. They may outgrow equipment, need new adaptations, change providers, switch medicines, etc. This means we as parents will be navigating through change, and our to-dos will reflect that.

We need to flip our way of thinking from trying to get it all done to pacing ourselves for the ebbs, flows, changes, and even the surprises that will undoubtedly be thrown our way.

When there are pressures coming down all around you and the pile of to-dos is miles long, you're still going to need to sleep. Yes, though the heat is on, you'll need to lay your weary head down and rest. Mama needs to make time to take care of herself right at the height of intense times.

As moms, we're accustomed to pushing ourselves until things are done before we stop. We're even accustomed to pushing ourselves to the brink of breaking. I'm not sure how this even makes sense, but somehow it does when we're trying to save our child. But how does breaking ourselves allow us to help them? Seriously, it's an oxymoron. It doesn't make good sense. But it's what we do.

If our body or our mind says rest, *we must listen!* Will we wait until we break down? Who will help our children then? Our bodies and our minds tell us things for a reason. Just because our child's rare disease says "go, go, go, gimme, gimme, gimme" doesn't mean our own bodies can accommodate these demands.

We have to make room for rest. When we're constantly operating at ninety miles per hour, we have to get in the slow lane from time to time and pull off the road so we can refuel. Human beings can't go full throttle all the time and still be effective. It's necessary to take a break to recharge and return a bit replenished so you can start again. Yes, it's hard to take a break when you feel like there's still so much to do. There is, and there probably will always be. So you're going to need to take a break despite that.

SOMETIMES GOOD ENOUGH HAS TO BE GOOD ENOUGH

Another thing I had to come to terms with was the fact that I wasn't going to be able to do everything the way I always did. I wasn't going to be the mom making the homemade Halloween costumes. (All right, who am I kidding? I was never that mom anyway. But this really solidified that I was never going to be that kind of mom.) I was not going to be making school lunches filled with sandwiches cut to look like dinosaurs. (If you're one of these moms, I'm completely jealous and utterly annoyed with you at the same time. ☺)

I've come to realize that there's only so much time in the day, and I have to choose where I want to put my time. I can either spend that extra twenty minutes I have calling to follow up on my son's piece of equipment that still hasn't arrived or make the dinosaur sandwiches. So at the end of the day, the sandwiches are square, but we got that piece of equipment handled.

You know what I like to call my dinners? "Get 'er done." Yes, I would love to be making four-course gourmet masterpieces, but it's just not gonna happen. My only requirements now are that meals are healthy and nourishing. So you wanna know what we're having for dinner, kids? Food. Here's a serving of "Get 'er done." Now eat it.

I learned that sometimes good enough is just going to have to be good enough. Find out what's important to you and spend the time on that. For some, it *is* cooking for their family. For some mamas, cooking is a beautiful expression of love. It's a joy for them to make a meal their family will savor and taste that love with every bite. It's a creative outlet and expression that refreshes them. Honestly, I think that's amazing (but, man, you're really making me look bad).

One of the things I do enjoy is having time to read with my kids, pray with them, and talk about the day with them before bed. But the great race to get them to bed is always looming, so I might have to give up something that's not as important in order to have that time before bed with them. Our days are so frantic, and I crave that time to connect. Yes, it's not perfect in any way, shape, or form, but I try to have that time at night with them because it feels important to me and is an expression of my love.

But I've learned that if I am running hard the entire day, rushing to appointments and therapies, coming home, helping with homework, getting lunches packed, cooking dinner, cleaning it up, and getting kids ready for bed, by the time I get to the nighttime part of the day, I am wiped. I have no mental or emotional capacity left to be present and engaged.

That means something else on my plate has to be good enough so I can have energy for the thing I truly adore. That nighttime ritual with my kids is important to me, so I try to give it precedence like the precious time it is for us.

I learned a long time ago to let go of some things. I just can't do it all. I do what I can and what's important to our family. Sometimes good enough is going to have to be good enough.

SOMETIMES YOU HAVE TO PUT YOUR HEAD DOWN AND GET IT DONE

Another thing a wise rare mama friend taught me is that there will be times when you'll have to hunker down and get things done, and you may have to fall off the grid for a while. This is survival mode, people. Sometimes you can't get around to everyone and everything. You want to, but you can't because you're waking up early and running hard all day long to appointments, on the phone with insurance companies and service providers, and attending meetings at the school. You're in and out of your car and don't have a minute to stop and answer the twenty texts you've received, so you think, *Okay, I'll answer them later.*

When you finally jam some dinner into your body, get your kids in bed, and sit down to catch up on paperwork and respond to all the emails and texts, you fall asleep with your clothes on, sitting up, paperwork in your hand. Survival mode! Your friends and family may wonder what the heck has happened to you because they haven't heard from you in weeks. You've gone MIA. This isn't by choice but by necessity. You would love nothing more than to get on the phone for an hourlong chat with your bestie—or even better, go to dinner or lunch in person—but you're under mounds of vital deadlines.

It's really hard because what you want to do and what you're able to do are two different things. However, sometimes you'll have to dig in, hunker down, go into your cave, disappear off the face of the earth, and get it done, because you're on a time constraint for something that trumps everything else. Do you want to be so out of touch? No, of course not, but sometimes there's no other way to do it all. This may make other people feel all sorts of ways, but it doesn't change the fact that you have barely any time, your child's health needs are pressing, and so is your own care.

Sometimes you're just going to let a bit of the world fall away for a little while. Sometimes there's no choice; you'll just have to pick back up when you can. It's okay. Really, friend, it's okay.

ENLIST HELP

I know we talked about building your support systems and asking for help when you need it, but I want to drive this home. You are not an island, and you were not meant to be one. Sometimes (most times) there is just no other way to do this than with help. So if you haven't gotten over that yet, get over it. You're going to need to enlist help. This is why I laid out the various in-home health and respite programs earlier. If you can get assistance with childcare, this is going to help you tremendously.

If you can delegate, do it. If you can afford to hire help, do it. Whether it's help with housekeeping, laundry, meals, or whatever frees up your time, you need all hands on deck. It's not a cop-out; it's a lifeline. Take it.

SAY NO TO OTHER THINGS SO YOU CAN SAY YES TO YOU

Here's a hard truth: Life is not going to stop while you're going through this. I'm not even talking about anything having to do with rare disease life. I am talking about just regular old life things. It's still going to send you a zillion to-dos, invitations, expectations, commitments, and obligations. They'll just keep coming at you like a freight train. Somehow life doesn't let you off the hook just because you have a child with a rare disease.

It's up to you to let yourself off the hook. That's right, you're going to be the one to grant yourself permission to change your commitments and your calendar. Trust me, no one else is going to do this for you. You won't even believe what other people are still going to expect and ask of you. Like I said before, they just don't know. They haven't been through it, so they can't know.

Yes, some things *you* have to do. But others . . . well, do you? Do you *have* to do them? What can you say no to? What can you let fall away? What can you take your focus away from?

Where is all of this time to handle all the responsibilities that come with a rare disease going to come from? Seriously, extra hours are not going to get handed to you along with the test results of your child's diagnosis. It's unfair, I know!

Where is the time to fit everything in going to come from? It needs to come from somewhere. And I'm saying that it can't come from your own care. Do you hear this, mamas? *Not from your own care!*

Whoa, you can tell I'm pretty fired up about this one. I'm not yelling at *you* so much as I am to the whole world. Do you hear this, world? We will no longer give away our own care to put something else before it! *No more!*

Now, let me be clear about something. This is tough for a mama like me. I have a servant's heart. I enjoy helping others. It's always been a part of my life. When someone asks for a volunteer, my hand darts up before I even realize it left my lap. Clearly, I enjoy it.

When Miles was diagnosed, Mason was in preschool. I remember finally gathering some of my wits about me to share with Mason's teacher what we'd learn about Miles's diagnosis and what we'd be facing. I wanted her to have an understanding of what was going on in our home so that she could keep her eyes out for any ways this was affecting Mason. She was a lovely woman, kind and caring, and a nurturing teacher. I was grateful Mason was in her class.

I felt like if I shared with her the depths of what was going on, she might be understanding if family members were helping get

Mason to and from school while we were at appointments for Miles, or if we had to miss certain events, or if I forgot simple things like signing this or that form. I guess I just wanted to make sure if it looked like we were losing our minds, she'd know the reason why.

Do you know the first question she asked me after she offered her condolences and prayers?

She asked me if I wanted to be the room mom.

In that moment, I remember thinking, *Huh? I'm trying to tell you that I was just delivered the worst news of my life, that I'm grieving, that I'm coming undone, that I'm up in arms worried about how this will also affect Mason. This is my SOS signal. How, of all things, could you ask me to take on another responsibility? How do I even look like someone fit to be room mom?*

You all remember what I told you about how I almost forgot to pick up Mason from school that one day, right? I mean, clearly, I was not room mom material at that point.

So of course, do you know what I said?

I said, "Sure, I'd love to do it."

Rookie move. Clearly, I had not learned to say no at that point. I mean, I wasn't lying, I would have loved to! But seriously, what was I thinking? I wasn't. I wasn't thinking; I was pleasing. I wanted her to like me. I didn't want to miss out on things like this for Mason because of Miles's diagnosis that was already stealing too much. And let's be honest, I was flattered that she thought of me as someone that she'd like to have as her room mom.

But there couldn't have been a more wrong time for me to take on that role. So there I was, sending out emails about class parties and events and reminding parents to bring their children's school supplies, while I could barely remember my own name. In other times, I think I could have room-mom'd with the best of them. And you know what? I think I somehow managed to pull it off in a way that was not all that terrible. But it came at a cost. And that was the cost to me, to my own care. Nothing like a ten-month commitment to teach me this lesson.

Maybe even if I was the right girl, it was most definitely the wrong time.

I know that now. But I wasn't listening to myself then.

Sacrificing my own care so I could still keep up with all of life's demands in addition to all of the rare disease demands was my solution. I was determined not to let this disease change me. I didn't want it to change my self-identity, so I was trying to keep up with everything I always had been. I was trying to be a good mom. Trying to be a good wife. Trying to be a good friend. Trying to be a good daughter. Trying to do everything for everyone all the time as best I could. But it wasn't working well. For anyone. Including me.

This is tough, my friends. We've spent our whole life building our identities and thinking of ourselves in a certain way. Taking on the identity of a rare disease mom may not have been something we saw coming. This doesn't mean you have to say goodbye to all that you were or change who you are altogether. This means you may have to do things in a different way.

Let me point out that there's a big difference between letting a rare disease change your core values and letting it change the way you logistically operate in the face of limited time. But I couldn't see that then.

What I understand now was that if I did things differently, it didn't mean I was changing the core of myself; it just meant I was learning to prioritize myself given the confines of the situation before me. Loving myself has always been one of my core values, so I don't know why I didn't see then that saying no was in fact a loving way to uphold the core value of loving myself. Perhaps because it conflicted with loving others, another one of my core values.

My wise mama told me once, "Nikki, there is a season for everything. When your kids need you, that's exactly where you are supposed to be. It's where you should put your time." My mom has a servant's heart like no one I've ever seen. That woman has a beautiful soul and gives of herself like no other. Coming from her, that meant a lot. And I believe it's sage advice.

Our children need us, and it's one of the most important places we can put our time and energy. But *we* need us too. We need to put time and energy into ourselves so we can pour into our children.

Find solutions that don't involve sacrificing your own well-being. Get intentional about where you put your time and energy. What fuels you? What serves you? What helps you uphold your well-being and that of your family? Those are the places you should be putting your limited time and finite energy.

There are a lot of things in the rare disease world that we have to do whether we like it or not. So in other parts of our life, we're going to need to say no to things we just don't want to do if we don't really have to do them.

We need outlets that are going to charge, uplift, and encourage us. We need conduits to relaxation, restoration, and recuperation. And, girl, we all need some places to just have some dang fun!

Run activities and invitations through a filter of restoration, joy, and excitement. Does this bring me joy? Does this excite me? Does this help restore me? If yes, then go. If no, then pass. We don't have gobs of time like we did pre-kids to be running around saying yes to every invitation we bump into because we have nothing better to do. If it's not an emphatic *yes*, then it's a *no*.

And speaking of nos, I'm going to come right out and say something else. When there is a choice, stop spending time with people who suck. Yep, I said it. Your time is just too precious now. Do you want to walk away from your one opportunity to socialize in weeks just to feel drained, irritated, offended, or wound up? Hard pass.

Say no to the jabbers, guilters, one-uppers, told-you-so-ers, bullies, braggarts, drama queens, jerks, manipulators, condescenders, controllers, and button-pushers. Hmm, there may be no one left. Kidding, but I'm pretty sure we all know at least one of these.

Listen, we all are going to have to do plenty of things in life that we don't want to do, with plenty of people we don't want to do them with; it's inevitable. But I'm saying when you do have a choice, choose who you spend your time with wisely and stop feeling guilty about it.

This is part of prioritizing ourselves and our own well-being. And it has to come from us. No one is going to do this for us. We have to set our own boundaries around our time and be the ones to enforce them.

Get crystal clear about what invigorates you and what you're going to say yes to. Write it down if you have to, so when something comes up that isn't possible for you to do and doesn't fall within your list of things that fuel you, you can quickly discern what to do with it. Say no to what you need to so you can say yes to you.

Mama, please—you have to say yes to you.

For what it's worth from a rare mama who's been there, I hope these takeaways about taking care of yourself shed some perspective for you. You're in charge of prioritizing and upholding your own well-being, and it's truly one of the most important things I could pass along from the list of things I wish I'd done differently.

It's never too late, and I'm starting now!

Just start now.

Rare Mama Truth

Clone wanted. Inquire within.

CHAPTER 19

Caring for the Whole Self

"When you recover or discover something that nourishes your soul and brings joy, care enough about yourself to make room for it in your life."

JEAN SHINODA BOLEN

Now that I've impressed upon you the importance of why you need to take care of yourself, let's take a closer look about how to promote wellness and uphold your well-being. When I talk about taking care of your overall well-being, I mean nurturing your whole self, including your mental, emotional, physical, and relational needs. I'm talking about finding a healthy balance in your mind, body, and spirit.

When you're time-starved, sleep-deprived, and anxiety-filled, this is extremely hard to do—but, mama, it's necessary for so many reasons. If you truly want to help your child, you'll need to invest time into taking care of your whole self. Because if mama goes down, the whole ship can sink. Let's talk about how to take care of each part of your well-being, including mental, emotional, physical, spiritual, and social.

MENTAL/EMOTIONAL WELL-BEING

It's common for the emotional strain of rare disease caregiving to become overwhelming. Many moms need help sorting through their feelings. At the same time, they worry that if they dive into their emotions too deeply, the whole well will explode, and they'll drown in their sea of sorrows. I can certainly understand that. But feelings and emotions are sneaky; they often surface whether you want them to or not. You may choose to shove them down, but at some point they'll bubble up and trickle out. They may even manifest themselves in other ways, such as physical injury or illness. So you may want to just deal with them outright.

A very wise doctor once told me that we can't live in a constant state of a stress and adrenaline rush. It's not sustainable. We can handle it for short bursts, but there needs to be a reprieve. We need the recovery period too.

How can we battle the effects of stress from caregiving? How can we nurture our mental and emotional well-being?

Some moms choose to spend time alone (easier said than done, I know)—reading, praying, meditating, writing, journaling, or being in nature, to name a few examples. Quiet time by themselves helps them refuel and reflect. This reflection time is so important when the world around you is moving at one hundred miles per hour. Time to slow down and reflect allows you to process what's happening and how it's making you feel. Sometimes you have to *feel* all your feelings in order to move through them.

Practices such as breathwork, muscle relaxation techniques, and meditating can give a sense of calm, peace, and balance that can benefit both emotional well-being and overall health. These practices can help us clear away the information overload that builds up every day and contributes to our stress, bring us to a place of clarity, connect with our intuition and our internal guiding systems, and let go of everything but the present moment.

Other moms pour their emotional and mental energy into meaningful action such as advocating for their child's disease or helping other moms and children with the same diagnosis. Some of these moms have told me that doing something proactive helps them feel less powerless over their child's condition. It helps them feel like they're contributing and making positive changes. It also helps them connect with a community of like-minded parents focused on the same goal.

Some moms seek support and comfort through family and friends. Talking with a confidante about how we're feeling and dealing can help release those emotions. Though our family and friends may not be able to completely identify with what we're going through, they can still be an ear to listen. Sometimes just voicing our feelings allows for a release of all the tension that surrounds them. Letting others around us know what we're going through on a daily basis provides opportunities for them to support us.

Many moms seek professional help. Since having a child with a rare disease comes with a whole new set of rules and way of doing things, and since rare disease caregiving can be overwhelming, it can be helpful to talk to a professional who can provide clarity. A therapist or counselor is an unbiased third party with whom we share our feelings and who can help us learn to cope with our new normal. If you think this may be helpful, seek out a family therapist who has experience with chronic illness. If you feel the emotional strain taking a toll, don't be afraid to ask for help.

Whatever helps you process and work through your emotions to keep you in the best mental state is worth the investment of your time. You'll be thrown so much information during this journey, and you will need clarity of mind to have good comprehension, judgment, and discernment. Your mind is a powerful tool that can be sharpened, tuned, and polished. It's an important part of your whole self that can help keep the other parts in balance.

> Change your thoughts and feelings from fear, ineptness, and confusion to bravery, competency, and ability.

As well, your thoughts and feelings often control how you see and interpret things. If you start to change your thoughts and feelings from fear, ineptness, and confusion to bravery, competency, and ability, you'll cultivate those very things in your life. Your mindset has the ability to shape your reality. Find ways and outlets that allow you to work through your emotions and keep your mental well-being balanced.

PHYSICAL WELL-BEING

Because the mind and body are interconnected and affect each other tremendously, it's important that we pay attention to the ways our mind can affect our physical health. Many moms feel the effects of the stress of rare disease caregiving on their bodies. According to the Mayo Clinic, stress can cause physical effects and changes such as headaches, muscle tension and pain, fatigue, stomach upset, change in sex drive, weight loss, weight gain, and sleep problems. [1]

In addition, because moms are caregivers and the caregiving requirements for a child with a rare disease are significant, a mom's body is often working overtime. We may be doing tasks that our child is unable to do. We may be lifting, transferring, holding, toileting, bathing, dressing, feeding, stretching, massaging, etc. This can put physical strain on our body. It's important to know this going in and come up with strategies for staying healthy. Mayo Clinic suggests getting regular physical activity, stretching to avoid injury, and practicing relaxation techniques such as deep breathing, meditation, yoga, tai chi, or massage.

Often, if we don't give our body a break, our body will make us take a break—be it from injury or illness. Then what? How will we care for our children if we're sick or injured?

Our bodies are our vessels, and they need certain basic things like sleep, exercise, and good nutrition. When we have a child with a rare condition, we're typically so focused on their well-being that ours can go right out the door. We may be running them around to physical therapy, swim therapy, and equine therapy, but we haven't done any exercise or physical activity ourselves in years. We may be working with occupational therapists and nutritionists to make sure our children have feeding abilities and are getting proper nutrition, yet there we are, grabbing a fistful of goldfish crackers and calling it lunch as we rush out the door to get to appointments. Of course, we know better, but we just don't have the time. This is our reality.

And sleep? Don't even get me started about sleep! Who can sleep when things around us are in chaos or we're wrestling with difficult information? Not to mention so many of us have children who are unable to sleep through the night due to their condition. And if they aren't sleeping, we aren't sleeping. Yet sleep is of the utmost importance. When we don't sleep, our bodies are tired, our mind is in a fog, and we have less patience and bandwidth for all the things we need to do. Getting enough sleep has a ton of benefits, including getting sick less often, lowering the risk for serious health problems, reducing stress, thinking more clearly, improving mood, and getting along better with people.

The truth is, with rare disease caregiving, it's extremely difficult to do the very things that will help us. But focusing on our own physical health has to be a vital part of our new routine. Just like you take good care of your child, take good care of yourself too, mama.

Keep your body stretched so it doesn't get tight. When it's tight, you're more prone to injury, especially if you're physically lifting or carrying your child. Move your body and get your blood pumping; not only is it good for your physical health, but it also releases endorphins, and that's good for you mentally. So much of this goes hand in hand. Eat a whole, balanced diet. I'm not talking about some gourmet dinner you have no time to cook; I mean be sure you get your vegetables, fruits, protein, and vitamins to ensure your body has the proper intake to fuel you.

Another powerful tool for taking care of our physical well-being is breathwork. Breathing practices and conscious control of one's breath are said to influence one's mental, emotional, or physical state, with a claimed therapeutic effect. Simple breathing techniques that consist of breathing in for five seconds and breathing out for five seconds are easy to execute during the day from wherever we are and can have enormous benefits to our overall well-being.

Give your aching paws a break. Rest. Put your feet up. Close your eyes when you can. Refresh. Take care of that precious vessel so it's in top working condition.

SPIRITUAL WELL-BEING

With so much stressful information and situations in your life, how will you keep your soul and spirit intact? How will you battle the thoughts that can turn you bitter? How will you keep your light shining in the darkness? Your spiritual well-being is an important part of keeping you balanced while you're caregiving.

Our spirituality can be a source of strength and solace. In the midst of medical treatments, endless appointments, and emotional highs and lows, spirituality and faith can become pillars of support for caregivers, offering a foundation to withstand the storms that come with caring for a child with a complex medical condition. This is a deeply personal journey, and for many, the intertwining of spirituality and caregiving becomes an integral part of finding meaning and maintaining resilience in the face of adversity.

One of the spiritual practices that can help with maintaining or improving your spiritual well-being is prayer. Prayer can foster a sense of connection to God, give you a stronger mindset, improve your outlook, help you maintain positivity, and give you hope. Prayer can also reduce feelings of isolation, anxiety, and fear. Prayer also has been proven to have many physical health benefits, such as regulating heartbeat and increasing lifespan.

Both prayer and the practice of meditation may become coping mechanisms, offering moments of reflection and connection with something greater than oneself. They can be important parts of finding the balance needed in rare disease caregiving. They can help feed our souls to stay light and bright in weary, dreary times.

I know we all come from different backgrounds and different beliefs. I don't know where you are in your spiritual journey, but let me ask you right now, if you haven't considered your faith, might you consider it now?

You can either let this experience diminish your faith or awaken it.

I have let this experience with a rare disease awaken my faith, and though I would never push my beliefs on anyone who's not interested, I do want to offer my experience for those who are. My faith has been an anchor in

> **You can either let this experience diminish your faith or awaken it.**

this stormy sea. I feel God's love more than ever before. That may seem strange to say, considering my child was diagnosed with a severe disease, but I have felt God's presence and His hand on my family's life. We've asked, and we've received.

I was always a woman of faith and a believer in Jesus. But leaning into and strengthening my spiritual life has helped me cope and given me more peace than I ever thought was possible at the most difficult time of my life.

Now, if you haven't noticed already, I'll admit that I am the type of person who likes to feel in control of my life (oh sweet, sweet control). But life with a rare disease has been a humbling reminder that I am not in control of many, many things. I've had to learn to surrender. It's my life's lesson, and I've had to learn it over and over again (and will probably continue to do so). Mostly because I am stubborn. But also because I keep going back to taking up the load myself, feeling that it all depends on me to figure it out and that the weight is on my shoulders to hold the whole thing together.

But the truth is that the greater my need to control things, the more overloaded, stressed, and empty I feel. I have learned that surrendering is an act of trusting God to take up the load. It's an invitation for Him to walk with me and *share* the load because it's too heavy for me on my own. In this way, when I surrender, I am not alone.

The act of surrendering doesn't come easy for me. In fact, the idea of surrendering may even sound funny coming from me because I've written a book about taking on rare disease battles. But I've learned this: There will come a time when I've done everything I can do. I've done the research, I've done the work, I've fought the fight, I've worked hard to turn the *no* into a *yes*, and I've put every ounce of blood, sweat, and tears into the battle. What else can I do?

I can "let go, and let God."

It's the hardest lesson for me to learn. But when I let go and let God, I am sharing the load. Instead of waiting until I'm so burned out and exhausted to turn to my faith, I've learned to surrender daily to God's plan and rely on Him for strength and peace.

When I'm troubled, when there's a situation that seems impossible, when there's a decision too weighty or a load too heavy, I've realized that the answer isn't always to do more or to press harder, but instead to lean into God's Word, to get quiet and still so I can hear God's voice. It's so counterculture, this idea of getting quiet right in the midst of a time that demands you to take action. But for me, it's in the stillness that I gain perspective to make decisions that are thoughtful, purposeful, and meaningful.

I've learned to pray my way through the day. At each point, at each turn, at each confusing decision, with each fearful step, during each hard circumstance, and with each sad or bitter thought—I pray it away. When I don't know the answer, when I don't know where to turn, and when there seems to be no way—I pray!

I've learned to pray and converse with God daily and express all my feelings, hurts, and hang-ups to Him. I expect Him to help me, trust that He will, and I give it all to Him.

I've been absolutely blown away by God's power and His ability to take my worries, confusion, and never-ending questions, and calm my soul in the midst of the storm. While the boat was rocking, while I couldn't find a paddle, and while I was scared I would fall overboard, He has helped me sit calmly through it. No, the storm didn't stop. It raged on through the night—dark, windy, and wet— yet there I sat. Right there in it. And you know what happened? Eventually, the wind ceased blowing, the sea calmed, and the sun rose. Yes, I was tired, wet, and wind-blown, but I lived *through* it with a peace that didn't come from my own making. I realized Jesus was driving the boat. He was the master captain.

And so, when I am going through a stormy time in my life, I have learned to focus on God instead of my troubles. He is able to stretch out His hand and walk with me through the raging waters. I can call to Him and ask Him to come into my boat. When I let Him take the helm, He calms the storms of life.

This awakening of my faith has helped me get up out of bed after an unimaginable diagnosis, make decisions that were too big for me to make on my own, brave procedures and surgeries that were too scary to face alone, and wake to face another day.

I'll never forget the day I gave it all to God. I remember running to the upstairs bathroom in my bedroom, far from my boys who were downstairs with my husband, locking the door, collapsing on my knees, weeping, and calling to God to save my son. I wept so hard I thought I might pass out. The dam had broken, the walls had ruptured, and my emotions came gushing out with a tsunami-like force. Curling into a fetal position on that cold bathroom floor in agonizing pain, a guttural animal-like wailing howled out of me, one I didn't recognize. And in those moments, I pleaded and cried out to God in the most intense, needy, and passionate surrender I had ever witnessed from myself. I gave Miles over to God. I told God I would trust Him. I would trust Him with my most precious gift. "He is Your son, You created him, and I know You love him. Now heal him, spare him, and save him," I begged God.

And I believe He did.

I have never cried like that before nor since. And on that transformative day, I lay there on that cold bathroom floor until I couldn't cry anymore. Then I sat up, and I prayed for strength. I prayed for the strength to be Miles's mother and do everything I needed for him. I told God there was no way I could do it without Him. I told Him how much I needed Him to guide me forward, to make hard decisions, to endure emotional distress, to fight for Miles's needs, to see him through painful medical procedures, and to push on despite my pain, fear, lack of abilities, and shortcomings. I asked Him to give me strength beyond measure so that I could help my son.

And I believe He did.

When the FDA approved the first-ever treatment for SMA, the same treatment my son had received for the two years prior through the clinical trial, my prayer was answered, and it felt like a miracle. It was *our* miracle, and it is our testimony.

I know that the strength I used to make our way forward was not my own; it was Jesus holding my hand through every step. There just isn't any other way I would have been able to take the steps I took. The strength I had felt divine. And God didn't just give me strength; He also gave me hope.

This hope has been the cornerstone throughout our journey, and it has marched us forward when at times it felt like all was lost. It helped guide us like a North Star as we faced the unimaginable, and it led us to possibilities we were told we'd never see come true.

Though my son is now on a lifesaving treatment, it doesn't mean our lives are without difficulty. Miles endures many effects of the disease. And so we continue on, and whenever I feel lost, overwhelmed, weak, or distraught—and believe me, the times are many—I turn back to God. I remember what He already did, and I remember what He can continue to do.

And though I often get ahead of myself and take up the armor to fight on my own, I am reminded that I was never meant to do this alone. So, I turn to Jesus over, and over, and over to continue to walk with Him every step.

I trust. I surrender. I pray.

If you haven't yet, might you consider strengthening your relationship with God and seeing if He provides you with that grounding anchor and the hope we all so desperately need?

I prayed yet again when I wrote this chapter (I pray for you rare mamas all the time). I prayed to God and asked Him what He wanted me to write, and what I heard was, "Just tell them I love them." If you are reading this and it's stirring something in your heart, then maybe it's meant for you. God loves you and is waiting for you.

SOCIAL WELL-BEING

Social well-being can be defined as the sharing, developing, and sustaining of meaningful relationships with others. This allows us to feel authentic and valued, and it provides a sense of connectedness and belonging.

According to the National Institutes of Health (NIH), social connections may help protect health and lengthen life.[2] Scientists are finding that our links to others can have powerful effects on our health. Whether with family, friends, neighbors, romantic partners, or others, social connections can influence our biology and well-being. Strong, healthy relationships are important throughout our life. They can impact our mental and physical well-being.

Many of us are social creatures and have a strong desire to be with others, to be connected, and to feel like a part of a group. Social outlets are part of our happiness and can positively impact our overall well-being. With the time involvements for rare mamaing being so high, it often leaves little time for social interaction. However, without social interactions, we run the risk of becoming socially isolated. This is different from choosing to enjoy solitude or alone time. Social isolation is withdrawing from relationships, which can lead to negative feelings and fears, which can become a self-enforcing spiral.

Mindfully carving out time for social interactions can help fend off isolation. For many of us, social outlets can help us focus on something other than our child's rare disease. It can allow us to take a break from the normal routine, normal worries, and normal responsibilities.

Spending time with our spouse or partner can allow us to reconnect and feel a stronger bond. These relationships are often the foundations of our family life. Spending time with family can allow us to feel a sense of support. Family members can provide encouragement, positive reinforcement, and a sense of being surrounded by others willing to help. Time with friends can give us an outlet for fun, camaraderie, relaxation, and rejuvenation. Belonging to a club with like-minded people can often help us engage in an activity other than caregiving. It can allow us to stay connected to our hobbies and passions. It can help remind us who we are outside of being a parent of a child with a rare disease.

If you're a social type of person and being social helps you feel a sense of balance and is a source of happiness, then intentionally seek out social settings, interactions, and outlets.

Listen, I know you probably already know a lot of these things, but sometimes because of our situation, we think the rules don't apply to us. Even though we know better, we ignore our needs and put ourselves last. Or we're so busy with rare disease caregiving that we just forget. Or there's so much to do that we don't prioritize ourselves. Sometimes we just need a reminder. Sometimes we just need permission.

Consider this your big, flashing reminder and your letter of permission:

Mama, your health and well-being are more important now than ever before. Just as your child is worthy of good care, you are worthy of good self-care. It's vital to spend time taking care of your well-being. By the authority of all the rare mamas who have gone before you, I hereby grant you permission to nurture yourself, and prioritize your well-being. Take good care of YOU!

Rare Mama Truths

Dear Self-Care, I miss you. I mean, I really miss you.
It's not that I don't love you. Oh, how I love you.
I promise I will find time for you tomorrow.
Love, A Rare Mama

CHAPTER 20

Creating a Self-Care Plan

"As important as it is to have a plan for doing work,
it is perhaps more important to have a plan for rest,
relaxation, self-care, and sleep."

AKIROQ BROST

f you've been picking up what I've been throwing down in the last chapters, maybe you're thinking, *Okay, yes, I understand* the *importance of taking care of myself. Thanks for the reminder and thanks for the permission, but how? When? How and when do I take care of myself when there's no time and there are so many other things that need to get done?*

We're up against a unique set of challenges. So what can we do? We can make a plan.

Just like we make plans for our children's care, we need to plan for our own. Just as we plan OT, PT, ST, behavioral therapy, etc., for our child, we need to make a plan for our own self-care. This isn't any rocket-science concept here, but maybe we don't ever think about it in this way. Sometimes we aren't as methodical with our own care, and the reality is that we need to be.

> Sometimes we aren't as methodical with our own care, and the reality is that we need to be.

We have to be a little more strategic in coming up with ways to get the breaks we need. We have to plan for them and schedule them into our life intentionally. Caregiving breaks have to be high on our priority list, just as high as the good care we are giving our children.

All right, mamas, let's do this once and for all. Let's create a plan to take care of *you*! How? First, we're going to figure out the types of self-care activities that are truly restorative to you and the things that are nonnegotiable. I think it's really important that we have a clear understanding of what works for us as individuals if we're going to get 100 percent on board. Next, we're going to uncover strategies to get our plan in place. Last, the execution part is up to you. Don't let me hear about you not executing. Ima havta come lookin' for you!

Get out a pen and paper or a digital notetaking device, and look at your calendar. We're going to do this right here and now. Yep, I'm serious. You need a plan—or this is just not going to happen. I feel strongly about this one. I've seen it. I've lived it.

Go on now. Get your gear. Go on. I'll wait. Mama, I'm not playing. Okay, got what you need? Let's begin.

STEP 1: UNCOVER YOUR UNIQUE SET OF SELF-CARE ACTIVITIES.

We're all beautifully unique and wonderfully made individuals. We have our own interests and passions. We have our own desires and dreams and our own goals and pursuits. Your self-care activities should reflect these.

You need to get extremely specific on what activities are important, essential, and enjoyable to you as an individual. Know thyself.

For example, for the sake of my physical well-being, I learned I need to stretch my body in the morning before I start transferring and lifting my son who is in a wheelchair. If I don't, I'm more prone to injury. I've already experienced injury from this lifting and transferring. I've torn the meniscus in my knee, and I've overused and injured my back. Good times. Because of this, I experience a lot of tightness in my knees, hips, and back. I need to stretch my muscles so they are loose and limber before I put them to use all day long. If I don't, I risk injury again.

Stretching in the morning has become my nonnegotiable. It started out as something necessary so I can help my son, but it's turned into so much more. I get up early in the morning before my children wake up, when its quiet in the house, the sun is rising, and the day is new. It's turned into my time to pray and plan my day, which also helps me emotionally and mentally.

I feel inspired during that early time of day. I often hear God's voice in the wee hours while I'm looking out at the sunrise. I do some of my best thinking and idea generating during that time. For me it's a beautiful way to start the day, and it's become something enjoyable that I look forward to and appreciate.

What about you, mama? What are your nonnegotiables?

Remember, self-care doesn't have to be something you loathe. In fact, a lot of your self-care should even feel like things you enjoy because then you're more apt to do them. Some of our self-care activities should consist of things that help us meet our well-being goals in each of the important areas such as physical, mental, emotional, spiritual, and social health, and others should consist of things that we just flat-out enjoy. Forget about what every published self-care list includes or suggests if it doesn't sing to you. If bubble baths sound boring, but listening to heavy metal music makes you feel alive—girl, do your thang. Hair-band it up!

Let me illustrate this with an example. You'll see exercise on every self-care list. Why? Because it's good for your physical health. Exercise has been proven to be beneficial for mental and emotional health too. Many people get a charge from exercising. The release of all those endorphins leaves them on a high. They just absolutely love exercising!

I am not one of those people.

Yes, I know I need to exercise to stay healthy, and I even need to do it to stay strong to lift my son who is in a wheelchair. Staying in good physical health is important to me, and it's one of my goals—so it's something I do. But it's not something I love. It may promote and support my physical health, but this one doesn't check the emotional or spiritual health box for me. After a workout, I don't walk away feeling emotionally restored and uplifted. I check it off as something I did for my physical health, but I still need something else for my mental, emotional, and spiritual well-being. I'll be very honest: I don't exercise as often as I should, and it often falls off my list when the days are busy (I'm still working on this). I know the reason underneath all that is probably because I don't love it. So I don't emotionally miss it when I don't get it. Does that make sense? Some things I do because I need them to support my health. Others I do because I enjoy them.

Here's another thing to know: We are going to implement different types of self-care activities depending on what goal we are trying to achieve, depending on where we are at in a certain life stage, and even based on what we need in a given day depending on our mood.

On some days when you're running around frenzied or you've been through a harrowing ordeal, you might need an activity or ritual that's going to calm you down in order to restore your sense of balance. On other days, when you're feeling low, sad, or isolated, you might need an activity that revs you up and plugs you in to get you back to center. You might need different things at different times. If we have ideas about the things that calm us and the things that charge us, then we can implement the various activities that will help on that given day.

Here's another thing: Sometimes we have the idea that self-care is some grand, luxurious, unattainable endeavor—a three-week trip to Tahiti with ten of your best friends, a weekend getaway to a five-star spa, a yoga/meditation retreat on the top of a mountain. While those sound incredibly amazing and enlightening, and perhaps would be extremely restorative, that restoration may first of all be unattainable, and even if it was attainable, it may be fleeting as we return to our daily lives. True self-care at its best is composed of actions we take on an ongoing basis to not only refuel once we're already drained, but also to help us proactively promote and maintain our well-being before we get to burnout. Taking vitamins each day, a fifteen-minute walk in the morning, journaling in bed before sleeping—these types of activities support and uphold our health on a daily basis.

> True self-care at its best is composed of actions we take on an ongoing basis.

We need to get extremely granular and figure out what things we love to do, what are our nonnegotiables, what calms us, what fuels us, and what meets our goals to promote each piece of our well-being—physically, mentally, emotionally, spiritually, and socially.

Now it's your turn to brainstorm and jot down what those things are for you. Ready to make your lists?

What Are Your Goals and Wants?

- Physical
- Mental
- Emotional
- Spiritual
- Social

What Are Your Nonnegotiables?

- What are your must-haves/must-dos?
- What are the things that can't fall away because they are just too important?

What Do You Enjoy?

- What lights you up?
- What makes your heart sing?
- What do you look forward to?
- What feels like you?

What Calms You?

- What helps you unplug?
- What helps you slow down?
- What helps you be still?

What Excites and Fuels You?

- What charges you?
- What revs you up?
- What energizes you?
- What gives you power?

STEP 2: IDENTIFY WHICH ACTIVITIES GO ON YOUR PLAN.

Now that you've got lots of ideas, which ones are you going to try to incorporate into your daily life? Which ones are going to make it on your plan? You can start small by adding one or two and then build over time. It doesn't need to be the whole enchilada all at once. No need to overwhelm yourself before you even start. You can keep your list to pull from and add more in the future. You can also keep your list handy so you can use activities interchangeably depending on your mood on any given day.

I recommend starting with something that only takes a short amount of time in your day so it's more doable. Maybe you just start with ten or fifteen minutes. Maybe after time you'll be able to increase. But just commit right now to something small. Practice first with one or two of these short activities. You can do something more involved as you work your way up.

Got one or two things in mind that you're going to add into your life? Okay, carry on.

STEP 3: IDENTIFY BARRIERS AND SOLUTIONS.

What are the specific barriers that get in the way of you doing these activities? We all know time is going to be a barrier. What else? Childcare, energy, money, space, distractions, interruptions, focus?

In the example of my nonnegotiable self-care practice of stretching, the specific barrier that got in my way was having someone to take care of my children while I was doing this activity. Every time I tried to stretch, someone would need something, and I would get interrupted. It was frustrating, and I'd end up getting unfocused to the point of often giving up on the stretching. I also figured out that stretching wasn't as effective if I didn't do it first thing in the morning because then I was using my body to lift before it was stretched. Wrong order.

But I couldn't give this up; it's a nonnegotiable. So I had to figure out a solution. My solution was to do this first thing in the morning before my children were up. This meant I had to wake up earlier to build it into my schedule, which also meant going to bed earlier. I know this is not a solution for all of us because some of our children are not sleeping through the night or require 24/7 care. We all have our unique set of circumstances. This is just my example to get your wheels turning.

Think through the barriers and then brainstorm some solutions. This is why we spent so much time in earlier chapters emphasizing getting support systems into place. We need help! We need help with the barriers that get in the way of caring for ourselves. We need solutions so that we can put our self-care activities into play.

You may not have a solution to the barriers right now. This may take a little time to figure out. That's understandable. But the point is to start thinking about it and to start proactively looking for solutions.

STEP 4: SCHEDULE IT ON YOUR CALENDAR.

Next, you're going to schedule this self-care activity on your calendar as if it were a nonnegotiable appointment. Yep, you're going to look at your calendar right now and figure out a little ten- to fifteen-minute block where you can schedule it in. We all know that we live by our calendars. Does it even exist if it's not on the calendar? No, it doesn't. Get it on there.

STEP 5: PRIORITIZE THIS APPOINTMENT.

See that blocked-out time on your calendar? You know what that block represents? A boundary. You're putting a little, hard-edged square with sharp, pointy edges on your time to fend off and poke anything that tries to get in. Think of that block as a brawny bouncer that won't let any schmucks in. Access denied.

Schedule everything else around that block. Just like you plan everything around your child's important appointments, you're going to do the same with your important self-care time. It's on your calendar as a reminder of time already dedicated otherwise so that if something else gets asked of you at that time, you can say no. As best as you can, don't change this appointment with yourself because of something else. Protect it. Defend it. It's a top priority.

Of course, there will be times when you just don't have a choice. There will be emergencies and health needs that rise up and trump this appointment. This is the way of rare life; we know how this goes. But this should be the exception, not the norm. If things keep trumping and bumping your planned time, you might need to rethink your strategy and find a different time or solution.

In my example of stretching, there were times when my son was scheduled for a 6:30 a.m. appointment at the hospital, which was two hours away. We had to leave our home at 4:30 a.m. Ouch! Guess what happened on those days? I couldn't feasibly wake up any earlier to have time to stretch in the morning before we left. It just wasn't possible. So on those days, I had to find an alternative—such as stretching the night before or stretching when I came home from the appointment. It wasn't ideal, but at least I found replacement options when one of these situations arose.

STEP 6: TEST, LEARN, AND REFINE.

Try it out for a week or two and see if it works. Give it a test drive and be an observer. Is it working? Is it having the desired effect of refueling you? Does it work in real life?

If it doesn't, make adjustments. Get the kinks worked out. Refine, refine, refine.

Be specific. Be methodical. Don't give up. This is worth it. *You're* worth it.

Okay, you've got your plan in hand? Hold on to it like it's gold. Because it is. It's your gold. It's your love letter to yourself. It's what helps you be you. And that, my friend, is one of the most vital parts of your fight plan!

Rare Mama Truth

I scheduled "me time" today. By "me time," I mean
I hid in the bathroom with a book and a granola bar
and pretended I was on a remote tropical island—
just me, a snack, and silence.

CHAPTER 21

Crafting Caregiving Breaks and Resets

"Taking care of myself doesn't mean 'me first.'
It means 'me, too.'"

L.R. KNOST

Mama, I'm rooting for you to get a little break here and there. I know you need it and deserve it, and though it's hard to do, we gotta, gotta, gotta get it!

So here are some ideas for getting a break from caregiving. I know these won't work for all of us. We all have our own set of unique circumstances. But perhaps you can find one or two caregiving breaks or resets from this list to adopt and add to your routine. Or perhaps none of them will work, but I'm hoping it will get you thinking and will spark an idea that *does* work for you!

CAREGIVING BREAKS

- Take a break while your child is at an appointment.
  Many of our children attend PT, OT, speech, behavioral therapy, or some standing appointment regularly. Often, we have to be a part of these appointments too. But if there is ever an opportunity that you don't *need* to be in the appointment, and you and your child are comfortable without you attending, use it as an opportunity for a little break. Go outside and take a walk, sit in your car and read, or catch up on the phone with a friend. We have to look for little opportunities in the day where we can grab a handful of minutes for ourselves.

- Eat dinner after your kids have eaten and are in bed.
  Choose one night a week when you feed the kids and put them to bed early. Then have dinner on your own or with your spouse or partner. Order or prepare a special meal and savor every bite with no interruptions. Use this as a time of solitude or a time to connect with your spouse or partner.

- Alternate wake-ups with your spouse or partner.
  If you have a spouse or partner, plan for one day you wake up with the kids and the other day your spouse/partner does. On the morning that it's your day off from waking up with the kids, use that time for whatever you like—sleeping in, a morning walk or workout, reading, meeting up for early coffee with a friend, pampering, etc. This may work best on non-work days. For example, if you or your spouse/partner work during the week, alternate days off on the weekend so you can each get an easygoing type of morning.

- Wake up an hour before the kids.
  If waking up early is not your thing, I get it, but maybe give it a try to see if you might like it. There is something about

getting up when the house is quiet and having a little uninter-rupted time for yourself to get your thoughts together before the chaos begins. Use this time to read, write, pray, meditate, do yoga, exercise, listen to a podcast, or have your coffee, and start the day refreshed. If your children aren't sleeping through the night, this one may not be doable for you right now, and that's okay. Sleep is vital, and we aren't going to skip out on that. If you're trying to wake up earlier, you'll need to go to sleep earlier so you still get the same number of hours of sleep. If you want to try incorporating this into your life, the best way to do this is to start with small incremental changes to back into the ideal time you want to start waking up. Start by going to sleep fifteen minutes earlier the night before and wake up fifteen minutes earlier the next morning. Try this for a couple of nights and then back up another fifteen min-utes, and another and another until you get to your ideal wake-up time. You're training your body clock for this new rhythm. After a while, your body will adjust to the time dif-ference and reset your internal clock to start waking at your ideal time.

- Find an older child to play with your child.
  Let's be honest—it's tough to find caregiving for our children. We have to be so selective. But sometimes you just need a few minutes to get a couple of things done. We all know that most kids love playing with other kids who are slightly older than them. So find a kid in your neighborhood, a friend's kid, or someone's older sibling, and hire them for a few hours to come and play and hang out with your child. You'll still be home and have eyes and ears on everything, but your child will be occupied and enjoying themselves, and this will allow you to read, catch up on emails, cook, etc.

- Trade time with another mom.
  Find another mom you trust and trade time when you watch each other's kids. One day you watch her kids, and one day she watches yours. It doesn't have to be an extended amount of time; perhaps it's just an hour or two. But that little break can help you immensely when you need a little time to yourself.

- Have someone take the kids out while you stay home.
  Sometimes moms just need to be in their own home, with some peace and quiet, in solitude without caregiving. Sometimes we don't feel like getting dressed and going out and running around. Sometimes we just feel like being home in our pajamas and on our couch with a good book or a mindless movie. Plan for a couple of hours where your spouse, family member, friend, babysitter, etc., can take the kids out of the house and keep them busy while you stay put at home. All. By. Yourself.

- Plan one night a week when you have the night off.
  Find one night during the week when someone else handles the entire night, including dinner and cleanup, bathing, bedtime routine, and everything else until lights out. Maybe your spouse handles this night, or you ask a family member to do this for you one night a week, or you hire a babysitter, or use respite. Having that one night where you know you get a break from the routine and have time to yourself will make a world of difference in your week.

- Make a standing date with girlfriends.
  There's nothing like our girl time. Laughing, consoling, venting, sharing inside jokes—it's good for our soul. We know

every time we see our girlfriends, we come away feeling uplifted. But when everyone is busy with kids, it's hard to make it a priority. Set up a standing date that allows everyone to make it a priority, get it on their calendar, and have childcare covered. Dinner the first Thursday of every month? Brunch the second Sunday each month? Cards at rotating houses on one Tuesday evening per quarter? Having time carved out that you can look forward to can do wonders for your psyche.

- Plan one day a month to yourself.
I know this one is easier said than done. Taking a whole day to ourselves may feel totally impossible or like a complete luxury. I get it. I know this may not work for everyone. For those of you who can pull it off, it will require a lot of planning—sometimes to the point that you may wonder if it's even worth it. Oh, mama, it just may be worth it! The feeling you'll have when you wake up and know that you have the entire day to focus on yourself will be priceless. So plan it a month or two out so you can attend to all the details of who will watch your child and the list you'll need to provide them with that includes all the information for the day. Then plan what you're going to do with your day— relax under a tree in a park, go shopping, have lunch with a friend, etc. The best part is you get to decide because it's "your" day! If one day a month isn't possible, then maybe every other month, or every three months—whatever you can do. And if it's not in the cards right now, keep it in the back of your mind so if there is ever an opportunity that arises you can take it! Oh, how I hope you can figure out a way to get that break!

FIFTEEN-MINUTE RESETS

What about the situations where we just can't get a big chunk of time to focus on ourselves? Oh man, do I get that. But we still need little breaks in the day to refuel, recoup, and reset. Here's the basic science: If our body and mind are in motion all day long and our adrenaline is pumping and telling us to run like a cavewoman from a wild animal chasing us, at some point, it's going to burn out. It cannot keep up at that constant pace. It needs to reset. If we don't make time to take a break, we will start to feel the emotional and physical effects of this constant state of "go."

So then, what can we do?

We can find fifteen-minute spots each day to build in little resets. We can take these short breaks to turn off our body and our mind and regroup. I'm telling you these short breaks can make a world of difference.

I would love to have a perfectly balanced daily schedule with an optimal amount of time each day to complete all my to-dos and the perfect amount of time to rest. But it's just not the way my life operates. Instead, I have to shove these little breaks into the day wherever I can. It's not perfect, but it certainly helps. It helps me change my state of mind back to calm (or calmer).

For now, try to start with one day at a time scheduling a fifteen-minute break. See how it goes, see how it feels, and see where in the day it works. It may take a little trial and error at first. Over time, perhaps you can build up and add another fifteen-minute break into the day. Then another one. Small steps here and there until you have a few resets that allow you to breathe and regroup.

I've put together the steps to get you ready for your reset along with several fifteen-minute refresh ideas that I chose specifically to switch off both your mind and body from their regular program.

I know you don't have hours on end, but I bet you can find fifteen minutes. Mama, I urge you to try this. I encourage you to do this for yourself. You are a beautiful mama doing beautiful work. Now love on yourself a little bit with a fifteen-minute break for you *today*!

Five Steps to Prepare for Your Resets

1. Look at your schedule and pencil in your break time for that day.

2. Choose the fifteen-minute break suggestion you're going to do.

3. Turn off your phone, social media, distractions, and anything beeping.

4. Clear your mind. This is your time; this is your space. No to-dos, no what-ifs. Tune it all out and only be in that moment.

Fifteen-Minute Reset Ideas

Here are some ideas to get you thinking and get you started, but the point is to find what sings to you. What is it that truly feels restorative to *you*? This is going to be different for all of us. Listening to fifteen minutes of soul, funk, or some gut-belting blues takes me out of my head and helps me lose myself more than fifteen minutes of calm, Zen meditation music ever does. But hey, that's just me! What is it for you? What will help you unplug, get lost, go within, be present, relax, or restore? Mama, grab yourself fifteen minutes of *that*!

- Walking—strolling outside in fresh air and taking note of nature
- Breathing—inhaling and exhaling to reconnect with your calm

- Stretching—lengthening your body to allow it to be loose and limber

- Sipping—savoring a hot cup of tea and literally doing nothing while you sit and sip

- Dancing—shaking it like you're at the nightclub, choosing your favorite pick-me-up song or a tune that takes you back to old times and dancing like you're crazy (you might enjoy this way more than you plan to)

- Journaling—writing down all your feelings and thoughts and getting them out of your head

- Praying—talking to God, thanking Him, and asking Him for what you need

- Meditating—clearing your mind and connecting to your highest self

- Acupressure—applying acupressure techniques to promote relaxation

- Reading—letting your mind escape to another place or time

- Lounging—positioning yourself flat on a bed or a lounger and just being still and off your feet

- Bathing—soaking in a bubble bath and feeling the textures of the water and bubbles

- Calming—using a calming app for soothing and bringing your pace down

- Massaging—using your hands, a foam roller, a tennis ball, or whatever you have

- Painting/Coloring/Drawing/Writing—creating to let your spirit fly free

This list could go on, but I think you get the point. And just to be sure, let me just say it again: Caregiving breaks are not going to happen without you making them happen. They just aren't. It's up to us, and us alone, to make them happen. So get creative and figure out ways to get that break, girl!

> Caregiving breaks are not going to happen without you making them happen.

Rare Mama Truth

A Well-Rested Rare Mama:
Noun. 1. A mythical being found in the land where fairy godmothers, mermaids, unicorns, and other fabled creatures exist.

PART VI

Rare Life

(OTHER BEAUTIFUL
AND ANNOYING THINGS)

CHAPTER 22

Allowing Joy

"Some days, joy is a gift. Other days,
it's an all-out battle. Fight on, girl."

UNKNOWN

One day you're going to feel joy again. It's crazy when it happens, but one day you'll look up and find that the beauty in your life and the joy are returning.

I don't know how to explain this, because when my son was first diagnosed, I wondered how I would ever even smile again. Joy seemed to be a thing of the past. But something happens along the way. Not only does your whole life change, but *you* also change. Once you've hacksawed your way through the jungle, overturned every leaf for answers, and left your blood, sweat, and tears along the way, something changes inside you.

Maybe it's because things have been so hard that when something good happens, it's an almighty hallelujah! Or maybe it's because your perspective changes and you realize that when something beautiful happens, it truly is a gift. Or maybe you're just so dang worn out and haven't slept for so long that you're starting to hallucinate. Whatever it is, I'm here to tell you that your broken heart will slowly start to beat again. You will find joy in something simple or even mundane.

When I was younger and before I had kids, I would hope and pray for something extraordinary to happen. Ordinary made me want to throw up. Contentment seemed like death. I wanted the unexpected, the rare, the exciting. What's next? What's next? But now I'm able to appreciate more of the plain and normal. Now I pray for a regular old day. No excitement, no drama; just easy, regular, and normal. Maybe that's pathetic. Or maybe that's genius. I'm not really sure, but I'm thrilled when the days are simple. It doesn't happen very often, but when it does, I relish it. I've also come to realize that I see joy in little things more than ever before.

Joy that Miles, despite his disease, gets to go to school.

Joy that Mason, despite growing up amid a million medical appointments, is a goofball with a funny alter ego named "Larry" who makes funny faces and gestures. Old Lar Bear always provides the best comic relief.

Joy that my husband and I can still tease each other and laugh at our own inside jokes.

Joy in little things. Or maybe they aren't little things. Maybe to our family they're big, amazing wins because we were told at one point that these might not happen. Either way, we're not taking them for granted.

I never understood that joy and pain could exist at the same time. It still pains me to see all that my son has to endure. I feel pain on a regular basis from all sorts of circumstances and situations with his rare disease. But I feel joy too. They are two parallel lines running through my life. I try not to let the pain overshadow the joy. The pain must not be ignored, but neither should the joy.

The truth is, the older I get and the more I learn about life, the more I understand this dichotomy. The more I see that joy and pain are intertwined. Like two branches that swirl and connect upward as they grow. In fact, this is exactly life—life and death, joy and pain, light and dark, spring and winter. They exist together.

My son's diagnosis was and may always be my darkest night. But I've learned this about the dark: it doesn't have to envelop you whole. Night makes way for the dawn. And seeking the dawn is not betraying the night.

There are seasons to sit in the suffering, and there are seasons to sit in the sun.

It's not negating the endured anguish and the wreckage of the aftermath. There are seasons to sit in the suffering, and there are seasons to sit in the sun.

Fall apart, grieve, endure, and then allow yourself to seek joy. Joy is a state of being that comes from within and is not dependent on the situations and circumstances around you. I found my joy after staring down a fatal disease that could rob my child of his life. Perhaps in this stare-down, I realized the fragility of life. And in that grief-stricken state, I chose to make the most of it. If it was going to be short, then I wanted my son to get the best of me. I wanted him to feel joy, and so I had to feel it too. It was a choice I made in how to live this life despite the blow it dealt us. But the perspective it offered was crystal clear. I had to choose joy.

Joy is a choice, my friend. I hope you choose it. I hope when you see it, you grab hold and smother it. I hope you spend a little time with it. When you see it again, I hope you grab it even quicker. Then you might even start looking for it. You may even start seeking it. You may even start feeling it. And there you have it. You're choosing joy over and over.

And joy is finding you. It's showing up for you—in the morning, at work, at the grocery store, in your dreams. You'll start to see things through a different filter. Instead of seeing what your life doesn't have, you'll see what it does. You'll start to see what you can make of it. You'll choose to make the best of it. Instead of seeing what your life lacks, you'll see what it offers. Instead of holding on to the life you thought you'd have, you'll embrace this life you were given.

> Instead of holding on to the life you thought you'd have, you'll embrace this life you were given.

You'll find that even though your child's life is different from what you expected, and they may lack things you wished for them, they have undeniable gifts and there's beauty in the simple moments with your family. Miles may not be able to do typical physical things, but I find his mind to be a wonder. He has a dry sense of humor and a wit that is well beyond his age. He is so crafty and feisty, and he is a ridiculously shrewd negotiator. He says when he grows up, he wants to be a "boss." I'll never let on and tell him that he kind of already is.

And Mason—the compassion from his heart makes me just want to cry. It's so beautiful how he loves so fully without hesitation or limit. He is teaching me many important things—love, kindness, empathy, humility, and the value of a generous spirit. I thank God every day for him and for choosing him to be my son.

I am so grateful for my husband. He has always made me feel loved, but watching how hard he works to better our family and how he continues to show us his love even during the high tides of stress is such a gift. Seeing who he is in the face of this storm, so strong and so sensitive at the same time, has given me even more admiration for him. My, how I'm opening my eyes to see all that is right before me! Beauty right here in the chaos. God is definitely helping me to see it. It's amazing what can happen when your lens starts to change.

You will laugh again. You will make a joke again. You will find your sense of humor again. You will. It may be gone for a short time, or it may be gone for a long time. But it will return. The feelings of desperation and despair can make way for more. Like each day, the sun will rise again after the darkness.

Rare Mama Truth

You know you're a rare mama when true joy
equals a full night's sleep and the rare,
blissful moment of peace where no one
needs you for at least ten minutes.

CHAPTER 23

Recognizing Chaos

"In the midst of movement and chaos,
keep stillness inside of you."

DEEPAK CHOPRA

Since I vowed to tell you the good, the bad, the ugly, and even some things you don't want to hear, let's get to one of the things you might not want to hear. On top of everything else you're going through, you're going to experience chaos.

Yes, just when you think you've finally made sense of this mess, chaos will arrive on the scene to stir things up. While you're smack dab in the middle of your crisis and your stress and your worry, life will throw you one more thing just to top it all off.

This has happened to my husband and me numerous times—so numerous that I'm writing a chapter about it! There have been times when we were doing our best to deal with some difficult news about Miles's health, such as the fact that he needed to have another surgery, and while we were trying to wrap our heads around it, come to grips with it, find our way through it, and move forward with it—the car won't start. An ordinary, everyday life annoyance gets thrown into the mix and just about puts us over the edge. So now instead of just focusing on the surgery, we're worried about how we're going to physically get to the surgery at a hospital two hours away, because our car isn't working properly.

Or our refrigerator would break down. Or a rat would crawl up into our car and die but not before eating through all the hoses and causing nine hundred dollars' worth of repairs. The hot water heater would go out. The drains in our house would clog. An owl would build a nest in our fireplace and spend all night hooting. The trees in our yard that were not supposed to bear fruit would suddenly bear fruit after eight years. (I'm talking so much fruit that there was fruit everywhere, damaging our car parked underneath one of the trees.)

You name it, the everyday life stuff will happen at the most inconvenient times and in the midst of your stress. Just when you think you can't take any more, more will get piled on. You'll make an appointment with a specialist and wait three months, and when the day finally arrives to go and see the specialist and get the answers you need, your child will be sick. Or your other child will be sick and need to stay home from school, and now you'll either have to cancel the appointment or scramble to find someone who doesn't mind watching a sick kid while you take your other child to the specialist. Or another family member will end up in the ER. Or you'll receive a stressful change at work. Or you'll owe taxes you weren't expecting. Or your babysitter will tell you she's moving. Or your pet will get sick. I'm not making this stuff up. Life will explode right in front of you as you're doing your best to keep it all together.

Life is a living and breathing thing of its own. It doesn't care about your plan. It doesn't care about your convenience. It doesn't sync its schedule to suit yours. And it doesn't care that you have a child with a rare disease. What a jerk.

Life is wild and free and unruly and not in your control. The only control you have over it is the way you respond to it. Sure, you can go ballistic, and sure, you have every right to do so, but it won't change anything, it won't stop anything, and it won't solve anything. So there you are.

> Life is wild and free and unruly and not in your control. The only control you have over it is the way you respond to it.

One time, in the height of a stressful stretch, I sprained my ankle. It was December, which is already a busy time for anyone preparing for Christmas, and pile on the fact that when you have a child with a chronic illness, you're often trying to see all your doctors and specialists and get equipment by the end of the year before your insurance deductible starts over again in January. Miles was in kindergarten, so he was only at school half the day, and Mason was in second grade. Miles and I had to pick up Mason and a neighbor friend's daughter from school, and I was rushing around so much that I slipped and fell on the two stairs that lead from my house to the garage. I mean, I went in and out on these same two steps every single day, twenty times a day.

But on this particular day, I slipped and fell and twisted my ankle. The pain was so bad that I almost threw up. I was supposed to lift and load Miles into the car and go pick up the other kids, and I couldn't even move. I twisted it so bad that I had to see a doctor, and I ended up having to do physical therapy twice a week for six weeks to rehabilitate it. So then, not only was I taking Miles to physical therapy, but I was going to physical therapy during the holiday season and at the height of an already stressful time dealing with Miles's medical needs. Overwhelm overload!

Another time, the night before one of Miles's big hip surgeries that had been planned for months, my husband, Tony, was taking Mason to my parents' house, where he was going to stay while we were at the hospital. I was at home going over the list of everything for the surgery when I got a call from Tony. He and Mason had been rear-ended. Yes, they were hit on the short, fifteen-minute ride to my parents' house. I just about lost my mind. I was already in an anxious state for the major surgery Miles was about to endure. But now I was worried about how Mason and Tony were doing. It was minor, thank goodness, and for the most part they were okay. But Tony told me he felt the impact in his back. The very back that was going to be needed to lift and transfer Miles for the next six weeks of his recovery since Miles's post-op instructions included no weight-bearing for six weeks.

Seriously, I almost came undone. I went into a spiral, worrying about Mason and Tony's recovery from the accident. And then I started thinking of all I would have to do to deal with auto insurance companies and manage this accident and the aftermath. In the end, it all turned out okay. Tony and Mason were not hurt, their backs were okay, and the car was fine. But it was enough to send me into a tailspin during an already stressful time.

Those are just a couple of examples, but I could share dozens with you. It's happened so many times that my husband and I can completely recognize when it's happening, and we can even laugh about it. You know the kind of laughter when you're so overtired and it's either you laugh or cry? Yes, that kind of laughter. We laugh about the sheer chaos of how life unfolds sometimes. Because what else are we going to do? We either laugh or cry. So we laugh.

Don't get me wrong, in the moment when it's happening, I straight-out lose my mind. I'll be going along, doing the best I can to deal with a stressful piece of information about my son's condition.

I'll be trying the best I can to keep all the balls in the air, keep my sanity, and keep my joy, and then I'll drop my key fob into a glass of water that's sitting in my car's cup holder and realize it's fried the fob and now my car won't recognize my smart key—so my car won't start. And that's when it happens—the wheels come off the bus, the train derails, the hinges come undone. I straight-out lose it.

If you were parked in the parking lot near me and looked over, you'd see a crazy woman sitting in her car pounding on her steering wheel, screaming to herself, and wildly pushing the ignition start button five hundred times. Then you'd see me start to laugh uncontrollably. I'd be laughing and snorting until snot came out of my nose and tears streamed down my face. You'd look over and think, *That chick has come undone!*

And you'd be right. Then after a bit, I'd calmly gather myself and call my husband and say, "Hey, it's me. I know you're right in the middle of preparing for that big meeting tomorrow with business contacts that are coming in from out of town, but when you have a chance, can you help me get the other key fob from home because I have to pick up the kids in an hour? HAHAHAHAHAHA!"

And my husband would say, "Yep, sounds about right. I'll figure it out. See you soon." And then later that night, we'd both rant and rave, sneer and snarl, and ultimately die laughing at the sheer hardness and madness and chaos of it all. I mean, you can't make this stuff up.

I share with you the inevitable and undeniable wild way of the jungle so that you too can recognize it when it happens. In all honesty, I wish I could wave it away for you and never let you experience any of it, but the reality is that you *will* experience it at some point during your journey. Now that you know about it, I hope you can recognize it when you see it.

The jungle is unruly, and at times it will feel like pure pandemonium. If it helps you feel any better, I can tell you this too shall pass. You'll get another key fob; you'll fix the refrigerator—or the broken hot water heater. You'll call pest control, you'll get your car serviced, and the plumber will unclog the drain. Some of these inconveniences are temporary. But the stress, financial impact, and havoc that they wreak at times when you don't *have* any time will feel like sheer madness. And it is. But you'll get through it. When it happens, I hope you can remember this part of the book and say, "Aha! This is what she was talking about!" I hope you can choose to laugh about it at some point too.

Rare life is wild. Get your game face on.

Rare Mama Truth

BEST DAY EVER!
What happened, you asked?
Absolutely nothing. It was thrilling!

CHAPTER 24

Considering Comparing

"A flower does not think of competing
with the flower next to it. It just blooms."

ZEN SHIN

M ama, can I just say right now, your life may look different from the lives of those around you. You may be the
only one you know who has a child with a rare disease.
Or you may be the only one you know with your child's particular diagnosis. Your journey is probably going to unfold differently
than those of your family members, friends, and neighbors. So take
heed about spending any time comparing your life to others; you're
playing a different game and by a different set of rules. You can't be
bothered trying to keep up with the Joneses when you're just trying
to keep your kid healthy. So do yourself a favor and don't compare.

I've had many a rare mama tell me that they fell into a depression seeing all their friends' kids do this or that and it reminded
them of all the things their child wouldn't be able to do. They would

look on social media and see their friends off on some outing or vacation, and it would fill them with envy or sadness as they realized they wouldn't be able to do those types of things with their child. Yes, comparing is a part of human nature, but heed my warning and don't spend much of your time here.

> **The comparing game is a losing game. Opt out of playing.**

There will always be someone smarter, richer, faster, better, or taking more fabulous trips than you. But the truth is, that's just the way life is no matter whether you're a rare disease mama or not. The comparing game is a losing game. Opt out of playing.

Let me take this one step further and say that there may come a point on your journey when you realize you can't do life the same as everyone else. Or perhaps you can, but it's exhausting, and it comes at a cost you're no longer willing to pay.

There was a distinct point on my journey when a shift happened for me. I realized that trying to make my life fit into a mold that wasn't shaped or designed for a family like mine was ludicrous. Instead of trying to reshape, restructure, reform, rewrite, or remodel us to fit a mold we were never going to fit, I decided we'd make our own way. We'd sing our own song. We'd beat our own drum. We'd honor our own journey.

This meant letting go of expectations and visions of how life "should be." We had to cast aside the "shoulds" and instead "do us." That meant finding and living out what truly brought us joy and served our family.

You know what else that meant? Not caring what anyone else thought about it.

This shift was life-giving. It freed me from trying to fit into a box I was not made to be in. And it freed up our family to live and enjoy the life we have, right as it is.

There's a saying, "A tiger doesn't lose sleep over the opinion of a sheep." True words. So reign over your domain in any way, shape, or form that serves you and your family. Because your way is good enough, and so are you. Beware of the trappings of things that make you feel as though you have to do life the same as everyone else. Your path is different, and that's okay.

You'll breathe a big whiff of fresh air when you realize you don't have to do it any other way than your own. Find your own way. Follow your own path. Be your own you.

You know what happens when you allow yourself to be who you are? It allows others to be who they truly are too. It draws people to you because they feel like they can be themselves around you. And don't we all just really want to be ourselves and be accepted for it? Don't you think authentic people are much more interesting?

I know you want your child to be allowed to be themselves; you don't want anyone to put your child in a box. And how can we teach our children to let their true colors fly and honor themselves and their beautiful differences? By modeling it for them.

Listen, sister, never in my wildest dreams did I see my life unfolding like this. It's still shocking when I really think about it. But what am I going to do? Bury my head in the sand because my road is different from everyone else's? Hide because maybe it's messy and unfamiliar? Over time I've come to terms with the fact that it's still my life, and I'm going to make it something beautiful.

Comparisons, I bid you adieu.

Find what feels right for you and your family and do it that way.

Live *your* life. Make *yourself* proud.

Mama, you do you.

Can't even keep up with the laundry,
let alone the Joneses.

PART VII

Practicing Prowess

CHAPTER 25

Building Resilience

"She is full of wounds, riddled with scars, but she
is still standing, and she is still beautiful."

R.H. SIN

When Miles was newly diagnosed, I met these amazing moms of older children living with SMA. One of the first things one of them told me was "You're going to be okay." At the time, I didn't know what she meant. While I was so appreciative of her advice and her confidence in telling me that, in my head I was thinking, *How am I going to be okay? I will* never *be okay! My son just got diagnosed with a severe disease. How could this ever be okay?*

Now years later, I know what she meant. She meant that while this situation is definitely not okay, we will find our way within it. She meant that moms are resilient. We will find our way to being okay. Maybe it's because we have no other choice. Or maybe it's because we were built for exactly this. Maybe we were built to love our child and be okay no matter what. Maybe this is precisely what it means to be a mother. A mother won't turn away. And so we find our way.

I am finding my way. And you are too. Because eventually it will become clear that you have a choice in how you respond to all of this. You're either going to decide to be okay or you're not. I mean, in truth, I will never be okay with the fact that my son, who had no say in the matter, has a disease. It's heartbreaking. But on a daily basis, I'm making my peace with it so I can live my life and so he can live his. I'm choosing to be resilient, and I'm learning how to stand in the storm. Because what's the other choice? Depression? Being comatose?

Believe me, I know that sometimes these feelings and reactions are beyond our control. Sometimes they are the body and mind's involuntary reactions to pain and loss. So sometimes, most times, we have to just get up and brush our teeth and put one foot in front of the other whether we're okay or not. Then get up the next day and do it again. The hard stuff may not go away or change, but we will change. We will build survival skills. We will grow. We will learn. We will get knocked down, and we will stand back up. We will build resiliency.

Psychologists define resilience as the process of adapting well in the face of adversity, trauma, tragedy, threats, or significant sources of stress—such as family and relationship problems, serious health problems, or workplace and financial stressors. Resilience involves not only "bouncing back" from these difficult experiences, but also growing personally.

While these adverse events are painful and difficult, they don't have to determine the outcome of your life. There are many aspects of your life you can control, modify, and grow within. That's the role of resilience. Becoming more resilient not only helps you get through difficult circumstances, it also empowers you to grow and even improve your life along the way. Resilience is the ability to adapt, learn, and grow in the face of adversity.

Harvard Business Review senior editor Diane Coutu looked at the nature of individual and organizational resilience. As one of Coutu's interviewees put it, "More than education, more than experience, more than training, a person's level of resilience will determine who succeeds and who fails."[1]

In her study, Coutu found that three fundamental characteristics seem to set resilient people and companies apart from others. The first characteristic is the capacity to accept and face reality. In looking hard at reality, we prepare ourselves to act in ways that allow us to endure and survive hardships; we train ourselves how to survive before we ever have to do so. Recognizing that setbacks are an inherent part of life is the first step. Resilient individuals first come to a place of acceptance. Then they take the next step anyway.

This is exactly what we discussed in chapter two, identifying our pain and grief, processing it, and accepting it. This important step of facing the realities of a diagnosis is critical in moving onward and ultimately leads to the building of resilience.

The second characteristic is that resilient people and organizations possess an ability to find meaning in some aspects of life. A clear sense of purpose acts as a compass during challenging times and provides direction and motivation, helping to weather the storms. Resilient people draw strength from their core values and overarching life goals. And values are just as important as meaning; value systems at resilient companies change very little over the long haul and are used as scaffolding in times of trouble.

As rare mamas, we have a profound sense of purpose—helping our child. This is what fuels us to get back up despite getting knocked down and move forward despite the hardships. Our love is the meaning behind every step we take and gives us the ability to do things we never thought ourselves capable of doing.

The third characteristic of resilience is the ability to improvise. Within an arena of personal capabilities or company rules, the ability to solve problems without the usual or obvious tools is a great strength. Resilience flourishes in the soil of adaptability. Life is dynamic and ever-changing. To build resilience, we must learn to navigate unpredictable currents of change with grace. Embracing change results in a more flexible mindset, allowing us to adjust our sails when the winds of life shift direction.

So much of rare mama life is plan, unplan, replan. I have learned that just as I've built my walls strong to withstand the storms ahead, I've also had to build them to be flexible. If we don't sway, we are at risk of breaking. And so I have learned to sway. I have learned to bend when I must in order to continue on.

You know how resilience is often built in rare mama life? By getting out of bed and taking your child to that appointment you're both dreading. Why? Not necessarily because you feel like the poster child for resilience, but because you love your child and want to help them, simple as that. So you get up and you do the thing you both don't want to do. Then the next day, you do it again. In fact, this is exactly how resilience is built. It's built daily as we take our children to OT, PT, obtain medical equipment, and all the things. As we're on the phone with insurance companies. As we face test results and receive information that is difficult to bear.

In the not quitting, not giving up, and in the carrying on, we are building our resilience. We are forging and refining and reshaping parts of ourselves every single day as we do the work to help our children. Just like our strength, one day we will realize we have become resilient as evidenced by all we've faced and accomplished, things that at the outset we may have thought impossible.

You know what else? Our children are learning resilience right alongside us. Some people learn resilience later in life, but our kids tend to learn it early. Because the truth is, life is not tidy. It's filled with challenges. At some point or other, we will all be faced with something that will knock us down, and we will have to get back up. When we learn resilience at an early age, it's a quality that sticks with us for life. Listen, I would trade my son not having a disease any day over learning resilience. But since I can't, I'm observing the role that learning resilience early on is playing in his character development. It's pretty remarkable the way this resilience is shaping him and how it's improving his mental toughness.

If accepting and facing realities, finding meaning and purpose, and adapting and improvising are the three fundamental characteristics of resiliency, then, rare mamas, perhaps we claim this label and own it, because this is in a sense what we are doing every day. We are the definition of resilient. In taking ownership of this characteristic, we can use it to give us a deep sense of knowing that we will endure.

> **Resilience is built over time, brick by brick.**

Perhaps some people are given more opportunities than others to build their resilience. Perhaps rare mamas are given more than their fair share of opportunities, but can you even build resilience any other way? Resilience is built over time, brick by brick. Each one strengthens the foundation. Sometimes the bricks are painstakingly heavy, but often those are the ones that can withstand the most torrential storms. We are laying our foundations and building our scaffolding.

My son's diagnosis has shaken my walls and tested my foothold in a thousand different ways. It has broken me open to reexamine all the pieces of myself and to see with different eyes, clearer perspective, and a certainty of purpose. I've had to put myself back together.

The rebuilding has not been easy, but it has left me different. It has allowed the refinement of many aspects of myself. It's pushing me toward a version of myself that has been built through fire, and as a result there are a lot of pieces of my character that are stronger than before. This new building I house myself in can withstand storms the previous version never imagined.

And so will yours.

I'm not sure about many things, but I am sure about this: I will find my way. I will stand in the storm. I am resilient.

The rains may continue, the fire will burn, the battle will rage on, and yet still here I am.

Here I am, despite it all.

Here I am, because I don't want this diagnosis to have the last say.

Here I am, because I don't want anything to steal my joy, because it's mine.

Here I am, because I still have a life to live.

Here I am, because it's my story, and I want to contribute to writing it.

Here I am, because I'm not what happened to me; I'm what I choose to become.

Here I am, because I love my son, and I want to be by his side.

I fight every day to say, "Here I am!"

I am weathered and worn, but I am still standing. I have an aching back, a bum knee, gray hairs, and an extra layer of cortisol around my belly, but I'm here! I did not go down in the fight. I have not been knocked out yet. Though I'm tired, I keep climbing back into the ring. The victories may be small, but they are sweeter than I ever could have imagined.

I just took Miles to another procedure. For the umpteenth time, we've gone to the hospital. He's gotten blood draws and other various tests, and I've tried to distract and comfort him while he undergoes the procedure. Is this easy? Nope. I hate hearing him cry. Does it raise anxiety in me every time I do it? Yep. But instead of working myself into a frenzy leading up to it, I try not to give it much power anymore. I just think of it as a necessary means to an end, and I focus on the fact that it's an absolute godsend that he is able to receive medical interventions that uphold his health. The significance is not lost on me. So we show up, and though it's hard, we are grateful. We get it done, and then we return to our life. In a handful of months, we'll go and do it again.

This is resilience. I am building mine every day, and you are too.

Rare Mama Truth

Where have I been? Oh, just here prancing
around, wearing my resilience like a cape
and conquering the day.

CHAPTER 26

Bringing You to the Fight

"A warrior believes in an end she can't see
and fights for it. A warrior never gives up.
A warrior fights for those weaker than herself.
It sounds like motherhood to me."

KRISTIN HANNAH

There is one last thing you need to bring to this fight—YOU! Bring whatever it is that makes you YOU.

Sometimes it feels like caregiving requires us to abandon who we are. Like we must relinquish our former identity. Taking on the identity of a rare mama doesn't mean you have to say goodbye to all that you were or change who you are altogether. It means you have to stay true to who you are even in this new role. It means accepting and embracing this new role and doing it your way.

Bring exactly who you are to this. Bring your gifts, your talents, and your strengths. Find ways to incorporate them into your fight.

Use what you have. Use what you know. Use whatever you have as a foundation and build upon it.

If you were always a funny person and humor was how you identified yourself and your place in the world, you don't need to lose your sense of humor just because you're a rare disease mama. As you go through the hardness of receiving a diagnosis, you may come close. I almost did, and I'm still fighting not to lose it. But I hope you eventually get to a place where you can use it. It may be just the thing that helps you get through.

Or maybe you were an artist, and now you have absolutely no time to do your art. It's your art that may help you through this. Maybe you're a project management genius. If so, bring that to the table and use it to manage this mother lode of a project put on your plate. If you have strong faith, bring your faith. If you're creative, bring your creativity. If you're an organization goddess, bring your organizational skills.

> Bring exactly who you are to this. Bring your gifts, your talents, and your strengths.

Bring exactly what you have to offer this fight so you can still thrive as a person. Use your unique qualities and gifts, whatever they may be, in this new role. Use whatever you have in your toolbox to do this your way.

Do not abandon your true self. Do not lose yourself entirely. You were beautifully and wonderfully made as the best mother for your child. Bring it all. We need your light and your voice and your secret sauce. You have something to offer to your child, your family, the rare community, and yourself. Bring it to the fight, mama.

Bring it.

Rare Mama Truth

Rare Motherhood: It's like being a nurse, a lawyer, a teacher, a PT, an OT, a nutritionist, and a therapist all rolled up into one but on little sleep, for no pay, and while wearing sweats.

CHAPTER 27

Rising to the Call

"Brave women are not born from
comfort zones. They are made in the fire."

VIKTORIA APANASENKO

As you head out into the rare world or continue along your rare path, there is one more important thing I want to discuss with you—only it doesn't have to do with systems and services or processes and plans. It has to do with who we become as mothers through this rare disease journey.

Here's the important and difficult question I want to ask: What will you allow to rise in your life when it's impacted by a rare disease? This is arguably one of the most important conversations in all of this book. And while each of us must define this for ourselves, I want to simply pose the question and make space for us to think about it both now and along the way.

All of us will undoubtedly be faced with a choice. Often it happens while we're so busy that we might not even notice it happening.

Sometimes it happens in the beginning, sometimes it happens much later, but at some point you'll see a choice before you. Let me explain what I mean.

> What will you allow to rise in your life when it's impacted by a rare disease?

When we receive a rare disease diagnosis for our child, we experience a fall of sorts. We plunge into a dark sea of anguish and loss. We grieve the loss of the life we thought our child would have, along with the loss of many hopes and dreams. We wrestle with the diagnosis; we learn, grow, and accept; and then we rise to help our child. After the fall, we rise.

But as we rise, might we consider *how* we do it? And might we consider *what* we will allow to rise within us?

Rare disease is going to force some things to rise whether we like it or not. Our anxiety can rise. Our fear can rise. A rare disease can raise depression levels, feelings of inadequacy, mistrust, isolation, and on and on. Often these are unconsciously happening as involuntary and reactionary responses to pain and desperate circumstances. But as you move through and notice the changes within you, might you notice what else rises?

Your compassion? Your patience? Does it raise your love to new levels? Does it allow you to raise your voice to advocate? Or raise your hand to help? What parts of your character will you let it cultivate?

This kind of intense pressure is going to refine you in one way or another. When we're held to the fire, how can we allow it to refine our character and transform us?

When there is a choice, what will you allow to arise within you? What will you choose?

Will you get to know yourself deeply and give yourself unconditional love?

Will you grant yourself grace? Will you know deep inside that you're doing your best and that's all you can do? That it's all any of us can do, and that it's enough?

What about your heart? Our hearts have taken a hit. Mine still feels bruised. But it's not broken. It still beats. And while I still have a heart that beats and while I'm still here on this earth, how will I cradle my bruised heart?

What about yours? Will you allow it to grow and heal? Will you allow it to still spread love? Maybe even more love than you ever knew was possible?

What about your soul? How will you feed it? Will you serve it music and art, food and friendship, sunshine and God? How will you replenish it?

Will you let this diminish your faith, awaken it, or strengthen it?

Will you be a conscious observer of where you are at points along the way? Will you check in with yourself? Will you nurture your sacred body?

Who will you be when control is unattainable and when living with unknowns is a new way of life? Will you plan what you can and yet remain flexible as all those plans may change? Will you rage against the changes, standing rigid and firm as storms crash against you? Or will you hold fast to the things that matter, like your values and your faith and your relationships—and with the other things, can you flow? Can you bend? Can you stay flexible so you don't break as you move through them? Can you hold things with an open hand instead of a clenched fist so the dirt and sand and rubbish can sift through and what remains are life's gems?

If this life of yours is unfolding differently than you expected, will you still require that it fit into the same mold? Can you change course? Find a new way? Adapt, lean in, embrace?

What if you fall apart? How will you put yourself back together?

Will you put yourself back together the same way? Or differently, knowing what you know?

As you put yourself back together, can you consider the scaffolding? What goes in? What stays out? Can you rebuild in ways that will serve you in the life you're actually living? Reconstruct in ways that honor the things that are most important to you, sometimes letting go of the rest? Instead of holding on to the life you thought you'd have, can you learn to embrace this life you were given?

Because this is still your one precious life. And it's still beautiful. Yes, it may also be terribly hard and messy, and many parts of it may just be downright unfair. But that's the thing about life. Lives are touched by disillusion, delays, divorce, disease, and even death. Lives are also streaked with sweetness, surprises, celebrations, and successes. Life is a dichotomy. There are losses, and there are new beginnings. There is hardship and heartache and there is also blessing and bliss. There is suffering and sadness, and yet there is joy and jubilation. It's a mixed bag.

There's a lot I still don't know, but I know this: Your life is still yours. You are still writing your story. And so I ask, how will you write it even now? What will you put in? What will you take out? What will you prioritize?

How will you measure your time here? Maybe the measure of a good life is different for lives like ours. Maybe we ought to change our metrics. Maybe it's about snuggles on the couch or sunsets on a Sunday. Slow moments with our family. Or our child's small victory that we weren't sure was possible. Maybe it's just holding each other dear. Maybe it's about connection versus achievement. Maybe it's not about productivity or measuring at all. Maybe it's about meaning.

Maybe life's meaning looks different than you ever thought it would. Because it's changed. Perhaps there will be encounters with people you never thought you'd meet. Perhaps there is a purpose that becomes clear. Perhaps it's most important that you just keep asking these questions. Or that you stay open—open to it all.

Maybe it's simply about love. The same love you started with. Because of love, from love, for love. Maybe you just keep coming back to love.

Only *you* can resolve what life's meaning is for you.

Only you can determine how to live despite the circumstances.

Only you can decide how to use this life you've been given.

Only *you* can consider who you become.

Only *you* can choose what you let rise inside of you.

A fall. And then a rise.

Will you answer the call to rise above?

Mama, how will you rise?

Rare Mama Truth

Rare parenting doesn't ask if you're ready—
it just calls, and you rise, and stumble
your way forward, fueled by love.

CHAPTER 28

Proceeding with Empowerment

"She is clothed in strength and dignity,
and she laughs without fear of the future."

PROVERBS 31:25, NLT

Well, mamas, it's time. Time to head off. I wish I could be by your side as you step forward to go and fight the fight of your life. I wish I could be next to you through it all. But the truth is, you don't need me. You have it all inside of you already. It's all there.

So I leave you with this little pep talk.

If I were there with you now, at the end of our little sit-down chat, I'd stand right in front of you, grab you by both shoulders, look you right in the eye, and say, "You can do this! Look at me. You can do this. Yes, it's hard. Yes, you are tired. Yes, you are sad. Yes, it sucks. But you can do it. I know you can. I believe in you."

It will test you. It will try you. It may almost break you. But it won't.

You will discover strength you never knew you had. You will learn grace you never knew was possible. You will become more powerful than you ever thought you could. You will see beauty you never expected. You will learn to trust your instincts. You will become the expert of your child. You will kindly sweep off the naysayers and lovingly let go of those you must.

You can do this.

You will be exhausted and yet live with exuberance at the same time. You will carry stress on your shoulders and still find the will to laugh at something funny or make jokes at the sheer hardness of it all. You will see light through the darkness.

This is our Rare Mama manifesto of empowerment:

My body may be tired, but my mind has become clear. There is still so much I need to learn and figure out, and though I don't have all the answers now, I can take comfort in knowing that I can be resourceful. I know how to ask for what I need, and I know how to get things done. I have honed my roar, and I know how and when to use it. I am learning when to fight, when to pivot, and when to let go. I still don't know what tomorrow's weather holds, but I will put my sunscreen on anyway. I know I still have mountains to climb, but I feel confident that somehow I will make my way up and back down again. I've failed, and I'm flawed, but I will keep trying my best and showing up to try again tomorrow.

Mama, keep noticing. Keep considering. Keep adapting. Keep loving.

Keep going.

Remain. Endure. Hope. Love.

> Go forward, rare mama, and be the empowered woman you are.

Because of love, from love, for love. May you always come back to love.

Go forward, rare mama, and be the empowered woman you are. Go fight the fight. Let your light shine while you do it and light the way for the other moms still finding their way through the darkness. Love hard. Dream big. Leave it all on the stage.

You are a fighter. You are a warrior. You are a rare mama rising. Now get out there and wake up and shake up the jungle with the sound of your mighty roar.

Stand empowered in your prowess!

Rare Mama Truth

It's time to step into the fight. You may never feel ready, but you are, in fact, ready! Begin.

APPENDIX

Rare Mama Musings

A collection of pieces and poems I wrote
to inspire, encourage, and uplift you.

ANATOMY OF A RARE MOTHER

The rare mother has . . .

Eyes that see through to her child's heart to know what they want or need even when they can't speak for themselves.

Ears that hear the yes when someone tells her child no.

A sense of smell that can sniff out when something's not right.

A **mouth** that boldly speaks on her child's behalf when it's necessary.

Lips that lull and soothe her child to sleep after one of their "hard" days.

A palate that makes the taste of each small victory oh so much sweeter.

A mind that is processing, filtering, and discerning all sorts of information, even when it's beyond her comprehension, if it benefits her child.

Shoulders to cry on that offer comfort and peace to her loved ones.

A back that lifts and transfers her child many, many times a day.

Hands that caress the forehead of her child, who is sick or in pain.

Arms that cradle her crying child, who is scared during a traumatic episode or medical procedure.

A stomach that bears hard news, tribulations, and disappointments.

Legs that run the extra mile to get whatever her child needs.

Feet that hit the ground running from the moment she wakes up in the morning until she lies down at night.

A temperament that can be as fierce as a lion or as gentle as a lamb.

A soul of an angel, always believing the best in her child.

A **heart** that won't stop loving no matter where this journey goes or what it takes along the way.

A RARE KIND OF LOVE

My sweet son, you may never know the depths of my love for you. Ours is a rare kind of love.

You may never know how many times I wept alone on the bathroom floor, curled into a ball, begging God to heal you. It was the only place I could be alone and lock the door so you wouldn't see me in this state of deep distress.

You'll never know how many nights I woke up to turn you in the middle of the night because you were too weak to turn yourself. And then how many hours I lay awake afterward, unable to fall asleep, filled with fear for your life.

You may never know the countless mornings I woke, overcome with dread, to take you to an MRI, or to meet with a team of specialists who would tell me everything that was wrong with you, or to an all-day surgery, or to yet another uncomfortable procedure.

You'll never know how hard it was to hold you down while you cried all the way through a painful medical treatment because I knew it was going to help save your life.

You may never know how I wrestled with difficult decisions for your health because no one could tell me definitively and with absolutes that one way or the other was the best route to choose.

You'll never know how badly my body ached in pain from injuries due to constant overuse. Or how hard it was to hear doctors telling me that my cortisol is depleted and that the stress is taking a toll.

You may never know how many times I felt like I was barely able to keep my chin above water, to keep our household functioning, to keep regular relationships intact, and to keep you and your brother experiencing somewhat of a normal childhood.

You may never know. The truth is, I hope you never will.

I don't need you to know. I didn't do it for that. I did it, and continue to do it, because I love you.

I do it because I want to see you healthy.

I do it because I want to see you happy.

I do it because I want you to have every opportunity to grow and thrive.

I do it for love.

This is the love of a mother. This is love in action.

It is this love that allows me to go and do the hardest things that I never thought I'd be able to do.

It is this love that permits me to wake up each day and do it again.

It is this love that lets me choose not to be a martyr because I don't want that for you.

You may never know because I don't want you to.

What I want you to know is that I love you.

Some days, when I am sitting next to you, doing the most ordinary thing like helping you with your shoes, you lean over and kiss me on my cheek. Or you turn my face toward yours and look at me and say, "Mom, I love you."

My child, I love you too. Oh, how I love you too.

This is a rare kind of love.

It's rare, complex, and beautiful, just like you.

I THOUGHT I'D TEACH YOU

I thought I'd teach you how to stand.
Instead, you taught me how to stand up for those who can't do so
for themselves.

I thought I'd teach you how to walk.
Instead, you taught me how to take a step even when I was
overcome with fear.

I thought I'd teach you to ride a bike.
Instead, you taught me how to ride waves of uncertainty and still
find joy amid the storm.

I thought I'd teach you how to kick a ball.
Instead, you taught me how to kick down doors of opposition to
advocate on your behalf.

I thought I'd teach you how to throw a punch.
Instead, you taught me how to roll with the punches without being
disheartened along the way.

I thought I'd teach you how to fly a kite.
Instead, you taught me how to soar with a broken wing.

I thought I'd teach you to climb a tree.
Instead, you taught me to climb mountains.

I thought I'd teach you all these things.
Instead, you taught me so much more.

I thought I'd teach you.
Instead, you taught me.

THE BOND

In the quiet of a shared breath, it begins,
A thread unseen but unyielding.
Through first cries and sleepless nights,
The bond strengthens.

In the gaze exchanged through hospital walls,
A silent promise etched in love.
Through pain endured and comfort given,
The bond strengthens.

From whispered courage before the unknown,
To holding hands in the darkest hours,
Through each trial, faced side by side,
The bond strengthens.

It is not fragile, though tenderly born,
Not visible, yet it binds like steel.
Each challenge bends it, yet it does not break—
The bond strengthens.

Mother and child, hearts entwined,
A connection forged in life's fiercest fires.
It grows, it roots, it becomes ever more.
The bond strengthens.

RARE DISEASE CLIMBING CLUB

I stood at the mountain, heart full of despair,
Unsure how I'd climb or what waited up there.
A broken beginner, no map in my hand,
Facing terrain I could not understand.

With too much at stake and no turning back,
I began the ascent as the odds seemed to stack.
The ground beneath shifted; my footing unsure,
Each step brought tears, yet I had to endure.

At first, it was lonely, just me and the peak,
The silence so heavy, I struggled to think.
But then, through the haze, I saw others near,
Their presence brought hope and diminished my fear.

They perched on the ledges, farther ahead,
With knowing eyes and words unsaid.
Their presence alone was a beacon of light,
Proof others had endured this arduous fight.

Through rain and through wind, I watched them ascend,
Their strength and resolve gave mine a new bend.
Each moment of doubt, I'd look to the sky,
Guided by faith and these angels on high.

Their sweat fell like rain from paths up above,
A sign of the battle, but also of love.
At times, it was tears they let cascade,
Reminding me struggle is how strength is made.

"Watch out for that hazard, take care on this ledge,
Go slow and use patience near that rocky edge."
They called out directions, they steadied my stride,
Their courage and strength became my guide.

They climbed not alone, but for someone they loved—
A child, a mother, a soul up above.
I answered their question, "Who drives you to fight?"
"My son," I replied; "he's my reason, my light."

With each step I climbed, I began to see
A bond in this journey, a shared unity.
And even though my path was my own,
With a club of climbers, I climbed less alone.

Below, I saw others just starting to rise,
Uncertain and lost, with fear in their eyes.
And just as others had done for me,
I shared my strength so they could see.

"Keep climbing," I shouted; "you're stronger than fear!
The path grows less jagged if you step over here."
I revealed what I'd learned to show them the way,
So the climb might be easier for them one day.

And when once I slipped, a voice from below
Reminded me softly, "You're not alone,
If you fall, we will catch you; you'll rise once again.
This mountain is tough, but so are we, friend."

And that's when I saw the beautiful glow,
Of the powerful circle above and below.
A chain of support, unyielding and strong,
Each climber pulling the next one along.

With unity's power, no climb is too steep,
A shared purpose sustains us; our connection is deep.
We rise together, united, aligned,
Mighty in numbers, rare strength combined.

Though the summit's uncertain, the climb must go on,
With courage renewed by the strength of this bond.
The mountain looms mighty, but so does the love,
In the hearts of the climbers in the Rare Disease Club.

JOB TITLE: RARE MAMA EXTRAORDINAIRE
Job Description:

Seeking a dynamic, highly adaptable individual to join the elite ranks of Rare Mamas. This position is not for the faint of heart (or the easily grossed out). If you've ever juggled an iPad, a clipboard, a snack pouch, and a kid while calmly answering a nurse's twenty-question lightning round, this position is for you!

Key Responsibilities:

- **Schedule Keeper Strategist:** Maintain a calendar so complex NASA would be impressed. (What do you mean therapy overlaps with the specialist appointment you waited six months for?)
- **Hospital Waiting Room Pacer:** Walk miles without leaving the building. Bonus points for soothing panicked relatives via text while speed-eating stale crackers.
- **Head Caresser-in-Chief:** Provide calming strokes and whispered reassurances on demand. May require nocturnal shifts.
- **Insurance On-Hold Champion:** Listen to hold music long enough to hum it in your sleep. Negotiating skills to rival diplomats required.
- **Therapist Whisperer:** Masterfully coordinate with physical therapists, occupational therapists, speech therapists, and occasionally a therapy dog, all while nodding along like you totally understand (spoiler: you do now).
- **Rare Condition Googler:** Discover answers to obscure medical questions in record time. Expertly sift through mountains of information to separate trusted research from questionable advice.
- **MacGyver in Residence:** Modify, adjust, and rig medical equipment to fit your child's unique needs and body like a

bespoke suit. Fashion solutions out of zip ties, pool noodles, and scrunchies.

- **Special Education Expert:** Navigate the labyrinth of IEPs, 504 plans, and school accommodations with the skill of a seasoned negotiator. Advocate for your child's unique needs while decoding acronyms, attending endless meetings, and ensuring everyone remembers who the real expert on your child is: *you.*

- **Transport Specialist:** Fit all necessary equipment into a vehicle like you're playing Tetris, ensuring everything survives speed bumps, sharp turns, and the inevitable *"Wait, where did I put that one toy that was supposed to distract my kid on the drive?"*

- **Home Adaptation Genius:** Retrofit bedrooms, bathrooms, and kitchens with rails, lifts, and ramps while maintaining enough floor space for race car tracks and tea parties.

- **Emergency Responder:** Handle malfunctions at the worst possible moments, like during a road trip or 3:00 a.m. wake-up call, with the poise of an ER doctor.

- **Awareness Builder and Advocacy Pro:** Educate the world one conversation at a time, whether gently correcting strangers' assumptions, passionately rallying for systemic change, championing rare disease awareness campaigns, or just convincing your insurance to approve that needed piece of durable medical equipment.

Qualifications:

- **Experience:** Previous caregiving experience appreciated but not necessary. On-the-job training includes crash courses in courage, patience, and hope.

- **Education:** Advanced degree in Mom-onomics with minors in Sleepless Studies and Problem-Solving Psychology. A PhD in "Why Everything Takes So Long" is a plus.

Skills:

- Ability to function on minimal sleep and maximum coffee.
- Multitasking at an Olympic level (able to balance a backpack, medical binder, and a child while also opening a door).
- Advanced proficiency in decoding medical jargon, side-eye, and silence that speaks volumes.

Compensation:

- Payment in hugs, milestones that make your heart explode, and smiles that mean everything.
- Benefits include superhuman strength, unparalleled resilience, and a VIP pass to a community of other Rare Mamas who just *get it*.

To Apply:

Don't. You're already hired.

HOLDING A CANDLE IN THE DARKNESS FOR YOU

If I could describe what it felt like after I received my son's rare disease diagnosis, I would describe it as the lights being shut off. I felt alone and scared in the darkness.

Or I would describe it as a rain cloud moving in directly over my head, taking away the light of the sun, and raining on me all day long, day in and day out, for months. I felt cold, wet, and dreary.

But then, there was a point when I couldn't stand the darkness any longer. There came a time when I missed the sunlight and longed to feel its warmth on my face. There was a moment when I couldn't take being wet and shivering in that cold anymore. Eventually, I had to get up and walk out of that darkness, out from under that rain cloud, and into the light. It was my turning point.

But to come to my turning point and to break through, I had to learn to sit with my child's rare disease diagnosis. I had to soak in all those scared and sad feelings. I had to feel them all. Though this was the most challenging time of my life, and though my heart was shattered, there were a lot of things that came from those days of sitting in that place. I had a lot of talks with God during that time. I did a great deal of soul-searching and self-discovery. Somewhere there, in that darkness, I found my highest faith and my truest self.

Sitting under that rain cloud and allowing the rain to wash over me was a mix of feeling like I was drowning and also as though I was being cleansed. It was the hardest surrender of my life. It was the ultimate acknowledgment that I was not in control.

You may be sitting in the darkness or under your own rain cloud.

My heart aches so badly thinking of another mother sitting alone in the darkness, grieving her child's rare disease diagnosis.

I know the pain. I can recall it like it was yesterday.

Every ounce of my being wants to grab my umbrella, hold it over you, wrap you in a warm blanket, and hurry you off into the sun.

But I know I can't.

As badly as I don't want you to hurt, I also know you may have to sit a bit in the darkness.

I understand that it's a necessary step in the grieving process that cannot be denied. Yes, it's dangerous to sit in the darkness too long, but it's also dangerous to skip over it altogether. We all have a time when we must just sit in it, and a true friend will sit with you in the darkness while you grieve. So, I will sit with you right here in it.

And though I cannot make the darkness cease, I can light a candle.

I can strike a flame so you can see that there is still light. I can create a spark so you can feel that there is still hope. This tiny light can serve as a reminder that the darkness doesn't have to consume you. As hard as a rare disease diagnosis is to process and as dismal and dreary as all may seem and feel, when you are ready, you will notice this little shining light. It may be small, but it still gives off a glow. That glow may not be enough light to illuminate the entire path before you, but it may be enough light for you to see the ground right in front of you. And that may be enough light for you to take a step. That one small step is all you need. Just one little step forward.

I will hold that little candle until my arm gets tired. I will hold it for as long as you need and as long as it takes. I will be silently praying for you, perhaps as you go through your own process and as you work your way through it.

One day, when you are ready, I know you will get up and walk out of that darkness and out from under that cloud. You will make a decision to go forward. And when you do, I will hand off the candle so you may use it to light the rest of the path ahead of you. I will pass it like the passing of the baton, from one rare disease mother to another, off to run the next leg of the race, off to do good work, off to take care of their amazing child.

I can picture you getting up, dusting yourself off, wiping away your tears, and walking right on out of there. And I will be thinking to myself, *There she goes. She did it. It was long and hard, cold and wet, but she did it.*

I'll be watching in awe of you as you set off on your way.

I will be fist-pumping and cheering from the sidelines.

But until then, for now, right now, I will hold a candle in the darkness for you.

WELCOME TO THE RARE MAMA SISTERHOOD

Dear Rare Mama,

Welcome to the club of rare disease mothers—the best club you never asked to be in. This is a place where you will find understanding, support, and the kind of companionship that only comes from shared experiences of raising children with rare diseases.

If your heart feels shattered, your world flipped upside down, and your breath stolen from your chest, you've found your people. We are here.

You're exhausted? We know.

You're terrified? We've been there.

You're overwhelmed, wondering how you'll navigate this? We've asked those same questions.

You feel ill-equipped? Sing it, sister.

Here, you are understood. Here, you can lay down your hurts, fears, and doubts. You belong.

Out in the big world, your story might feel one-of-a-kind, incomprehensible to others. But in the rare mama community, your emotions are not only understood—they're shared. The anguish of hearing your child's diagnosis, the fear of the unknown, the grief of letting go of a different future—these are things we've all felt.

We rare disease mamas know the breaking of a heart, the aching of a soul, the crushing of a spirit. We've trembled, stumbled, and unraveled. We've faced situations so unfair, so far beyond our control, that they defy comprehension. We've seen ourselves truly shaken.

And yet, here we stand.

You know what else we've seen? We've seen our tired bodies pick ourselves up and carry on. We've watched our hearts expand in ways we didn't know were possible. We've discovered reserves of strength, resilience, and love that have carried us forward.

As rare mothers, our children's diagnoses may vary, and our journeys may look different, but what binds us is the unshakable love we have for our kids. That love is what gives us the strength to rise, even when we feel like we can't. It's what carries us forward, step by step, on this unexpected path.

You may feel small and rare right now, but know that you are part of a much larger community of rare-disease mothers—millions of us across the globe—fighting for our children, advocating for their needs, and finding ways to thrive in the face of the unimaginable.

You've joined a sisterhood of compassionate, courageous, and determined women who are here to support you, cheer you on, and remind you of your incredible strength. Together, we are powerful!

Let me assure you—none of us were ready for this journey either. And yet, here we are, standing alongside you as living proof that you *can* do this. We know that you will find your way, just as we are finding ours. You will discover strength you didn't know you had, and you will see your love for your child transform you in ways you never imagined. We already know all the good you will do.

This is not an easy road, but it's one you don't have to travel alone. This community of rare mamas has journeyed down the path you are walking, and we are returning to light the way. Track our popcorn trail. Follow our footprints.

Take our hands; let us lead you down the pathways we've tread before you and give you all we know to make your journey just a bit easier. Let's walk this road together!

Welcome to our sisterhood. We are waiting for you. We are rooting for you.

We see you, we believe in you, and we stand with you!

We are welcoming you with open arms, beloved sister.

In it together,

Nikki McIntosh

Fellow Rare Mama

Additional Resources

I began compiling a list of resources to include here, hoping to provide a quick reference for the many wonderful organizations that exist to support you and your child. From financial aid and education to government programs, adaptive recreation, clinical trials, and more, there are many resources available. However, since the rare disease landscape is constantly evolving, I wanted to ensure that this list remains dynamic, relevant, and current.

I decided that such a resource list would best serve the Rare Mama community as a living, breathing document updated regularly to reflect new opportunities, organizations, and support systems. So, I created an online resource hub at raremamas.com. Check it out!

Scan the QR code below or visit raremamas.com
to explore the latest resources.

Acknowledgments

This book felt like a divine seed planted in my heart, and bringing it into the world was like the birth of another child. God, thank you for meeting me in the early hours of the morning to help me put words to the page and in my quiet moments of desperation when all I could do was write. Thank you for entrusting me with this message and giving me the strength to see it through. Jesus, you are my hope, my light in the dark. Only you could transform my hardest moments into something meaningful. I am overwhelmed with gratitude for this purposeful work, a heart that burns with passion to pursue it, and the beautiful blessing it is to me.

To all the rare mamas, I want to thank you for the inspiration, the fellowship, and the love. It is a privilege to hear and share your stories and an honor to walk alongside you. I pray this book serves and blesses you. You are loved.

To my parents, you've taught me what it means to live with strength, faith, loyalty, and love. You have always supported my life's endeavors, and this book is no exception. You are my unwavering rocks, endlessly listening, allowing me to lean in when I need emotional support and sound guidance, offering helping hands, swooping in to take care of the kids, and showing me the meaning of unconditional love. Thank you for loving us so well and making us feel seen, heard, and held. A million thanks wouldn't be enough. Viva La Familia!

Mom, thank you for being my guiding light and greatest teacher, showing me through your life what it means to love deeply, serve selflessly, and live with fearless faith. I admire you endlessly—your resilience, your grace, the way you lead with love, and, of course, your zest for life and legendary dance moves. Thank you for every lesson, every sacrifice, and every moment you gave to shape my heart. You are the mother every girl dreams of and the friend everyone hopes for—I'm blessed to have you as both. And since you're too humble to ever allow me to say all of this to you in person, I had to capture it in print—na na nana na! Mom, seriously, thank you. When I grow up, I want to be you.

To Tony, my affectionate, generous, and loving partner in this life (not to mention my hot hubby). From reading early drafts to keeping the kids busy so I could write, from encouraging me to keep finding a way when obstacles arose to being the first to beamingly call me "author," you have supported me every step of this journey. Thank you, love, for always believing in my dreams and helping me bring this book baby into the world. From our wedding day to today, "these are the hands" that have remained clasped tightly in mine— through high tide and low tide. May we always hold on tight. I love you, I love you, I love you.

To my children, you are my heart and my soul, and I love you fiercely. Mason, my heart—your endless compassion, humble strength, quiet grace, funny faces, and fly dance moves bring light and laughter into my life. You embody everything beautiful about this world—love, kindness, and empathy—and I'm constantly learning from you. The only thing bigger than your heart is your purpose. I can't wait to see how God uses your gifts.

Miles, my soul—you were born on my birthday, and you are my forever gift. Thank you for everything you are: feisty, determined, quick-witted, and a shrewd negotiator who tries to outfox me every day. The tenacity, bravery, and fierce spirit you exude continually strengthen my own. We have important work to do together—Eye of the Tiger.

To my husband's parents, thank you for bringing me into your family. Thank you for surrounding us with support and love, which have meant the world to us and made such a difference in our lives. The way you love our children fills us with joy. We are forever grateful for your generous, giving hearts. I feel blessed to call you family, and I'm so thankful to have you in our lives.

So much love and thanks to all our family: Amy, Bob, Bud, Colin, Devon, Donna, Eli, Gary, Griffin, JoAnne, Joe, Josie, Judy, Kirk, Liz, Madelyn, Myrna, Quinn, Ryan, Sam, Sawyer, Stella, Susie, Trevor, Tripp, and Wyatt, and all of our grandparents, uncles, aunts, and cousins, who have supported our journey, championed our cause, and loved on our children. Thanks for all the various ways you've shown up for us. Having a loving tribe to uphold our family has been a beautiful gift and carried us through. We adore you, and our gratitude is immeasurable.

Thank you to the Templin and Wilkinson families for staying close and letting us lean on you when we needed to—and the times have been many. Your steadfast friendship has been a sanctuary in the hardest years and every year since. When you find friends who are there for you during both your highest highs and lowest lows, you know life has given you a gift. Also, when you can sit around and laugh at yourselves wearing wigs together, that's pretty great, too.

J'ne, from your willingness to read a big ole, first-draft, printed Word doc (that's love!), to encouraging me at every step on the way to launching this book. You are a friend who listens with her whole heart, shows up without fail, and stands by loyally and compassionately through every triumph and trial. Your faith inspires me, your selflessness humbles me, and your wisdom guides me. You are a true-blue, rare gem of a friend.

Miriam, from the very beginning of this project, you have been a beacon of encouragement, a pillar of support, and a reliable sounding board. Your deep empathy for others shines through in everything you do, and your radiant energy lights up every room you enter. Thank you for always showing up—whether to help carry the weight or to celebrate the victories—and for being such a beautiful, supportive friend.

Thank you to The OG Bias, who, when I shared that I wanted to help other rare mothers without pause, all jumped with offers to share your skills and talents. Traci, for lending your brilliance and expertise from positioning statements to name-crafting. Those early brainstorming sessions will always be cherished, and I am forever grateful. Stacey, my fellow rare mama, and my first podcast guest, thank you for allowing me to practice on you and for your camaraderie in our unexpected, rare sisterhood. Laurel, my birthday buddy, and soul sister, for connecting me to resources that helped initially when this was just a seedling. Kath, for your kindness, compassion, and encouragement—your quiet strength is always present. Bias, you are my diamonds, and I shine brighter in your presence, reflecting the light you bring into my life. Thank you for being a constant source of laughter, strength, and sparkle.

To The Lovely Birds, Heather Netzer, Jenny McGraw, Brittany Daniel, and Cynthia Hauser, for being unwavering friends, from the carefree red-carpet days of our twenties to the many seasons that followed—marriage, motherhood, and milestone moments—we've shared countless memories and weathered life's ups and downs together. You have been supporters, cheerleaders, and cherished friends (plus, your beauty tips are second to none). Love you, lovely birds!

Thank you, Greenbelt crew, for the love and friendship from the beginning days of raising our babies to launching them into adolescence. Thank you for supporting our family and our SMA events and for the Greenbelt hangouts, dance parties, and laughter along the way. G, thank you for the support and many discussions about this project over the years.

Jeff and Ann Marie Jennison, you walked the rare road before us, and we look up to you. From that first Global Genes event, where we stood in awe as Ann Marie spoke, to rallying the cousin crew and showing up for us at our first SMA event, to learning how you raise your children and the way you model faith in Jesus. Thank you for being lighthouses in our lives. We thank God for blessing us with you as family.

Thank you to Annie Micks, Christy Distler, Chris Ferebee, Gabriel Corral, Matt Emerzian, and Stefanie Zeltner for your support of the *Rare Mamas* project and for using your time and talents in various ways for which I am forever grateful.

Trupti Patel, "Trups," your heart is boundless, and your care is nothing short of extraordinary. You have become a trusted confidante, a wise mentor, and a cherished friend. Anyone who can put up with my kid (and me!) for years and still stick around is, without a doubt, a true angel on earth. We love you, and you are now family.

Shirin Ihani, for your skills, talent, dedication, and expert guidance, but even more so for your caring, compassionate heart. Miles and I are not the easiest pair, yet you always show us grace and understanding. Your talent was apparent from the start, but learning from you as a woman and mother along the way has been an unexpected gift.

Heartfelt thanks to the many people who have used their gifts to help our son and make his journey more joyful, including Brienne Amoroso, Brenda Penrose, Chris Ackerman, Chuck Hobbs, Dave & Jill Lefever, Erika Markel, Gina Forney, Heatherann Kaczmarczyk, Keith Orahood, Kim Munsell, Kristen Nelson, Kristy Norgren, Megan Keithly, Rachele Cippola, and Tiffany Sampson.

So much gratitude to Kenneth Hobby, Colleen McCarthy, Mary Schroth, Shannon O'Brien, Jamie Gibson, Jesse Aynes, Kyle Houlihan, Dany Sun, Nick Farrell, and the entire team at Cure SMA. Thank you for your tireless dedication to supporting the SMA community and your unwavering commitment to curing spinal muscular atrophy. Your work has profoundly changed the face of SMA, offering hope, resources, and a future once thought impossible. You are not just a patient advocacy group—you are a beacon of excellence, setting the gold standard for what patient-centered care and advocacy should look like. Your work has paved the way for groundbreaking treatments and transformed what it means to live with SMA. I am deeply grateful for each of you—for your leadership, your support, and your humanity. Thank you for everything you do and for the difference you continue to make every single day.

To the teams at Ionis and Biogen, and especially to Kristina Bowyer and Gail Hartin, thank you for the incredible work you do in changing the course of diseases and saving lives. Your groundbreaking innovations and tireless dedication are reshaping what is possible in medicine, offering hope and new beginnings to families like mine. Beyond your scientific brilliance, you have been a source of support to the SMA community and to our family. Your commitment goes far beyond research; it is deeply personal, and your kindness and care have made a lasting impact on our lives. I call you changemakers, but I am blessed to also call you friends. There are no words powerful enough to express the depths of our thanks. How does one say thank you for saving their child's life? I don't know, but thank you.

To the extraordinary doctors who have touched our son's life in such a profound way: Dr. Wendy Mitchell, Dr. Ramos-Platt, Dr. John Day, Dr. Perry Shieh, and Dr. Chamindra Laverty. Your expertise, dedication, and exceptional care have forever impacted Miles's life—and ours—in ways we can never fully express. Thank you for everything you have done and continue to do for SMA patients. You are our heroes!

The rare world is a better place thanks to others who use their talents and shine their lights so generously. Thank you to rare peers who have become beloved friends: Brittany Cocilova, Carri Levy, Daniel DeFabio, Effie Parks, Jessica Fein, Nasha Fitter, Nicole Johnson, and Patti M. Hall. The instant kinship we share has been one of the greatest gifts of this rare journey.

Big thanks to all the women who have entrusted me to share their stories, including Amanda Brundage, Anne Jacobs, Ashley Bristow, Caitlin Eppes, Carol Gelbard, Caroline Cheung-Yiu, Cathy Oh, Chardell Buchanan, Colleen Gagnon, Danyelle Sun, Deb Ayres, Dr. Katia Moritz, Dr. Kim Aldinger, Dr. Tara Zier, Kelly Cervantes, Kristen Gray, Margot LaFreniere, Maria Hadjidemetriou, Marissa Penrod, Mary McHale, Megan DeJarnett, Melissa Hioco, Monica Poynter, Niki Markou, Rachel Neimeyer-Sutherland, Ramya Ramaswamy, Shelley Meitzler, Tameka Diaz, and Teri Furey. Thanks for sharing not only your knowledge but your hearts!

Maggie Langrick at Wonderwell Press, thank you for your dedication to books that help, heal, and inspire. Your belief in the need for this book and your confidence that I was the right person to bring it into the world means more than I can express. Your passion for stories with purpose is matched only by your sharp intellect and warmth. Thank you, Maggie, for believing in me, this book, and the power of words.

Dee Kerr, from the very beginning, your enthusiasm for this book has been nothing short of infectious. Thank you for your endless encouragement, thoughtful feedback, unwavering faith, and kind soul. You share my passion for helping rare moms, and your steadfast belief in why this book absolutely must exist has been a gift.

Thank you to the entire team that helped launch this book, including Adrianna Hernandez, Brittany Jones-Pugh, Claudia Volkman, Laurie MacQueen, Maxine Marshall, and Rachel High. I am grateful to work with such a talented, intelligent, and passionate group whose unwavering support and expertise brought this vision to life with great care.

This book exists because of the love, inspiration, and support of so many. I am endlessly grateful for each of you. My cup runneth over.

Notes

INTRODUCTION

1. "Rare Disease Facts & Statistics," National Organization for Rare Disorders (NORD), https://rarediseases.org/ understanding-rare-disease/rare-disease-facts-and-statistics/.

2. "Rare Disease Facts," Global Genes, https://globalgenes.org/ rare-disease-facts/.

CHAPTER 1

1. *English Oxford Living Dictionaries*, s.v. "prowess (n.)," https://en.oxforddictionaries.com/definition/prowess.

2. *English Oxford Living Dictionaries*, s.v. "empowered (n.)," https:// en.oxforddictionaries.com/definition/empowered/.

CHAPTER 2

1. Larry Alton, "The 7 Most Stressful Life Changes (and How to Cope with Them)," *Inc.*, November 19, 2018, https://www.inc.com/ larry-alton/the-7-most-stressful-life-changes-and-how-to-cope-with-them.html.

2. "Spinal Muscle Atrophy (SMA)," Curesma.org, https://curesma.org/ about/.

3. "Grief," *Psychology Today*, https://www.psychologytoday.com/us/ basics/grief#the-process-of-grief.

CHAPTER 3

1. "Your Powerful, Changeable Mindset," The Stanford Report, September 15, 2021, https://news.stanford.edu/report/2021/09/15/mindsets-clearing-lens-life/#:~:text=Research%20shows%20that%20mindsets%20play,more%20resilient%20to%20life's%20challenges.

2. Carol S. Dweck, PhD, *Mindset: The New Psychology of Success* (New York: Ballantine, 2016).

3. Ibid.

4. "Winston S. Churchill > Quotes > Quotable Quote," Goodreads, https://www.goodreads.com/quotes/721301-fear-is-a-reaction-courage-is-a-decision.

5. *English Oxford Living Dictionaries*, s.v. "hope," https://en.oxforddictionaries.com/definition/hope.

CHAPTER 6

1. Qian Sima Confucius, *The Wisdom of Confucius*, Modern Library (1938).

CHAPTER 7

1. "Care Mapping," *Cristinlind.com*, https://cristinlind.com/care-mapping/.

CHAPTER 10

1. "Child Life Services," American Academy of Pediatrics, https://publications.aap.org/pediatrics/article/147/1/e2020040261/33412/Child-Life-Services?autologincheck=redirected.

2. "Why Child Life," Association of Child Life Specialists, https://www.childlife.org/practice/why-child-life.

3. "Preparing for Your Child's Hospital Stay," UCLA Health, https://www.uclahealth.org/mattel/preparing-for-your-childs-hospital-stay.

4. "Depression and Anxiety in Patients with Different Rare Chronic Diseases: A Cross-Sectional Study," National Library of Medicine, https://www.ncbi.nlm.nih.gov/pmc/articles/PMC6382125/.

5. Leslee T. Belzer, S. Margaret Wright, Emily J. Goodwin, Mehar N. Singh, and Brian S. Carter, "Psychosocial Considerations for the Child with Rare Disease: A Review with Recommendations and Calls to Action," National Library of Medicine, June 21, 2021, https://pmc.ncbi.nlm.nih.gov/articles/PMC9325007/.

6. "Living with a Rare Disease - Experiences and Needs in Pediatric Patients and Their Parents," Orphanet Journal of Rare Diseases, https://ojrd.biomedcentral.com/articles/10.1186/s13023-023-02837-9

CHAPTER 11

1. "Kids' Waivers," https://www.kidswaivers.org

CHAPTER 13

1. The chart sourced from https://drcnh.wpenginepowered.com/wp-content/uploads/2023/04/Education-Series-IDEA-v-504-Table.pdf.

CHAPTER 14

1. "When Family Doesn't Understand," *Muscular Dystrophy Association*, https://www.mda.org/sites/default/files/publications/LearningtoLiveP-195.pdf.

CHAPTER 16

1. Y. Rum, S. Genzer, N. Markovitch, A. Perry, A. Knafo-Noam, and J. Jenkins, "Are There Positive Effects of Having a Sibling with Special Needs? Empathy and Prosociality of Twins of Children with Non-Typical Development," *Child Development*, 2022, The Society for Research in Child Development, Inc.

2. Committee on Psychosocial Aspects of Child and Family Health, American Academy of Pediatrics, 2014.

CHAPTER 18

1. The National Alliance for Caregiving, in partnership with Global Genes, "Rare Disease Caregiving in America," February 2018, https://www.caregiving.org/wp-content/uploads/2020/05/ NAC-RareDiseaseReport_February-2018_WEB.pdf.

2. "Caring for Your Mental Health," National Institutes of Health, https://www.nimh.nih.gov/health/topics/caring-for-your-mental-health#:~:text=Self%2Dcare%20means%20taking%20 the,illness%2C%20and%20increase%20your%20energy.

CHAPTER 19

1. Mayo Clinic Staff, "Stress Basics," https://www.mayoclinic.org/ healthy-lifestyle/stress-management/basics/stress-basics/ hlv-20049495.

2. "How Does Social Connectedness Affect Health?," Centers for Disease Control, https://www.cdc.gov/emotional-wellbeing/ social-connectedness/affect-health.htm.

CHAPTER 25

1. Diane Coutu, "How Resilience Works," *Harvard Business Review*, May 2002, https://hbr.org/2002/05/how-resilience-works.

Author Photo by Stefanie Zeltner, Joie de Vivre Photography

About the Author

NIKKI MCINTOSH is the founder of Rare Mamas®, a resource and community dedicated to empowering mothers of children with rare diseases. Through her platform and the "Rare Mamas Rising" podcast, Nikki provides strategies, strength, and support to others navigating similar challenges. Her mission stems from the profound need she felt after her son was diagnosed with a rare disease, fueling her with a passion and purpose to offer a lifeline of hope and connection to other rare moms.

Before launching the Rare Mamas platform, Nikki worked as a Fortune 500 advertising and marketing executive for over 18 years. Never one to shy away from adventure or developing new skills, Nikki trained in and performed improv at the world-renowned Second City Training Center in Chicago before moving to Los

Angeles and becoming the director of strategic planning for a prominent city magazine.

In 2013, Nikki's second son, Miles, was diagnosed with spinal muscular atrophy (SMA), a rare neuromuscular disease. Thrust into the rare disease world, and spinning with doctors' appointments, therapies, and caregiving, Nikki left her career to take care of her son full-time as his condition necessitated. Today, as the founder and creator of Rare Mamas, Nikki supports fellow mothers of children with rare diseases, and sheds light on the challenges they face through writing, speaking, interviews, and podcasting.

Nikki is a sought-after guest speaker and a trusted voice in the rare disease space. From speaking on panels for leading U.S. rare disease organizations to facilitating breakout sessions for disease-specific events, and educating patient advocacy groups and biotech executives, Nikki amplifies the voices of rare mothers and passionately advocates for the rare disease community.

Nikki lives with her husband, Tony, and sons Mason and Miles in Southern California.

To connect with Nikki, visit raremamas.com.